THE TEXAS TRIANGLE

Number Twenty-Seven:
Kenneth E. Montague Series in Oil and Business History

The Texas Triangle

AN EMERGING POWER IN THE GLOBAL ECONOMY

Henry G. Cisneros, David Hendricks,
J. H. Cullum Clark, and William Fulton

Texas A&M University Press
College Station

Library of Congress Cataloging-in-Publication Data

Library of Congress Control Number: 2021932165
Identifiers: LCCN 2021932165 | ISBN 9781648430091 (cloth) |
ISBN 9781648430114 (ebook)
LC record available at https://lccn.loc.gov/2021932165

Maps are by William Tipton of Compart Maps in Ventura,
California.

This book is dedicated by the authors
to the future of the great state we live in and love.

CONTENTS

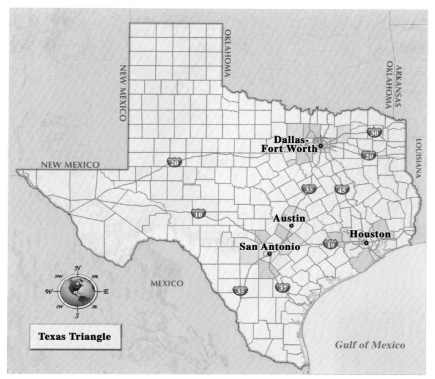

The Texas Triangle comprises 35 of the state's 254 counties. The 35 counties are in Texas' four largest metropolitan statistical areas: Dallas–Fort Worth, Houston, Austin, and San Antonio.

PREFACE

Henry G. Cisneros

The purpose of this book is to draw attention to an urban phenomenon of importance to Texas, to the nation, and to the world. That phenomenon of interwoven population growth, economic power, quality education, business leadership, and fiscal significance is the Texas Triangle, the network of three metropolitan complexes that together are reshaping the destiny of Texas and adding a strong pinnacle in the global system of economic megacenters.

The Texas Triangle consists of three metropolitan complexes: Dallas–Fort Worth at the northern tip, Houston-Galveston at the southeastern point, and Austin–San Antonio at the southwestern edge. It consists of four US Census–designated metropolitan statistical areas, or MSAs (Dallas–Fort Worth, Houston-Galveston, Austin, and San Antonio), and includes thirty-five urban counties that comprise those MSAs. The Texas Triangle soon will include four of the ten most populous cities in the United States (Houston, fourth; San Antonio, seventh; Dallas, ninth; Austin, presently eleventh but on a trajectory to grow to tenth; and Fort Worth, thirteenth). Each Triangle metro individually has a gross domestic product (GDP) the size of a respected nation, and together they generate the fifteenth-largest economy in the world.

Urban researchers who measure indices of economic interaction among metropolitan areas report strong transactional and ongoing bonds among the Texas Triangle metros. This sense of economic cohesion is further enhanced by the fact that nowhere else in the United States are there such large metros so proximate within a single state—that is, pulled together by the unifying legal and policy framework of one state.

That the significance of this complex is defining the identity and global perception of the new Texas is undeniable. The Triangle's national importance in generating new urban places, corporate leadership, research breakthroughs, educational excellence, and cultural innovations means that the Texas Triangle anchors a powerful urban dynamo in the geographic center of the United States' Sunbelt, akin to Chicago's national role in the last century. And in an era when international trade and cultural exchanges are best understood as transactions between de facto global city-states, the Texas Triangle takes its place among the most important economic engines in the world. By harnessing the Triangle's unprecedented pace of income and wealth creation, the Triangle cities can set important examples of human capital investment, inclusive growth, and quality urban place-making; they can also provide models for spreading opportunities to smaller cities and to the rural areas they influence.

The audience for whom this book is written includes Texans who want to understand the full dimensions of the phenomenon they are experiencing, national leaders who work to sustain the United States' economic juggernaut, and international investors who seek the strongest opportunities for economic growth in the world.

I have observed the emergence of the Texas Triangle as a cohesive force since, as mayor of San Antonio from 1981 to 1989, I joined in collaborative efforts with other Texas cities, including as president of the Texas Municipal League and as president of the National League of Cities. As secretary of the US Department of Housing and Urban Development and in more recent business and civic roles, I have worked with every mayor, city government, and chamber of commerce and most of the universities in every Texas Triangle city. I have observed the continuous strengthening of each urban area and the steady interweaving of interests and potentials that deserves explanation and warrants exhortations to action.

In the spirit of assembling the expertise of professionals who have similarly worked in the Texas metros and who have written about the larger potential, this book is a joint effort to combine the perspectives of Dallas–Fort Worth, Houston-Galveston, and

Austin–San Antonio. The principal organizer and interpreter of the research for this book is David Hendricks, who distilled insights gained over forty years as a business writer, business editor, and city government reporter for the *San Antonio Express-News*. David is a graduate of the University of Texas at Austin (UT Austin) and has covered Austin from the Express-News Capitol Bureau.

Cullum Clark is a member of the economics faculty at Southern Methodist University (SMU) in Dallas and is director of the Bush Institute-SMU Economic Growth Initiative at the George W. Bush Presidential Center also in Dallas. Cullum has been deeply involved in the public life of Dallas over his lifetime. His family roots in Dallas include his mother, Lee Cullum, and her tenure as a legendary journalist for the KERA public television station, the *Dallas Morning News*, and the *Dallas Times Herald*.

Bill Fulton is the president of Rice University's Kinder Institute for Urban Research in Houston, an urban policy center created to study the metropolitan growth challenges of the Houston area. Bill is well suited for the role of urban advocate, having been publisher of the California Planning & Development Report; mayor of Ventura, California; and city planning director of San Diego.

Together we have worked to describe the trajectories of each of the Texas Triangle metros in which we respectively live and work and integrate them into a larger dynamic of functioning cohesion and effective collaboration. We hope that the result is better understanding of an important moment in the United States' continuing urban development and a broader realization that community-building advances in the public interest become more likely when the trajectory of economic prosperity is matched to an informed sense of the possible and to abiding faith in human progress.

A lone star might be the symbol of Texas, but the urban Triangle dominates the state's economy.

THE TEXAS TRIANGLE

The Origins of the Texas Triangle

In 1966, lawyer Herb Kelleher met one of his clients, pilot / investment banker Rollin King, for a drink in the San Antonio downtown bar at the venerable St. Anthony Hotel. Kelleher was looking to start a business, and King had noticed that Texas business executives were often willing to charter planes to fly between large cities in the state because airfares charged by major airlines were so high. Kelleher and King were both entrepreneurs, and they discussed starting an airline to serve an in-state market, much as Pacific Southwest Airlines had done in California.

The legend is that King drew a triangle on a cocktail napkin, showing how the new airline would connect the major markets in Texas.

Like so much mythology about Texas, this legend is only partly true. King did not draw a triangle on a cocktail napkin that day.[1] But he did hatch the idea with Kelleher, who went on to be the airline's CEO. The following year, they incorporated what is now Southwest Airlines, and four years after that, Southwest became the first substantial discount air carrier—connecting Houston, Dallas, and San Antonio. It's now the third-largest airline in the United States, carrying more passengers than even United Airlines.

Kelleher and King are emblematic of the people who have created modern Texas. They grew up elsewhere—Kelleher in New

Jersey and King in Ohio—but headed to Texas as young men to make their fortune. They went not to a rural area or a small town but to a big city. They were, in today's parlance, entrepreneurial "disruptors," challenging a well-established system of air travel in the service of a new idea and fighting a four-year legal battle against established airlines—Continental and Braniff—before starting service. And they understood that Texas' prosperity depended not on rural areas and cowboy mythology but on an interconnected urban economy based in four large metropolitan areas. In other words, they understood that the Texas Triangle is—as urbanist Joel Kotkin put it decades later—the "economic guts" of the state.[2]

Indeed, in starting Southwest Airlines, Kelleher and King practically invented the idea of the Texas Triangle. Dallas–Fort Worth and Houston were both large, prosperous metropolitan areas, but their economies were separate. (In those days, business leaders in the two cities tried hard to stay out of each other's way.) San Antonio was a mostly military town. Austin was a small state capital with a university.

But in the half century since the Triangle was supposedly drawn on the cocktail napkin, these four metropolitan areas have grown rapidly in population, and their economies have become increasingly interdependent. Since Kelleher and King invented the idea of the Texas Triangle, it has become one of the fastest-growing and most economically powerful regions in the world.

Population

Today, some nineteen million people live in the Texas Triangle—defined as the thirty-five counties that make up the metropolitan areas of Houston, Dallas–Fort Worth, San Antonio, and Austin. (There are other metros within the Triangle, such as Waco and Bryan–College Station, but they are not included in this definition.) That's about two-thirds of the people who live in Texas—and almost the size of metropolitan New York City.

What's more, in the last decade, 85 percent of the population growth in Texas has occurred in the Triangle. Dallas–Fort Worth and Houston have added more people than any other metropolitan area in the nation, a little more than one million each. Austin and San Antonio added almost another one million between them. The Triangle includes five of the thirteen biggest cities in the nation (Houston, San Antonio, Dallas, Austin, and Fort Worth)—the densest concentration of large cities in the nation. At about 15 percent per decade, its population is growing much faster than any other major urban combination in the United States, including California and the Northeast Corridor. The Triangle is especially strong in migration from other states, rivaled only by South Florida and Northern California. It also has a high concentration of young people compared to other megaregions in the United States.

Mighty Economics

Economically, too, the Texas Triangle is a powerhouse. The four metropolitan economies had a combined GDP of approximately $1.3 trillion in 2018—about 6.3 percent of the US economy and almost 70 percent of the Texas economy.[3] The Triangle is bigger than the regional economies of Los Angeles, Hong Kong, London, or Paris; it's double the size of the Chicago region's economy. If the Texas Triangle were a separate country, it would have the fifteenth-largest economy in the world, larger than the economies of Indonesia, Turkey, Saudi Arabia, or the Netherlands. Compared to other US megaregions, the Triangle has been adding jobs quickly—83 percent over the past thirty years compared to 35 percent for other megaregions, on average, according to an analysis conducted by our team. (This gap is narrowing. Since 2010, the Triangle has increased jobs by 21 percent compared to 15 percent for the other megaregions on average.)

If it were a nation, the Texas Triangle would rank as a prosperous one, establishing new levels of quality of life that can provide models for other urban areas across the nation and world. The Triangle can be a model in another way, too, as a platform to extend new catalysts for economic progress to the state's smaller metropolitan areas and rural areas. If the state takes the right steps, the Texas Triangle can help overcome the urban-rural divide that confronts the nation as a whole.

Corporate Cluster

And the Triangle is not just a gigantic economic outpost. It's a center of corporate decision-making. Forty-nine of the Fortune 500 companies—almost 10 percent of them—are based in the Triangle, about as many as there are in all of California and almost as many as in New York State. At least five of the biggest companies on the Fortune 500 list are in the Triangle—ExxonMobil (second largest) in Irving, AT&T (ninth) in Dallas, Phillips 66 (twenty-third) in Houston, Valero Energy (twenty-fourth) in San Antonio, and Dell Technologies (thirty-fourth) in Austin. Other widely known companies include Southwest Airlines (Dallas), American Airlines (Fort Worth), USAA (San Antonio), ConocoPhillips (Houston), and Halliburton (Houston).

Furthermore, as economists Robert W. Gilmer and Samuel Redus have pointed out, the Triangle's metropolitan economies are deeply intertwined, thus strengthening the power of the Triangle as an economic region.[4]

According to an analysis of goods exports from the Brookings Institution, the Triangle's metro areas are each other's biggest trading partners by far—and the volume is high. In 2013, Houston's goods trade totaled almost $8 billion with Los Angeles, $2 billion with Chicago, $19 billion with China, and $40 billion with the other Triangle metro areas. Dallas–Fort Worth's numbers were very similar.

San Antonio's traded goods totaled $1 billion with New York, $2 billion with China, and $35 billion within the Triangle. Austin traded $5 billion in goods that year with China and $16 billion within the Triangle.

According to the Brookings data, the only other place in the country where there is so much commerce among so many different cities located in the same region is in the Northeast Corridor, which has a much bigger population. As Gilmer and Redus put it, "The four Texas cities have come together to form a great economic engine that serves Texas and much of the southwestern United States. . . . This engine has four cylinders that work in close coordination to power the Texas economy."[5]

But the Texas Triangle, mainly through its enormous airports in Houston and Dallas–Fort Worth and through the Houston Ship Channel, has become a global trading force too. Texas has long been the number-one US foreign trading state, and all four Triangle metro areas rank high among US metros in foreign trade.

This all points to the Texas Triangle as a powerful addition to the United States' network of metropolitan complexes that serve as economic engines and cultural centers.

Urban World

We live today on an urban planet. For the first time in history, more than half of the world's people live in cities—and virtually all of the world's population growth will take place in cities for the foreseeable future. Every human problem is now an urban problem, and every human opportunity is now an urban opportunity. The future of humankind will be decided, for better or worse, in urban areas.

At first glance, Texas may not appear to be a logical candidate to participate in this new urban world. After all, the whole mythology of Texas—reinforced constantly in popular culture through stories like Larry McMurtry's *Lonesome Dove*, icons like Willie Nelson, and movies like *Giant*, based on Edna Ferber's unflattering 1952 West Texas novel—is decidedly rural. Nor, at first glance, is the Texas Triangle a logical candidate to create an interconnected set of urban economies with an impact across the newly urban world.

Moreover, the transition to the "New Texas" is not without tension. Although 85 percent of the state's population today is urban—that is, living within what the US Census defines as the state's twenty-five metropolitan areas—the state's political decision-making too often lags behind in recognizing this reality. As recently as 2019, a visitor secretly recorded a private meeting at which then House Speaker Dennis Bonnen, from the town of Angleton, south of Houston, threatened to make the 2021 legislative session "the worst ever" for cities.[6] The recording also revealed Bonnen's desire to punish House members who helped defeat a bill to curtail lobbying by cities and counties.

But sheer demographic and economic numbers leave no doubt that the sometimes antiurban attitudes of some state lawmakers are increasingly out of date. The central message of this book is that the Texas Triangle defines the "New Texas" and will play a dominant role in determining its economic future, its demographic patterns, and its political priorities. And we suggest that it's very much in the interest of the state as a whole to encourage the continued growth and success of the Texas Triangle.

Urban Specialties

Unlike the Northeast Corridor or the urban regions of coastal California, the Triangle metropolitan areas don't share a common geographical bond. Dallas is a regional center located on the arid prairie in North Texas with deep economic ties to Oklahoma and other surrounding states. Houston is an energy center located on the humid Gulf Coast with deep economic ties to Louisiana. San Antonio and Austin are nestled on the edge of Texas' pretty Hill Country, but they were traditionally small cities without much economic diversity.

Nor are they all that close to each other. Dallas, Houston, and San Antonio—the three cities that were supposedly drawn on the cocktail napkin by Rollin King—are all between 200 and 270 miles away from each other, a three- to five-hour drive depending on traffic. (That's why the Southwest Airlines triangle worked—the three cities are just far apart enough that flying is an attractive alternative to driving.) Austin is a similar distance from Dallas and Houston, although it's only about 70 miles from San Antonio, and there's a growing economic corridor in between. (Fort Worth is only 35 miles from Dallas and has long been integrated into the Dallas–Fort Worth economy.)

Yet despite its rural image, Texas today is an urban state that rests primarily on an urban economy. That urban economy is centered on the Texas Triangle, a place receiving more population growth by birth and migration and more business investments than any other economic region in the nation.

Houston remains the world capital of energy and has the second largest port in the nation as measured by tonnage; it serves international markets. Even though Dallas–Fort Worth is growing just as fast—and has an energy sector as well—it functions more as a major regional center for the central part of the United States, with a large presence in transportation (because of Dallas / Fort Worth International Airport [D/FW]), distribution, and finance. San Antonio is still a military town, but it has a strong transportation and goods distribution connection to South Texas and Mexico. (San Antonio also has strong ties to Houston; the two are often viewed as one market for regional services ranging from newspapers to food markets to beer distribution.) In addition to being a capital town and a university town, Austin has emerged as the most important high-tech center in Texas—and perhaps the most important one anywhere in the country outside of California.

Probusiness

All this economic growth is built on the foundation of a probusiness philosophy—largely embraced by both Republicans and Democrats—that's different from the philosophies of the coasts. On the one hand, Texas is very much a low-tax/low-regulation state. On the other hand, the government has invested heavily in economic infrastructure—especially transportation infrastructure—to facilitate economic growth.

Texas is one of the few states in the nation, and the largest, that does not levy a personal income tax. That's one of the biggest attractions for corporations and wealthy individuals moving into the state. (The *New York Times* recently reported that young, wealthy tech entrepreneurs are increasingly moving from California to Texas and selling their stock only after they make the move to avoid California state income tax.)

The Triangle is one of the most affordable booming metropolitan regions in the nation. According to Zillow, Houston and San Antonio's median home prices are well below $200,000, while Dallas–Fort Worth is in the ballpark of $240,000. Even Austin, at $368,000, is half the price of most of the hot coastal metro areas. Overall, the Triangle's housing prices are 57 percent of the weighted average of all US megaregions, according to our analysis, and the issuance of new building permits is much higher than in any other megaregion. That's in large part due to the fact that unlike the coastal areas, Texas still has lots of land left—most of it flat and privately owned. However, real estate development is also less regulated in Texas than it is on the coasts, so housing and other real estate projects are approved and constructed much more quickly. (Houston famously is the only large US city with no zoning, but development projects move quickly in most other parts of the Triangle as well.)

At the same time that Texas has fostered growth in the Triangle through a probusiness approach to taxes and regulation, the Triangle itself—through actions of the state, its local governments, and its business leaders—took the initiative in building the big infrastructure required to support economic growth. Investments in water, power, broadband, and essential public facilities such as higher education campuses remain high priorities for both state and local governments. Perhaps most impressive, however, is the Triangle's transportation infrastructure.

The highway system built and maintained by the Texas Department of Transportation—popularly known as TxDOT—is the envy of the country, but the network of ports and airports within the Triangle may be the most important and impressive economic growth machine the state has created.

It all started more than a century ago, when business and civic leaders in Houston agreed to fund half the cost of converting a twenty-five-mile stretch of Buffalo Bayou into the Houston

Ship Channel. (The federal government paid for the other half.) Constructed a few years after the devastating 1900 Galveston hurricane, the ship channel created a whole new way for cargo to move in and out of the United States—and it remains a critical piece of economic infrastructure to this day. The Port of Houston is today one of the biggest ports in the nation, and the ship channel now contains an enormous portion of the nation's energy and petrochemical industry.

Meanwhile, in the last half century, the Triangle has led the country in expanding airport infrastructure. At a time when virtually no new airports have been opened in the nation, the Triangle has opened three since 1969—while also dramatically expanding a fourth and using two others to maximum capacity.

In Houston, a group of business leaders purchased one thousand acres north of the city in 1957 and held the property for almost a decade until the city of Houston was prepared to finance and construct what is now known as George Bush Intercontinental Airport. In the 1960s and 1970s—under the leadership of Dallas mayor Erik Jonsson, who said the prairie city needed to have "a port to the ocean of the air"—Dallas and Fort Worth resolved a long-standing competitive dispute and built D/FW Airport, today one of the most important airports in the middle of the continent.

Austin repurposed the closed Bergstrom Air Force Base into an airport in 1999. San Antonio added a terminal in the 1980s to expand from eight to twenty-seven gates. And Houston Hobby Airport and Dallas Love Field are busier than ever, with Hobby having recently completed a major expansion to accommodate international flights. (Hobby is an important symbol of economic expansion in the Triangle; it actually closed after the airport now named for George Bush opened in 1969 but reopened in 1971 to accommodate—you guessed it—Southwest Airlines' Texas Triangle flights.)

D/FW is the fourth busiest airport in the country, with thirty-one million boardings in 2017, while Bush is fifteenth, with eighteen million. Austin, San Antonio, Hobby, and Love all saw between five million and eight million boardings in 2017, ranking them in the top fifty airports in the United States.[7] Together, these six airports located in the Triangle's four metro areas accounted for some seventy-six million boardings in 2017—about 9 percent of all boardings nationally. The only region in the country that saw more boardings was the Northeast Corridor, which, again, has a much higher population. Both Southern California (including Los Angeles–area airports and San Diego) and Florida (including Miami, Orlando, and Tampa) have fewer boardings than the Triangle.

All of this economic infrastructure is drawing an enormous number of people to Texas, including work-ready in-migrants from other states and ambitious immigrants from around the world. Texas has added more than 3.5 million residents since 2010—the most of any state—and is now home to twenty-nine million people, more than any state except California. As stated earlier, 85 percent of all that population growth occurred in the Triangle—about three million people altogether. Overall, the Triangle grew by almost 15 percent between 2010 and 2018. By comparison, other large metro areas such as New York and Los Angeles grew by 3 to 4 percent in the same time period.

Furthermore, some of the fastest-growing suburban areas in the country are in the Triangle. For example, Hays County—on the I-35 corridor between Austin and San Antonio—grew by 40 percent during that time. Hays County, with San Marcos as the county seat, often ranks as the fastest-growing county in the country. Fort Bend County, in suburban Houston, has grown by 33 percent since 2010 and now has about the same population as San Francisco. Collin County in suburban Dallas—home to Plano and McKinney—is now adding as many people per year as Harris County, where Houston is.

Moreover, this population growth represents a healthy mix of natural increase (births minus deaths), migration from other US states, and international immigration. And as with the economy, different parts of the Triangle complement each other when it comes to population growth.

More than 1.1 million people from elsewhere in the United States have moved to the Triangle since 2010—about 40 percent of the total population increase. Two-thirds of those folks have gone to either Dallas–Fort Worth or Austin. Meanwhile, more than a half-million people have emigrated from other countries—and half of them have gone to Houston, which has become one of the nation's most diverse cities in the last three decades.

The probusiness climate and the constant flow of work-ready people into the Triangle have created a "virtuous cycle" of businesses flowing in as well. Among the global headquarters in the Triangle today are the global headquarters of Occidental Petroleum in Houston and national operational headquarters, such as those of Toyota USA in Plano and Mitsubishi Heavy Industries America, Inc. in Houston. Just like so many people from so many places, all three of these companies have moved to the Triangle in the last few years—Occidental and Toyota from Los Angeles and Mitsubishi from New York.

AT&T's Move

One other company that moved into the Triangle—and has now decided to stay—is the new AT&T, formerly Southwestern Bell Telephone Co.

Southwestern Bell was the smallest of seven regional Baby Bells that had spun off after the breakup of the Bell System in 1984. The company had been based in St. Louis for decades and, in fact, had roots in Missouri that dated back a century.

But in 1992, Southwestern Bell moved to San Antonio. At the time, company officials foresaw Texas as its best growth market and liked San Antonio's proximity to Mexico, where it was investing in the national telephone company. The city also offered an existing, nearly empty modern office tower alongside the scenic San Antonio River Walk downtown for the headquarters.

While in San Antonio, Southwestern Bell began an aggressive series of acquisitions of other Baby Bells, including the giant BellSouth and the shrinking, long-distance company AT&T. These acquisitions nearly put Ma Bell back together again, making the company a Dow 30 Industrials member. Over the years, the company changed its name to SBC and then to AT&T, reassuming its legendary stock ticker symbol, T.

In 2008, shortly after the introduction of the company's landmark partnership with the Apple iPhone product, AT&T moved its corporate headquarters again—but not outside the Triangle. Instead, AT&T moved its headquarters to a skyscraper in downtown Dallas that had long been Southwestern Bell's regional headquarters. Corporate leaders said the move was a simple business decision to gain better access to business partners and technology companies in Dallas—as well as access to both current and prospective employees in the fast-growing Dallas–Fort Worth metro area.

Potential Pitfalls

Any review of the promising prospects of the Texas Triangle also must consider factors that could limit the attainment of its full potential. History is replete with examples of seemingly inevitable economic juggernauts that were derailed or diminished by manmade errors or natural setbacks. An honest assessment of the Texas Triangle's trajectory requires that we consider the pitfalls on the path ahead.

An obvious hurdle would be a massive global recession that undermines the dominant sectors of the Texas Triangle metros. The cycle of worldwide economic expansions and recessions will undoubtedly continue, but the increasingly diversified economies of the Texas Triangle metros have demonstrated that they can grow faster than the nation as a whole through normal business cycles. That said, the Triangle—like all regions of the world economy—is vulnerable to deep global economic downturns, such as the COVID-19 crisis of 2020. And despite the growing diversity of the Triangle's regional economy, it's still particularly vulnerable to major setbacks in the oil and gas industry, as the world also experienced in 2020.

Another risk is that public policy failures, particularly at the level of the state government, might retard the growth trajectory of the Texas Triangle metros. Toxic partisan infighting between

Democrats and Republicans in Austin could entangle the state's leading cities and metros with new restrictions on their ability to manage ongoing growth. A breakdown in what has been a broad consensus in favor of growth-oriented policies could exact a steep toll on the Triangle metros. The red state / blue state contentiousness has been sparked, in great measure, by electoral politics that have led to instances of petty squabbles, with conservative lawmakers using social issues, such as transgender bathroom rules, to distract from the needs of urban Texas. But as the Texas metros grow in political power and electoral clout, it should be clear that the fight is greater than that. The state should focus on fortifying the areas and sectors that drive Texas' economic growth and provide avenues for rising prosperity everywhere. For instance, the legislature might become more reluctant even than it has been to invest in urban and suburban schools, leading to growing shortages of skilled workers. Faced with growing fiscal pressure from competing priorities, the state might fail to invest in infrastructure improvements necessary to the Triangle's future growth. Failure to prepare for future pandemics or climate change might undermine the Triangle's future. Among the United States' leading cities, Houston is one of the most vulnerable to hurricanes and rising sea levels. All the Texas Triangle cities face long-term challenges from hotter weather, drought, and increasingly destructive storms.

For now, the state's small-government policy orientation, its first-rate physical infrastructure, and its tremendous human energy have created an economic juggernaut that's now claiming its place among the great commercial regions of the world. The United States can look to the Texas Triangle for future breakthroughs in innovative products and creative services, but the world needs to see Texas for what it is—not the Wild West throwback still common in outdated stereotypes of the state but an increasingly urban economy looking to the future.

The Texas Triangle among the United States' Megaregions

U rbanist scholar Richard Florida has coined the idea that the most important geographic units driving the US economy today are neither states nor cities but megaregions.[1] The United States' megaregions are vast urbanized areas, in some cases crossing state boundaries, with multiple large metropolitan areas in relatively close proximity to one another. As Florida has shown, the megaregions are where the action is. They are the country's most powerful geographic engines of innovation and growth and its most potent magnets for talent. The consulting firm McKinsey makes the case in a report on the future of the US economy that thirty metro areas—including all four metros of the Texas Triangle—are pulling away from the rest, and almost all of them are in the top eight megaregions.[2]

Within each megaregion, the major metro areas have far stronger economic connections to one another than to metros elsewhere in the country, and they increasingly resemble each other in demographic and economic respects. As a result, each megaregion has its own distinctive "personality." And more, the United States' megaregions are competing with one another—for talent, for business, and even for political and cultural influence in the nation and throughout the world.

To understand the emerging urban model represented by the Texas Triangle, it's helpful to look at the Triangle in comparative perspective. We've assembled a new dataset on the country's eight leading megaregions: the Texas Triangle, plus the Northeast Corridor, the Urban Midwest, the Urban Southeast, South Florida, Southern California, the Northern California Bay Area, and the Pacific Northwest. In each case, we've included every metro in each area that makes the list of the United States' top one hundred metro areas by population, fifty-one metros in all, which means we can look at how the Texas Triangle compares to the other seven megaregions. Together, the top eight megaregions as we define them account for half of the United States' population and more than half of its economy.

The eight US urban megaregions, as defined by MSAs, are as follows:

Texas Triangle: Dallas–Fort Worth, Houston, Austin, San Antonio

Northeast Corridor: New York City, Washington, Philadelphia, Boston, Baltimore, Providence, Hartford, Bridgeport-Stamford, Worcester, New Haven, Springfield

Urban Midwest: Chicago, Detroit, Pittsburgh, Cleveland, Columbus, Cincinnati, Indianapolis, Milwaukee, Dayton, Akron, Toledo

Urban Southeast: Atlanta, Charlotte, Raleigh, Greenville, Columbia, Greensboro, Winston-Salem, Durham–Chapel Hill

South Florida: Miami, Tampa, Orlando, Lakeland-Winterhaven, Cape Coral–Fort Myers, Northport-Sarasota

Southern California: Los Angeles, Riverside–San Bernardino, San Diego, Oxnard-Ventura

Northern California: San Francisco, San Jose, Sacramento, Stockton

Pacific Northwest: Seattle, Portland, Spokane

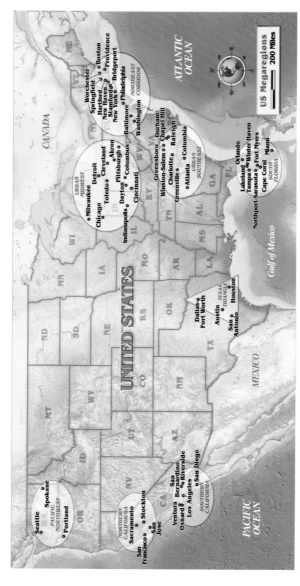

The Texas Triangle is one of eight megaregions, or clusters of large US cities. The megaregions each have their own economic dynamics and characteristics.

Looking at these eight megaregions together, two conclusions about the Texas Triangle stand out. First, the Triangle represents a thoroughly distinctive set of demographic and economic realities—a model unlike any other. Second, the Texas Triangle metros—like the metros in the other seven megaregions—are more similar to one another than they are to places anywhere else, despite their different histories.

Table 2.1 summarizes how the four Texas Triangle metros, and the Triangle as a whole, stack up against the population-weighted average for the United States' seven other leading megaregions on a set of demographic and economic measures.

Shifting Demographics

Consider the Texas Triangle's demographics. The Triangle metros collectively experienced population growth from 2000 to 2017 far ahead of any other region besides the Urban Southeast, which matched the Texas growth rate. In aggregate, the Triangle's population grew 47 percent from 2000 to 2017. By contrast, the weighted average growth rate for the other seven megaregions was approximately 18 percent. The Urban Southeast outgrew the Texas Triangle over the 2000–2017 period as a whole by one percentage point, but the Triangle pulled ahead of the Southeast over the past decade—17 percent to 16 percent between 2010 and 2017—and far ahead of the other six megaregions.

The Texas Triangle stands alone among the eight megaregions in attracting very strong net migration both from elsewhere in the United States and from abroad. The Triangle and the Urban Southeast have had by far the greatest percentage contribution from net domestic in-migration since 2000, while four of the eight megaregions have experienced more out- than in-migration. Meanwhile, the contribution from immigration to overall population growth rates in the Triangle since 2000 has been just behind that of South Florida and Northern California but easily ahead of the other five megaregions.

Table 2.1

| | Texas Triangle | | | | | Weighted average | Weighted Avg., Other Seven Leading Megaregions |
	Dallas–Fort Worth	Houston	San Antonio	Austin			
Median age (2017)	34.9	34.4	34.7	34.7		34.7	38.3
Population growth (2000–2017)							
Overall	43.4%	46.2%	44.5%	69.3%		47.1%	17.7%
Contribution from domestic migration	13.2%	9.6%	20.3%	36.8%		15.1%	−3.4%
Contribution from immigration	10.4%	12.7%	4.6%	9.7%		10.4%	8.4%
Population shares (2018)							
White	46.3%	36.1%	33.6%	52.0%		41.6%	52.4%
Black	15.4%	16.9%	6.4%	6.8%		13.8%	14.3%
Hispanic	28.9%	37.3%	55.4%	32.5%		35.8%	21.4%
Asian American	6.7%	7.8%	2.2%	5.8%		6.4%	8.7%
Population shares, twenty-five and over, with . . . (2017)							
Bachelor's degree or higher	34.6%	32.4%	28.1%	44.8%		34.1%	37.1%
Graduate or professional degree	12.0%	11.7%	10.2%	15.7%		12.1%	14.8%
GDP per worker, $000s (2017)	$149	$163	$124	$144		$150	$158

	Texas Triangle				Weighted average	Weighted Avg., Other Seven Leading Megaregions
	Dallas–Fort Worth	Houston	San Antonio	Austin		
Median household income, $000s (2017)	$67	$64	$57	$74	$65	$71
Industrial diversity index (Moody's, 2013)	0.80	0.59	0.81	0.67	0.71	0.65
Poverty rate (2017)	11.3%	13.9%	14.5%	10.4%	12.6%	12.2%
Economic freedom index (SMU Bridwell, 2012)	7.80	8.00	7.47	7.65	7.81	6.43
Wharton land-use regulation index (2006), lower = less restrictive	−0.19	−0.30	−0.24	N/A	−0.24	0.46
Avg. annual housing permits, 2008–17, as share of 2010 housing stock	1.50%	1.73%	1.00%	2.18%	1.59%	0.61%
Median home price to income ratio (2018)	3.9	3.7	3.9	4.1	3.8	5.1
Average commute time in minutes (2017)	28.6	29.9	26.5	27.0	28.6	30.5

Sources: American Community Survey and Population Estimates Program, US Census Bureau; US Bureau of Economic Analysis; Moody's; SMU Bridwell Institute for Economic Freedom; Wharton Residential Land-Use Regulation Index, 2006; Demographia Annual International Housing Cost Survey, 2018.

The Texas Triangle has by far the youngest population of the eight megaregions, with the lowest median age—34.7 years in 2017 compared to a weighted average of 38.3 years for the other seven megaregions—and the highest population share consisting of households with children under the age of 18. The Triangle has a much lower white population share than the average for the other seven megaregions—41.6 percent compared to 52.4 percent—and a higher Hispanic share, at 35.8 percent, than any other megaregion besides Southern California. Fully 49 percent of Texans below the age of 19 are Hispanic, and another 12 percent are Black, suggesting that the Texas Triangle represents a harbinger of an increasingly multiethnic future throughout the urban United States.

According to a 2019 study by WalletHub, Houston and Dallas ranked as the first and third most socially diverse of the top sixty-one cities in the United States. Fort Worth, Austin, and San Antonio were eleventh, nineteenth, and twenty-fifth. WalletHub measures diversity across a range of ethnic and socioeconomic variables by the Herfindahl-Hirschman index, a statistical method that gives a low score to cities whose population is highly concentrated in a single, homogeneous group and a high score to cities whose population is spread across a number of different groups. WalletHub then combines its multiple diversity scores for each city into a composite weighted average score.[3]

The exceptional ethnic diversity of the Texas Triangle metros is likely to present both opportunities and challenges in coming decades. Diversity—including the large immigrant communities in each metro area in the megaregion—will make the Triangle metros more creative, entrepreneurial, and culturally interesting than metro areas that are more homogeneous, based on history's lessons on the benefits of urban diversity. At the same time, social scientists have shown that highly diverse localities tend to invest less in "public goods" like education and social services than more homogeneous places, reflecting people's tendency to identify less with other people of different racial identities from themselves.[4] Perhaps the greatest future challenge for the Triangle will be to capture the benefits of extraordinary racial diversity while navigating its social and political complexities.

In education attainment levels, the Texas Triangle ranks slightly below the average of the United States' eight top megaregions. Among people over twenty-five, 34.1 percent have a bachelor's degree or higher compared to a population-weighted average of 37.1 percent for the other seven megaregions. And 12.1 percent have a graduate or professional degree compared to 14.8 percent for the other seven megaregions. The Triangle performs ahead of Southern California and South Florida on these metrics but well behind the top-performing Northeast Corridor, Northern California, and Pacific Northwest. It's also moderately behind the Urban Southeast, where the Raleigh, Durham, and Atlanta metros are ahead of all four Texas metros in attainment rates.

But a deeper dive into the data uncovers nuanced differences in education performance within Texas. When disaggregated, the education attainment levels of the white, African American, and Asian American populations are higher than average compared to those of their counterpart populations in the other eight regions. The performance of the Hispanic population in Texas, however, is lower than that of the Hispanic populations in the other regions, on average. This difference is profoundly important because of the larger and growing share of the school-aged population that Hispanics represent in Texas. The causes of this underperformance can be traced to limited English proficiency in certain neighborhoods and communities, insufficient access to English as a second language instruction in school districts, and the side effects of higher poverty rates.

It is clear that Texas must address these underlying issues if it is to achieve its overall education objectives and prepare its workforce of the future. The educational preparation of the workforce will heavily influence family income levels and economic performance in the state.

Higher Than Average Job-Market Diversity and Economic Mobility

Turning to economic measures, the Texas Triangle ranks just below the weighted average for the seven other megaregions in both its GDP per worker and in growth in GDP per worker since 2001. The Triangle likewise slightly trails the seven-region average in median household income: roughly $65,000 versus $71,000 in 2017. The Triangle has outperformed the Urban Midwest, the Urban Southeast, and South Florida on each of these measures of prosperity, but it has performed below top-performing Northern California and the Pacific Northwest. It's also just behind the Northeast Corridor.

The Triangle's relative position in GDP per worker and household income partly reflects the extraordinary diversity of its regional economy. The four Triangle metros all rank high or very high on a Moody's index of industrial diversity, which uses a Herfindahl-Hirschman index assigning low scores to places in which employment is highly concentrated in a single industry and high scores to places where people work in a wide variety of industries. Each of the Texas Triangle's metros has become more economically diverse over the past two decades. By contrast, the urban economies of Northern California, the Pacific Northwest, the Northeast Corridor, and the Urban Midwest are much more concentrated—the first two in technology, the Northeast in finance, and the Midwest in manufacturing—and have generally become more concentrated since 2000.[5]

At the level of individual jobs, the Texas Triangle has a much lower share of its workforce in computer-related occupations than Northern California or the Pacific Northwest and a lower share in finance than the Northeast Corridor. It also has a lower-than-average share in certain other high-value-added occupations, such as life sciences, design, and media. On the other hand, the Triangle has a higher-than-average share in manufacturing and is still a large provider of relatively high-paying jobs although much lower than that of the "Rust Belt" Midwest.

The Triangle's great economic diversity means that it performs below the megaregions that have been highly concentrated in the "right" sectors in recent years, particularly information technology and finance, but well ahead of those concentrated in declining industries, like basic metals and machinery in the Midwest and textiles, furniture, and tobacco in the Southeast. Diversity also acts as a hedge against troubles in any one sector of the economy, which is why the Triangle metros held up better than most during the severe recession of 2007–9. The Triangle metros have also seen lower unemployment rates and a faster jobs recovery than most other megaregions during the COVID-19 recession.

The Texas Triangle's modest lag in GDP per worker and household income also reflects the region's demographics. Its workforce is relatively young and with lower education attainment compared to those of other megaregions.

Again, a closer look at the numbers sheds further light on how the Texas Triangle's economy is performing. The Triangle actually has significantly *higher* median income levels than the seven-region average when adjusted for educational levels. That is, people in the Triangle with an associate's degree achieve higher median incomes than the average for similarly educated people in the other megaregions, and the same pattern holds for residents with bachelor's degrees and graduate or professional degrees. Lower-than-average overall incomes, however, are a result of lower education attainment levels, which in turn reflect gaps in educational performance and differences in access to academic programs for the state's ethnic minority and immigrant populations.

Seen together, the data on lagging education attainment levels among the Texas Triangle's minority communities and the Triangle's outsized success in attracting migration from elsewhere point to an important conclusion: more than other US megaregions, the Texas Triangle has been "importing" the highly educated workforce that has been helping power its economic growth from other parts of the United States and abroad. Early evidence indicates that the COVID-19 crisis has accelerated the movement of highly skilled people from the large cities of the East and West Coasts to the Texas Triangle metros. But the data also suggest the Triangle urgently needs to create a more balanced model of human capital development, growing more of its future workforce through formal education and adult up-skilling programs for homegrown Texans. The early success of San Antonio's "Project QUEST" program at Our Lady of the Lake University provides an example that all the Texas Triangle metros might emulate and scale up.

Upward Mobility

The Triangle scores higher than the average for the other seven megaregions on a widely cited measure of upward mobility developed by Harvard economist Raj Chetty.[6] Based on Chetty's research, people who grew up in families with relatively low income in the Triangle metros are earning more today than otherwise comparable people who grew up in the Northeast Corridor or South Florida and far more than comparable people from Southern California, the Urban Midwest, or the Urban Southeast on this metric. The Triangle scores somewhat behind the Pacific Northwest and Northern California.

The Texas Triangle is roughly in line with the average for the other seven megaregions in its population share living below the poverty line and its share earning middle-class incomes.[7] However, these statistics don't adjust for the very different costs of living in different regions. If adjusted for the Triangle's relatively low housing costs, the Triangle would clearly have lower poverty rates and a more robust middle class than more expensive megaregions, particularly Northern California, Southern California, and the Northeast Corridor.

So the Texas Triangle has been unusually successful in building a prosperous economy in which a young population can achieve upward mobility and a middle-class way of life. And it's done so without placing all its eggs in one basket, such as the technology sector or Wall Street finance.

Fast-Growing Housing Supply and Affordable Home Prices

Relatively cheap land and attainable housing have been key ingredients in the Texas Triangle's success story for generations. Median home prices in the Triangle metros were 54 percent below those of the eight-region average in 2010. Home prices in the Triangle moved up sharply over the last decade under the pressure of massive in-migration but remained 43 percent below the eight-region average in 2017. Rent levels, meanwhile, were 16 percent below the eight-region average as of 2017.

One would expect regional home prices to vary with regional income levels, so the slightly below-average income levels of the Triangle partly account for this gap. But adjusting for income, the Triangle has maintained a tremendous advantage even as home prices have surged throughout the urban United States. Median home prices in the Triangle stood at 2.9 times the region's median household income in 2010 compared to an average of 4.3 times for the other seven megaregions. By 2018, the Triangle's price-to-income ratio increased to 3.8 times, but the average ratio in the other seven megaregions rose significantly as well, to 5.1 times.[8]

Housing is far more attainable in the Texas Triangle for middle- and lower-middle-income families in particular. As of 2018, 19.5 percent of Triangle families who own their own home were "housing cost-burdened" by federal government standards compared to 25.1 percent for the eight megaregions as a whole. A decade of steep rent increases left 38.5 percent of renters cost-burdened in 2018, but even on this measure, the Triangle maintained better affordability than most other megaregions, where the percentage of cost-burdened renter households ranges from 40 to 49 percent. The Triangle has consistently maintained an enormous advantage over all three West Coast megaregions as well as the Northeast Corridor and South Florida.

A crucial underpinning of the Texas Triangle's relative affordability has been a two-decade housing supply boom far outstripping what's taken place in other megaregions. The pace of annual new housing permits, measured in relation to the total housing stock in 2010, has been more than two and a half times the average for the other seven megaregions—and fully three to four times the pace of Northern California, Southern California, and the Northeast Corridor. That said, new construction in the Triangle metros has slowed somewhat since 2016—particularly in the core cities of Houston, Dallas, and Austin—adding to upward pressure on housing prices. As we explore in later chapters of this book, rising home price-to-income ratios throughout the Texas Triangle pose a growing obstacle to upward mobility for moderate- to lower-income Texans. Also, rising prices have started to erode the Triangle's large housing cost advantage relative to the large coastal megaregions over the years since 2016, calling into question one of the Triangle's main drivers of inbound migration and economic growth.

Mobility

Average daily commute times, a measure of urban congestion, have risen moderately in the Texas Triangle metros over the last decade, to 28.6 minutes each way. Again, however, the Triangle has maintained a quality-of-life advantage, as the average for the other seven megaregions has risen more, to 30.5 minutes. The West Coast megaregions have experienced especially severe deterioration in commuting times over the last decade, making transportation issues one dimension of the decision for families leaving the West Coast for the Texas Triangle or smaller Mountain Time Zone cities. The Triangle's edge in commute times, despite the vast physical distances over which many urban Texans travel to work, reflects the region's better-than-average mobility infrastructure. Sustaining this advantage in the face of rapid growth in the population of the Triangle metros represents one of the chief challenges for Texas and its large cities in the decades ahead.

Cost of Doing Business

The Triangle also maintains a competitive edge in cost of doing business, based on a Moody's index. While overall business costs have risen in the Triangle over the last two decades, they remain 6 percent below the average for the other seven megaregions.[9]

The Texas Triangle metros are distinctive, moreover, in their public policy orientation. The Triangle scores far and away higher than any of the other seven megaregions on an index of "economic freedom" developed by SMU's Bridwell Institute for Economic Freedom, measuring the size of government, tax rates, and labor policy. The Triangle's lead has been growing over the last two decades, as "economic freedom" scores have declined elsewhere—particularly in the Northeast Corridor, the Urban Southeast, and the West Coast megaregions.[10] The region's edge in business taxes has expanded as well, helping drive a continuous inflow of businesses relocating from high-tax megaregions, particularly in California.[11]

The Triangle also maintains the most permissive land-use rules of the eight megaregions, based on an index by the University of Pennsylvania's Wharton School of Business.[12] While the expansive land supply surrounding the four Triangle metros has contributed to Texas' reputation for low barriers to entry for home builders, pro-growth policies in Texas generally have clearly made a substantial difference too. Business-friendly land-use regulations, expedited permitting processes, and investments in transportation infrastructure have largely allowed the housing supply to keep up with booming demand and help explain the housing affordability advantage of the Texas Triangle metros over other megaregions.

Quality of Life and Social Services Challenges

While Texas leads the nation's megaregions in many positive respects, it is also true that the Texas Triangle ranks relatively low in several important categories of public quality-of-life and social services measures. Texas generally scores lower among the states in measures of the population covered by health insurance and in per-capita education investment. Statewide data show that 20.2 percent of Texas adults lacked health insurance in 2018 compared to 10.0 percent of US adults. Texas currently spends $8,619 per student on education, 32 percent below the national average of $12,756 per student. These below-average performances in statewide spending on health care and education impact the accessibility and quality of those social services in the Texas Triangle metros. For instance, the Triangle's relatively large population without health insurance is straining hospital emergency rooms. Spending on the state's Medicaid program for lower-income residents has grown from 25 percent of the state government's budget in 2010 to almost a third today, crowding out investment in education and other state priorities. And inadequate spending on schools makes it likely that the Triangle will fall further behind other megaregions in education attainment levels over the next two decades unless it makes a significant course correction.

Other measures of quality of life also expose gaps between the Texas Triangle metros and the other megaregions in the nation. The Triangle, for example, lags behind all the other megaregions except for the Urban Southeast in urban greenspace, according to the Trust of Public Land's "Parkscore."[13] The Triangle also ranks below the eight-region average on measures of its portfolios of research universities and hospitals developed by the George W. Bush Institute.[14]

As the Texas Triangle metros work to address these and other shortcomings, they share an advantage over other megaregions attempting to enact urban policies to benefit their regions. The Texas Triangle exists completely within a single state and therefore operates under the same framework of legal guidelines, regulatory measures, fiscal expectations, and leadership structures. That means that as Texas cities seek to align their internal initiatives with state policies, they are negotiating with the same state entities and can together make a coherent case for the Texas Triangle metros.

No other US megaregion has multiple metro areas as large as the Texas Triangle metros—Houston, Dallas–Fort Worth, and Austin–San Antonio—aligned in such proximity and located in one state. For instance, the Northeast Corridor has five of the United States' top thirty metros in relatively close proximity—Washington, Baltimore, Philadelphia, New York, and Boston—but they are in four different states and the District of Columbia and do not operate under a single state's policy umbrella. The Urban Midwest, Urban Southeast, and Pacific Northwest megaregions are also spread across multiple states and thus face additional complex layers of state policy coordination and politics. The metros of the South Florida megaregion are all in Florida, but the policy issues confronting Miami in South Florida are very different from those challenging Tampa and Orlando, in the middle of the state. The Southern California megaregion and the Northern California megaregion are both in California, but the two regions, which are 381 miles apart, have historically had vastly different policy concerns, divergent economic bases and competing political relationships.

The Texas Triangle metros start with more similar interests and more interconnected economies than those of any other large megaregion, which creates opportunities for tighter policy coordination. The test for the future will be whether the Triangle metros and the state of Texas can forge a mutually beneficial agenda based upon the growth needs of the Triangle cities and their residents and the economic and fiscal interests of all Texans.

Shared Patterns of Texas Urbanism

Virtually all the distinctive characteristics of the Texas Triangle we identify in this chapter are true of each of the four Triangle metros individually. There are a handful of exceptions: Austin has considerably higher education attainment levels and a much greater percentage of its workforce in computer-related occupations than the other three. Houston's economy is less diverse, with its heavy energy focus, and San Antonio has much lower business costs and commute times than the rest of the Triangle. But the similarities among the Houston, Dallas–Fort Worth, San Antonio, and Austin metros far outweigh the differences, particularly once we compare them to metros elsewhere in the United States.

In sum, the modern-day Texas Triangle stands out as unique among the United States' megaregions. It is younger, faster-growing, less white, more Hispanic, slightly less educated, more economically expansive and diverse, more lightly taxed, more permissive in its land-use and business regulation policies, and more affordable for families and businesses than most of its megaregion peers. In these respects, the Triangle conforms to a number of widely held stereotypes about Texas.

But our analysis also shows—and this book aims to document in depth—that the Texas Triangle increasingly defies many common stereotypes. While the image of Texas as a low-tax, low-service, low-amenity state is partially accurate, it's a mistake to suppose the Triangle owes its economic success to having a cheap, if undereducated, workforce. As we've pointed out, the Texas Triangle's white, African American, and Asian American populations have higher education attainment levels than their peers in the other megaregions, and people earn more than their peers with comparable education attainment elsewhere, on average. The Triangle outperforms all other megaregions on Chetty's measure of upward mobility and has lower poverty rates than most peer regions after adjusting for lower costs of living. Our analysis further suggests the Texas Triangle enjoys better mobility infrastructure by some measures than most other top megaregions.

And as we show in the following chapters, the popular image of Texas as a deep red bastion of ideological conservatism bears little relationship to the emerging urban realities of the Texas Triangle. Political trends in Texas are similar to those in most other states: rural and small-town counties are deep red, the core urban counties of the state's large metro areas are increasingly deep blue, and the vast suburban regions of the Texas Triangle are trending from red to purple. The core cities of Houston, San Antonio, Dallas, Fort Worth, and Austin have long traditions of electing pragmatic, business-friendly centrists as mayors. Suburban counties in the Triangle have always leaned more conservative than the urban cores. But they've also been among the most growth-oriented communities in the nation, and their rapid growth is reshaping them into highly diverse, politically moderate places.

At the same time, it's also a mistake to assert—as national media commentators sometimes do—that urban Texas is becoming more like urban centers on the coasts as it grows larger and more ethnically diverse. On the contrary, the Texas Triangle metros are growing apart in some important ways from regions like the Northeast Corridor and Northern California. The Triangle is becoming more economically diverse as the coastal regions mostly grow more concentrated. Gaps between the Triangle and its coastal peers on economic policy, housing, and infrastructure are expanding, not shrinking. Despite the relatively young and diverse populations in the four Triangle metros—and their solidly blue political complexion in national elections—they have sustained their pragmatic style of local politics as coastal metros become more progressive.

A Distinctive Emerging Model

The Texas Triangle, then, is emerging as a truly distinctive geographic unit, quite different from the state's own historical experience and unlike other US megaregions. It represents a model for how to accommodate rapid population growth and growing ethnic diversity while sustaining economic dynamism and keeping middle-class lifestyles more in reach than they are in most other places. The Triangle also bears watching as a harbinger of challenges other US urban regions will face as they become more diverse, particularly in education.

The rest of this book tells the story of how the Texas Triangle came to be and explores what the rise of this emerging urban megaregion means for the people of Texas—as well as for the United States and the world.

The Texas Triangle's Position in the Nation and World

T he Texas Triangle sits tall in the saddle when its economy is placed in context, measured by its place in the economy of the United States and compared to other economies in the world.

The number to remember is $1.3 trillion. That was the size of the Triangle economy, or the GDP, in 2018 of the thirty-five urban counties that comprise the metropolitan areas at the three corners of the Texas Triangle.[1] From 2017 to 2018, the Texas Triangle economy increased by about $30 billion.

GDP is a measure of the total value of goods produced and services provided in a country, or defined place, during one year.

In the Texas Triangle's north corner, the Dallas–Fort Worth MSA had a GDP of $535.5 billion in 2018, the fourth-largest metro economy in the nation, according to the US Bureau of Economic Analysis. Dallas–Fort Worth represented 2.8 percent of the US economy.

In the Texas Triangle's southeast corner, the Houston-area economy was $490.1 billion in 2018, the seventh-largest US metro area's economy. The Houston–The Woodlands–Sugar Land area represented 2.6 percent of the US economy.

In the Texas Triangle's southwestern corner, the Austin–Round Rock economy in 2018 was $148.8 billion. The San Antonio–New

Braunfels economy was $129.3 billion. Together, the Austin and San Antonio MSAs combined for $278.1 billion, representing 1.5 percent of the US economy.

Pulling the metro economies of the Texas Triangle together resulted in a $1.3 trillion economy in 2018, the thirty-five counties accounting for 6.9 percent of the US economy, according to the latest data from the US Bureau of Economic Analysis. The entire state of Texas represented 8.7 percent of the US economy with a GDP of $1.84 trillion in 2018.

Economic Sizes

The world is made up of numerous megaregions. When it comes to the world's largest urban areas and biggest clusters of large cities near each other to form cohesive economic regions, the Texas Triangle ranks among the largest economies anywhere, in terms of GDP. Table 3.1 shows a comparative listing of large global economic regions, ranked in economic size.

If the Texas Triangle were a country, it would have been the fifteenth biggest national economy in the world in 2018, according to GDP estimates published by the World Bank,[2] the United Nations,[3] and the International Monetary Fund. The point is that the Texas metros are a significant global economic force.

The rankings become clearer when compared to individual country economies. On all lists, the Texas Triangle would have outranked Mexico, Indonesia, Turkey, the Netherlands, and Saudi Arabia as well. In fact, the Texas Triangle's economy was about twice as large as Saudi Arabia's or Switzerland's from 2016 to 2017.

If Texas as a whole was a country, it would rank a few slots higher than the Texas Triangle. Texas would have been the tenth-largest national economy on the World Bank's and United Nations' most recent lists. The Texas economy was larger than Canada's on the World Bank and United Nations lists.

These rankings do not mean the Texas Triangle is the largest US urban network. The New York–Newark–Jersey City MSA alone

Table 3.1

GDP at nineteen global economic regions (billions)

Northeast Corridor*	$ 3,712
Tokyo-Osaka-Kobe	$ 2,674
Urban Midwest	$ 1,862
Southern California	$ 1,484
Texas Triangle**	**$ 1,303**
Hong Kong–Shenzhen–Guangzhou	$ 1,044
Northern California	$ 929
Shanghai-Suzhou-Wuxi	$ 881
Greater London	$ 880
Greater Paris	$ 850
Urban Southeast	$ 841
Milan-Turin	$ 748
South Florida	$ 704
Rhine–Ruhr Valley	$ 574
Pacific Northwest	$ 554
Greater Beijing	$ 441
Singapore	$ 350
Greater Rome	$ 167
Greater Mumbai	$ 151

* Includes Boston, New York City, Philadelphia, Baltimore, and Washington metropolitan areas.

** Includes Dallas–Fort Worth, Houston, Austin, and San Antonio metropolitan areas.

Source: Various latest-available estimates dating between 2014 and 2018. US estimates are from 2018. Another way to put the Triangle's economic heft into context is to compare it to other notable economies in the world.

had a 2018 economy of $1.72 trillion, which is slightly smaller than the economy of the entire state of Texas. The New York City area by itself accounted for 9.6 percent of the US economy in 2018 compared to the Texas Triangle's 6.9 percent.

We can consider the New York City area the economic center of the Northeast Corridor megaregion, the region stretching from Boston to Washington, DC. The metro area economies of the Northeast Corridor megaregion as a whole added up to a GDP of $3.7 trillion in 2018. That comes close to Germany's $3.86 trillion on the International Monetary Fund's GDP list. If the Northeast Corridor is compared with entire country economies, it would be fifth largest and measure up well as a member of the G7 group of national economic powers. The Northeast Corridor is clearly the United States' largest urban agglomeration. But other interwoven metros exist across the nation.

Let's look at the US West Coast. The Southern California megaregion had a GDP of approximately $1.5 trillion in 2018. The dominant metro area in Southern California, Los Angeles–Long Beach–Anaheim, had accounted for $1.1 trillion of this total. The Northern California megaregion had a 2018 GDP of $929 billion, about $400 billion smaller than the Texas Triangle.

In the nation's heartland, the Urban Midwest megaregion had a 2018 GDP of approximately $1.9 trillion, the second largest in the United States. Spanning seven states with very different demographic, economic, and political realities, the Urban Midwest megaregion is arguably less of a cohesive geographic unit than the Texas Triangle or, for that matter, the Northeast Corridor, Southern California, or Northern California.

The main point here is not to assert that the Texas Triangle is today larger than these other megaregions. But it is to say that the Texas Triangle, which has not generally been considered within the United States or abroad as an economic unit in this context, has arrived. It is the fourth-largest interlinked urban engine in the United States. It is cohesive, globally linked, stocked with solid companies with long trajectories ahead, and the beneficiary of steady investment in modern infrastructure. In addition, it is the fastest-growing urban megaregion.

To sharpen the worldwide standing of the Texas Triangle further, eye-opening comparisons may be drawn between the economic sizes of the Triangle's individual metro areas not only with other global urban giants but also with entire countries.

The economy of the Dallas–Fort Worth metro area, for example, was almost the same size as that of Sweden, according to the International Monetary Fund's 2019 estimate.

The Houston-area economy was about the same size as Belgium's, according to the United Nations.

The Austin-area economy was bigger than Kuwait's, according to three lists. San Antonio's economy was about the same size as Ukraine's. The Austin–San Antonio metro areas combined, the southwestern corner of the Texas Triangle, have a total economy about the size of Egypt's.

Comparisons of economies to those in other large cities also are illuminating. The economies of both the Dallas–Fort Worth area and the Houston area each were larger than the Greater Mexico City economy, even though the Mexico City area has a population of more than twenty-one million.[4]

The Dallas–Fort Worth and Houston areas, moreover, each have economies larger than the ones in Shanghai, Hong Kong, and Beijing, China.

The Austin area's economy was about the same size as the one in Athens, Greece. The San Antonio area's economy, smaller than Austin's, was still nearly as big as the one in Abu Dhabi of the United Arab Emirates.

Exports

A large factor in an economic region's economic wealth is its foreign exports. Exports sustain economies by bringing capital from outside the region, which, of course, offsets the losses of capital sent from a region through imports. Exporting is a key factor in a region's GDP. Exports establish that a metro is engaged in the world around it instead of just "doing its own laundry" economically.

Each of the Texas Triangle metros is a net exporter on a significant scale. Texas, as a whole, was the leading export state in the nation in 2017 with $264.1 billion, or 17.7 percent of the US total.[5] Each of the Texas Triangle metros was among the top fifty exporters among US metro areas in 2016.

Houston is the giant of Texas exporting, the nation's number-two exporter with $84.1 billion in goods exported in 2016.[6] The Dallas area, number nine in the nation, was the second-largest exporting metro with $27.2 billion. The Austin area, number twenty-six in the United States, exported $10.7 billion that year. San Antonio, number forty-nine in the nation, exported $5.6 billion.

Altogether, the Texas Triangle metros exported $127.6 billion in goods in 2016, or about half of the Texas total.[7] If the Texas Triangle were a state, it would be the nation's third-largest exporter, after second-place California and ahead of Washington State and New York.

Texas exports petroleum oils, liquefied propane, computer parts and accessories, aircraft and aircraft parts, integrated circuits, modem devices, and machinery for making semiconductors and cotton, among other goods and agricultural products.

Of the goods shipped from the Houston area, the largest volume went to Mexico, followed by Canada, China, Brazil, the Netherlands, Japan, Singapore, Saudi Arabia, South Korea, and Colombia.

Judged by measures of economic power and exports, the Texas Triangle is a leader and clearly belongs in a global hierarchy of urban leaders.

The Texas Triangle's Rising Migration Crescendo

People are streaming into Texas as never before and more than anywhere else. And when they move to Texas, almost all of them are moving to the Texas Triangle.

Even Texans who live outside the Triangle are moving to the Triangle metropolitan areas, intensifying the state's urbanization.

The evidence is widespread. A series of population reports issued from 2017 to 2018 tell a common story of the Texas Triangle as a strong draw for new residents.

In 2017, the Texas Demographic Center at the University of Texas at San Antonio issued a series of four reports on Texas migration patterns: "In the early twenty-first century, Texas has become a leading destination for both international and domestic migrants. Together, these migration flows are adding around 250,000 new residents to Texas each year. In addition to the quarter of a million new Texans close to a million resident Texans move within the state each year," the first of the 2017 reports stated.[1]

In 2018, the Federal Reserve Bank of Dallas (Dallas Fed) published a report titled "Gone to Texas: Migration Vital to Growth in the Lone Star State." Authors Pia Orrenius, Alexander Abraham, and Stephanie Gullo observe that "the state's 1.8 percent average annual population growth is about double the nation's 0.9 percent."[2] According to the authors, "For most of the 20th century, international and domestic migrants streamed into California in a seemingly endless flow. International immigrants still do, but in every year since 1991, net domestic migration to California has been negative, with a significant share of Golden State residents leaving for Texas. In the post-recession period—2010 to 2017—Texas was the recipient of 920,000 net domestic migrants, equal to 3.6 percent of the state's 2010 population. Texas was the second-largest net recipient of domestic migrants" numerically.

But also in 2018, the US Census Bureau released its 2017 population estimates for US MSAs, counties and cities that made it clear Texas had become the nation's top destination state. The Census reports came after the Dallas Fed published its article.

In March 2018, the US Census released a report, "New Census Bureau Population Estimates Show Dallas-Fort Worth-Arlington Has Largest Growth in the United States." The report stated that the Dallas–Fort Worth metro area had grown by 146,238 people between July 1, 2016, and July 1, 2017.[3]

The Houston–The Woodlands–Sugar Land metro area was number two with a population gain of 94,417 people over the same period. The Austin–Round Rock metro was number nine with a gain of 55,269 people.

The Census report was accompanied by a graphic titled "Texas Keeps Getting Bigger," which listed the top fifteen US counties in numeric growth from July 1, 2016, to July 1, 2017. Eight of the fifteen counties were in the Texas Triangle.[4] These included all of the core counties in the Texas Triangle metros, plus several of the ring, or suburban, counties, as shown in table 4.1.

In percent growth, Texas had three counties of the fastest-growing counties among the top five in the nation between 2016 and 2017, according to the same US Census report. Comal County (New Braunfels) was number two with 5.1 percent growth, or a gain of 6,867 people. Hays County (San Marcos) was number four with 5 percent growth, or 10,140 more people. Kendall County (Boerne) was number five with 4.9 percent growth, or 2,062 additional people.

In a separate report issued one month later in April 2018, the US Census Bureau listed the nation's one hundred fastest-growing

Table 4.1

Texas counties led US population gains, 2016–17

Maricopa County, AZ	73,650
Clark County, NV	47,355
Riverside County, CA	36,744
Harris County, TX	**35,939**
Tarrant County, TX	**32,729**
King County, WA	32,687
Bexar County, TX	**30,831**
Dallas County, TX	**30,686**
Denton County, TX	**27,911**
Collin County, TX	**27,150**
Hillsborough County, FL	26,939
Orange County, FL	25,377
Wake County, NC	23,060
Fort Bend County, TX	**22,870**
Travis County, TX	**22,116**

Source: US Census Bureau, 2017 population estimates, July 1, 2016, to July 1, 2017.

counties by percentage with a population of ten thousand or more between July 1, 2016, and July 1, 2017. Even in this deeper list, Texas dominated with twenty-three counties among the top one hundred.[5] Twenty of those twenty-three counties were in the Texas Triangle. Florida had ten counties on the list. California had one.

The US Census Bureau went further by ranking the top one hundred US counties in percentage population growth between the 2010 US Census official count, dated April 1, 2010, and the bureau's July 1, 2017, estimate. Texas had twenty-one counties on that seven-year growth list, eighteen of them in the Texas Triangle. Florida had ten counties on the list. California had none.

The evidence of the rising migration to the Texas Triangle kept mounting. One month later, in May 2018, the US Census issued another report—"Census Bureau Reveals Fastest-Growing Large

Cities." This report ranked numeric population gains by cities, measuring growth within specific city limits.

The number-one city was San Antonio with a gain in population of 24,208 between July 1, 2016, and July 1, 2017.[6] San Antonio's 1.6 percent growth rate for that twelve-month period translated into net population growth of sixty-six people per day in San Antonio.

Four other Texas Triangle cities were among the top fifteen fastest-growing cities, as shown in table 4.2.

According to Texas State Demographer Lloyd Potter during the 2018 Texas Demographic Center annual conference,

San Antonio was adding more people than any other city in the country in that year. It was the first time San Antonio has had

Table 4.2

The fifteen US cities with the largest numeric increases, 2016–17

San Antonio, TX	24,208
Phoenix, AZ	24,036
Dallas, TX	18,935
Fort Worth, TX	18,664
Los Angeles, CA	18,643
Seattle, WA	17,490
Charlotte, NC	15,551
Columbus, OH	15,429
Frisco, TX	13,470
Atlanta, GA	13,323
San Diego, CA	12,834
Austin, TX	12,515
Jacksonville, FL	11,169
Irvine, CA	11,068
Henderson, NV	10,534

Source: US Census Bureau, numeric population increases between July 1, 2016, and July 1, 2017, populations of fifty thousand or more in 2016.

that distinction. One-third of cities adding people more than any other are in Texas (five of the fastest-growing top fifteen). That is not an insignificant thing. Notice who is not on [the list]. Houston has been one of these that has been at the very top [of population growth rankings]. Houston added a little more than eight thousand people (between 2016 and 2017). That's a dramatic shift for Houston. Why is that happening? My speculation is that it would have to do with the downturn in the price of oil. This is before [Hurricane] Harvey [which flooded Houston in August 2017]. Harvey is not represented here at all.

The same report listed the most populous cities in the United States as of July 1, 2017. For the first time, the Texas Triangle had five cities among the largest fifteen cities in the nation. Fort Worth in 2017 had edged out Indianapolis, Indiana, to reach number fifteen. Fort Worth later rose to number thirteen.

California had four cities among the top fifteen largest in the nation in 2017—Los Angeles, San Diego, San Jose, and San Francisco, in order of ranking. No other state had more than one city ranked. But it should be noted that the populations in the five core Texas Triangle cities in the top fifteen totaled 6.99 million people, far fewer than the nation's number-one city on the list, New York City, with 8.62 million people under one mayor.

In June 2018, the Texas Demographic Center issued new population estimates for Texas metro areas as of January 1, 2017, which also showed the population growth in those metro areas between

Table 4.3

Texas Triangle metros population gains and percentages, 2010–17

Dallas–Fort Worth–Arlington	894,403	13.9%
Houston–The Woodlands–Sugar Land	874,841	14.8%
Austin–Round Rock	347,123	20.2%
San Antonio–New Braunfels	299,395	14%
State of Texas	2,913,772	11.6%

Source: Texas Demographic Center.

the revised 2010 US Census and January 1, 2017, as shown in table 4.3.

While the state of Texas population grew by 11.6 percent overall during the 2010–17 period, only seven of the state's twenty-five metros exceeded that percentage. All four Texas Triangle metro areas grew more than the state average, led by Austin–Round Rock's 20.2 percent population growth.[7]

The rising population numbers for the Texas Triangle metros are huge and impressive. But where did all this population growth come from?

The question of Texas' population change was explored in-depth during the 2018 Texas Demographic Conference held in Austin. Natural increase, the difference between births and deaths, accounted for 52.5 percent of the increase in population statewide between 2011 and 2017. Net domestic migration, the number of people moving to Texas from other US states minus the number of Texans leaving for other states, accounted for 19.8 percent of the state's population rise. In more practical terms, in 2018, about five hundred more babies were born daily in Texas than the number of people who died, and about five hundred more people, domestically and internationally, were moving to Texas than the number who were moving away, according to the Texas Demographic Center. The international and domestic migration numbers made Texas the fastest-growing state in numeric growth and percent population growth between 2010 and 2017, according to the Texas Demographic Center, citing US Census Bureau estimates.[8]

Texas grew by 2.91 million people over the seven years from 2010 to 2017, an 11.6 percent increase. California grew by 2.28 million for a 6.1 percent change. Florida's population rose by 2.18 million for an 11.6 percent increase. The national population percent increase was 5.5 percent.

Most of the domestic migration, from other states, flowed into the Texas Triangle's suburban counties that ring the large cities, according to the Texas Demographic Center. The center cited the top fifty counties in the nation for percent growth between 2015 and 2016. Eleven of the counties were in the Texas Triangle. The percentages of the population growth during that period from

Table 4.4

Percent of migrant growth in Texas counties among the top fifty in US population growth, 2015–16

Kendall (Boerne)	95.9
Comal (New Braunfels)	88.5
Bastrop (Bastrop city)	83.5
Hays (San Marcos)	82.2
Rockwall (Rockwall city)	82.2
Kaufman (Kaufman city)	81.3
Ellis (Waxahachie)	78.1
Williamson (Georgetown)	74.1
Fort Bend (Sugar Land)	59.4

domestic migration to the following counties was staggering, as seen by the examples in table 4.4.

In other words, almost all the population growth in those counties came from people moving to Texas from other states. And several of these counties were among the fastest-growing in the nation.

"All of these counties are growing," Potter said during the conference. "If you drive through them, you see all kinds of indicators of infrastructure development. There's a lot of detour signs, orange cones, big-box stores, sitting in traffic in a lot of them if you are anywhere close to rush hour. These places are growing really fast. Growth from domestic migration puts an instant demand on infrastructure, and infrastructure takes a long time to plan and to put into place. You have to issue bonds. You have to plan the whole thing. You have to hire and contract, to build highways, to build schools, and so on."

Between 2011 and 2017, Texas led both Florida and California in total population change each year, according to the Texas Demographic Center. California led Texas and Florida in natural increase each year, with Florida showing very small numbers in births, which could be explained by its popularity as a retirement state. California also led against Texas and Florida in annual increases in international net migration. From 2011 to 2014, Texas led Florida in domestic net migration, but Florida led Texas from 2015 to 2017—a shift that, Potter said, can be explained by low oil prices that slowed the flow of energy workers into Texas' drilling fields. From 2011 to 2017, California lost more people each year to other states than it gained from other states. "Many of them are moving to Texas," Potter said.

Push, Pull

"There's an incredible dynamic that's been at work in Texas generally and especially in the Triangle at least for the past forty years," notes Bernard Weinstein, SMU economist and associate director of SMU's Maguire Energy Institute in Dallas. Weinstein continues,

> I've lived here since 1975, and the population of D/FW has doubled. I'm sure that's true of Austin and Houston, and San Antonio and Austin are growing together. It's been a combination of push and pull factors. When I moved here from New York I was impressed by how different the political environment was. Everybody you met, whether in the business community or the political community, would tell you their number-one priority was business and economic development. That hasn't changed in forty years. That's the mantra of business leaders, chambers of commerce, every governor regardless of party. They've been focused on economic development, job creation, bringing businesses here from every part of the country, every part of the world. That hasn't changed.

In the interview, Weinstein goes on to describe why numerous Californians and New Yorkers have moved to Texas:

> It's the combination of push and pull. The push factors of California, and this would be true of New York and other high-cost states, are the high cost of living, high taxes, lots

of government regulation, housing costs, utility costs, traffic problems, lots of disamenities. Manhattan is booming. [But] you look at New York state overall, their economy is going down the toilet. New York State has been losing people for twenty years. Even the New York metropolitan region is losing people. But there is the facade of Manhattan. Everyone wants to be there. There is lots of construction. The pull factors [drawing people to Texas are] the positive public policy that results in fairly low taxation (although when you put state and local taxes together, we're in the middle of the pack), but we have no personal income tax. We have high property taxes. For high-income individuals, that lack of a personal income tax is a big draw. It is even a bigger draw because of the [US president Donald] Trump tax cut because it limits the income-tax deduction for state and local taxes. You might have been in the 13 percent marginal income tax bracket in California, but you could write it all off. You now can write only some of it off. [There's] the ease of starting a business and doing business. We have good infrastructure here. We all complain about roads and traffic, but if you moved here from New York or California, you don't complain about the traffic in D/FW. Our infrastructure is in relatively good shape. It's not as important a factor as it used to be, but being a right-to-work state was a plus for Texas, but unionization has left the private sector. Utility costs are cheaper here. People don't leave California because of the weather, but people do leave the Northeast because of the weather. They want that more temperate climate. So it's a combination of push factors in some parts of the country and pull factors. Growth begets growth. One of five new jobs created in the United States was in Texas during the last decade. That generates interest in investing here.

Age, Ethnic Dynamics

The ages of the people moving to Texas are revealing. Most of the people who arrived in Texas between 2005 and 2013 were in the eighteen to forty-four age range, 55.9 percent. Another

15.1 percent were in the forty-five to sixty-four age range. Together, 71 percent of the people moving to Texas during those years were working-age people. Only 5.2 percent were in the retirement-age range, sixty-five and older. Only 23.8 percent were children under the age of eighteen. Most of the arrivals were men in the working-age range. For example, in 2013, men moving to Texas from other states in the eighteen to forty-four age range numbered 52,202. Women totaled 30,691. Only in the retirement-age range, sixty-five and older, did women outnumber men in 2013.

Ethnically, Anglos are moving to Texas in higher percentages than the existing state population. According to a Texas Demographic Center report, "From 2005 through 2013, Anglos comprised 54.3 percent of all domestic in-migrants but only 46.2 percent of the Texas population. Hispanics made up the second largest of domestic migrants in Texas. However, unlike Anglos, the 22.4 percent Hispanic share of domestic in-migration was less than this group's 36.8 percent share of the total Texas population."[9]

Where are the transplants to Texas from other states moving from?

"California is our biggest sender, followed by New York and Louisiana. There's been significant flows from Louisiana historically. Illinois, the Chicago area, have had people moving to Texas," Potter explained.

The Dallas Fed mostly agreed in its 2018 "Gone to Texas" article: "In the post-recession period (starting in 2010), 12 percent of domestic migrants to Texas came from California, followed by Florida (6 percent) and Oklahoma and Louisiana (both 5 percent). These are gross (not net) measures of migration. Migration from populous state in part reflects their larger populations; California is 12 percent of the U.S. population, so it's not surprising that 12 percent of migrants to Texas come from there."[10]

Further evidence of Texas' popularity for outside residents came in early 2019, when Phoenix-based U-Haul reported that Texas led the nation in 2018 in the number of U-Haul truck shipments into the state versus the number leaving the state.[11] Texas also led the nation for 2016 and 2017. Texas increased its arrivals of U-Haul rentals by 5 percent from 2017. Most of the U-Haul rentals came to the Houston, Dallas–Fort Worth, and Austin areas, all in the Texas Triangle. The states with the most U-Haul rentals leaving versus those arriving were Illinois, California, and Michigan. The rankings were based on more than two million one-way U-Haul rentals during 2018. A U-Haul press release states, "While migration trends do not correlate directly to population or economic growth, U-Haul growth data is an effective gauge of how well states and cities are attracting and maintaining residents."

One thing is for sure: Texas does not have to pay people a cash incentive to move there. Vermont, on the other hand, does. In 2018, Vermont approved legislation that would pay up to $10,000 to one hundred people starting in 2019. The Remote Worker Grant Program would cover costs to people already employed out of the state to move to Vermont and do their work there. In 2018, Vermont had sixteen thousand fewer workers than it did in 2009, according to the governor.[12] The Vermont population in 2017 was 623,657, number forty-nine in the nation and about sixty thousand people fewer than in the Texas city of El Paso.[13]

Employment Factor

This all adds up to one main message: people were coming to Texas to work.

The Texas Workforce Commission has reported numbers confirming the large labor demand in Texas. The top six Texas counties in the number of help-wanted job listings during February 2017

Table 4.5

Dallas County	72,737
Harris County	59,990
Travis County	41,262
Bexar County	32,372
Tarrant County	25,077
Collin County	14,968

were in the Texas Triangle, and all had open-job listings of more than ten thousand, as seen in table 4.5.[14]

The job openings often require skills and pay well. Truck drivers were most in demand in help-wanted advertising during a ninety-day period ending in February 2017. Also among the top

Table 4.6

Number 2	Registered nurses
Number 3	Retail supervisors
Number 6	Software application developers
Number 7	Office supervisors
Number 10	Web developers
Number 11	Computer system network administrators
Number 12	Computer system analysts
Number 16	Accountants

Source: Texas Workforce Commission.

twenty occupations with the most help-wanted ads were higher-skill, higher-paying positions, including those shown in table 4.6.

"Domestic migration is driven by demand for labor. We have a lot of people moving into the state because our population in Texas is not growing fast enough. If Texas had not been becoming more diverse in terms of race and ethnic composition, we'd be in big trouble economically. We probably would not have grown and been growing the way we are now without our increasingly diverse population," Potter said.

"What motivates domestic migration?" the Dallas Fed article asks rhetorically. "Surveys such as the Current Population Survey ask people who moved why they did so. Just over half of cross-state movers to Texas relocated for a job (53.1 percent), another 24 percent for family reasons and 20 percent for cheaper housing or other amenities such as a shorter commute."

"Family reasons" are tied indirectly to job opportunities. When one member of a family finds a new job in another state, their family members usually follow. This could include immediate family members, retired parents, and other relatives.

According to Potter,

> There are people coming to Texas from other states because of economic opportunities and, of course, they bring family members, and then there are people moving here to retire. Sometimes they [retirees] would be joining family members who are here. You have maybe someone who came here for a job and then their parents come here to retire. They are needing assisted living or coming to spend more time with the grandchildren, that kind of thing. We see that being a factor. There is a pretty good proportion of migration that happens for family reasons. That is on the backside of economic migration.

When people moved to states other than Texas, only 43 percent said it was for employment, the Dallas Fed article adds: "Employment opportunities in Texas are a clear draw. Besides adding jobs at a rapid clip, employment growth in the state has been widespread across industries and has required a wide skill distribution. Since the end of the Great Recession, every major industry has added jobs led by 35 percent gains in professional and business services, 22 percent in construction and 33 percent in leisure and hospitality."

The jobs have been available almost entirely in the urbanized part of the Texas, especially the Texas Triangle metros, Potter said during the 2018 demographics conference, referring to a map: "Here's the population triangle. The points of the triangle are really where the population dynamics are very vibrant, especially in terms of growth."

The story in much of rural Texas is different, Potter added:

> There are a number of our counties, about ninety, that are losing population. All of them would be classified as rural, certainly nonmetro. They are not growing in employment opportunities there. The economies tend to be agriculturally oriented, but agriculture is increasingly becoming capitalized. There is consolidation of ranches and farms, so there is less demand

for labor in much of rural Texas. Young people that are born there [have graduated] out of high school. They are either going to look for work, and they won't find it in their county of origin, or they will go to the population triangle or one of these population centers out west, or they are going to go to school, but there's probably not even a community college in many of these counties. You have the continued urbanization of the population. The other piece of this is after young people move out and are entering the reproductive ages, they are not having their babies back in their counties of origin. They are having their babies in the population triangle or urbanized areas. They have left behind their moms and dads, which affects the aging structure. In about a third of the counties, you have natural decrease. There are more deaths than births occurring in about a third of these counties. Every year, there [are] a couple of other counties that shift over to that decrease component.

Eighty-two of Texas' 254 counties are urban, and the state has twenty-five MSAs. In 1910, the state's population was 24.1 percent urban. By 2010, it was 84.7 percent urban, creating what the Texas Demographic Center calls "a growing population divide."

"There is a general pattern where migration, mostly originating outside of Texas, is adding substantially to the populations of the state's largest [metro areas]," according to the third migration report released by the Texas Demographic Center in October 2017. "The non-metropolitan areas also have rates of natural increase that are much lower than those of the [metros]. These differences between the metropolitan and non-metropolitan areas suggest a future where the state's population becomes increasingly urbanized and regional patterns of population growth become more disparate. This could leave large areas of Texas with more limited access to employment, medical care, educational opportunities and other goods and services. . . . External migration is sharpening the existing demographic differences between the urban and rural areas of Texas."

This trend is not new in Texas, but urbanization has occurred at greater volumes in recent decades as the overall state population expanded. Families have transitioned from making a living off undeveloped land, on farms and ranches, to starting careers in the knowledge economy inside paved, urban jungles. This trend of urbanization at the expense of rural areas has been rife with human drama. This has long been noticed by Texas artists. Texas novelist Larry McMurtry, a native of Archer County, addressed the changing culture of Texas and the restlessness of its rural youth in the 1960s in his early fiction such as *Horseman, Pass By* (later made into the movie *Hud*), *Leaving Cheyenne*, and *The Last Picture Show*. In more recent years, movies based on Cormac McCarthy novels also portrayed rural restlessness and sometimes desperation, especially *No Country for Old Men* and *All the Pretty Horses*. These stories, and others, raised awareness worldwide of Texas as a place of painful cultural and economic transition as the population growth of Dallas, Fort Worth, Houston, San Antonio, and Austin began to kick into high gear.

One sign that rural Texas areas are losing population to the urban Texas Triangle is that Dairy Queen restaurants—an iconic small-town cultural restaurant chain for the state since 1950 where rural Texans gather for coffee and meet after Friday-night high school football games—are going dark. They are closing in small towns. In October 2017 alone, twenty-seven Dairy Queens were shuttered in Texas. Dairy Queen headquarters is in Minneapolis, Minnesota, but Texas has six hundred of its restaurants. The *Houston Chronicle* newspaper in 2018 featured the closing of one Dairy Queen in San Augustine, in East Texas between Nacogdoches and the Louisiana border: "Dairy Queens, as it happens, are not disappearing from Texas—they're just moving. They're expanding in major metropolitan areas like Houston and Dallas, reflecting the growing urbanization of the state. Rural Texas is shrinking, the Dairy Queens boarding up, the small towns becoming smaller. Back in 1971, about 2,500 people in San Augustine welcomed the new Dairy Queen; about 1,900 remained to see it go."[15]

International Immigration

Net international migration, or immigration, accounts for even more population growth in Texas than net domestic migration growth, with immigration accounting for 27.7 percent of population growth in 2017 compared to domestic migration growth of 19.8 percent, although the balance between the two categories has shifted back and forth since 2011.

International immigration is an entirely different dynamic from domestic migration in Texas, and the sources of international immigration have evolved in surprising ways also.

International immigration is divided into two categories, authorized immigration and unauthorized immigration, Potter explained in an interview:

> Authorized immigration is less driven by economics. Usually it has to do with family reunification. You will have someone who is here maybe foreign-born and has legal status, whether a green card or something, that enables them to sponsor family members. That is where much of international flow comes from.
>
> We have unauthorized international immigration as well. The bulk of that, generally speaking, is economically driven, coming here from Mexico, to work. There are refugee flows. A lot of people equate that with illegal immigration, but it is not illegal immigration if they are coming here claiming asylum. In the common vernacular, it is kind of the same thing.

The Dallas Fed article points out that illegal immigration declined after the 2007–9 Great Recession: "Migrant apprehensions along the Southwest border have declined 75 percent from their peak of 1.6 million in 2000. About 52 of the foreign-born population in Texas is from Mexico. Other growing flows include high-skilled immigrants from China and South Asian nations."

According to the Dallas Fed, "The total undocumented population in Texas is an estimated 1.65 million, about 6.1 percent of the state's population, with large shares from Mexico and Central America."

"That's not insignificant," Potter observed during the demographic conference. "When you see twenty people in Texas, one of them is unauthorized."

The sources of international immigration have changed. In 2005, Latin America was the source of 69.4 percent of noncitizen immigrants to Texas. A decade later, in 2015, that percentage had fallen to 44.1 percent. Taking up the difference was the increasing number of Asian immigrants to Texas; they accounted for 17.3 percent of immigrants to Texas in 2005. A decade later, the percentage had risen to 35.8 percent.

"That's a big shift in a relatively short period of time for migrants. We are seeing a dramatic increase in immigrants from Asian countries. China and India are the two biggest senders," Potter said during the 2018 Texas Demographic Conference.

In the San Antonio area, immigration flows from Mexico and Central America (37.9 percent of its total immigration) barely outnumbered Asian flows (36.5 percent) between 2010 and 2014, according to the Texas Demographic Center, citing US Census Bureau data from its American Communities Survey reports.

But Asian immigrants dominated the Austin, Dallas–Fort Worth, and Houston metros during the same period. Dallas–Fort Worth saw the most Asian immigrants, at 43.9 percent of its total immigration, with the Houston area drawing 38.2 percent and Austin at 37.9 percent. In those three metros, Mexico and Central American immigration all were less than 30 percent.

A clear urban-versus-rural division exists on the preferences of where immigrants settle in Texas, depending on their origins. According to the Texas Demographic Center's fourth migration report, released in November 2017, immigrants from Mexico and Central America between 2010 and 2014 accounted for 69.1 percent of all immigrants to rural Texas. The percent for urban Texas was only 33.1 percent from Mexico and Central America. In urban Texas, Asian immigrants dominated with 37.6 percent. The Texas Demographic Center also noted that foreign immigrants were more likely than domestic migrants from other states and from rural Texas to settle in the core counties of the large metro areas because of housing availability, employment opportunities, family ties, and social networks.

According to the Texas Demographic Center report, "The mixing of people from various origins is often a catalyst for social change. In contemporary Texas, the state's large metropolitan areas are the focal points of this fusion. . . . In time, this [population] redistribution has the potential to realign existing political and cultural boundaries within Texas' largest urban areas."

As the population of the Texas Triangle has expanded, the Triangle has become more diverse ethnically, bringing different ideas and approaches to commerce. Because of the combination of births, domestic migration, and international immigration, the Texas Triangle has positioned a faster-growing labor force than the United States as a whole.

The Dallas Fed article makes the difference clear: "The Texas Demographic Center's projections suggest that if migration into the state continues at the 2000–2010 pace, the working-age population will increase 1.8 percent annually through 2035. Pew Research Center projections for the United States, meanwhile, suggest that immigration at current levels will be enough to counteract the trend of retiring baby boomers and lead to a modest 0.3 percent annual growth rate percent of the working age population."

How Texas Grows More Rapidly Than Other States

"**W**hen you think about why some states grow faster than others, you basically have to answer two questions: Where do people want to live, and where can companies maximize profits? The cost of living and the cost of doing business play a big role in that. Texas always has had an advantage," said Federal Reserve Bank of Dallas Senior Economist Keith Phillips in 2018.

The key word from that quote might be *always*. Economic and population growth in Texas, especially in the Texas Triangle, has been a long-term phenomenon for at least fifty years. For most of that period, for example, Texas outperformed the United States as a whole in job creation.

Texas employment rose at an average annual rate of 4.5 percent between 1960 and 1980, while the US rate increased by 2.7 percent, according to the Dallas Fed. Over the next twenty-year period ending in 2000, the gap narrowed, with Texas employment growing by 2.4 percent compared to the nation's 1.9 percent. After 2000, until about 2015, the US average annual employment rate was just 0.4 percent, while the rate in Texas grew at 1.6 percent.[1]

"Taken together, this works out to about a 1 percentage point growth advantage over the nation since 1960. The recent oil boom and Texas' avoidance of a housing bust have been offered as ways to explain Texas' recent strength. But these factors—while undeniably contributing to Texas' economic resilience over the past few years—cannot account for a consistent growth advantage over 50 years," writes Jason Saving, a Dallas Fed senior research economist.

Housing

Population growth has been one propellant for economic growth, which we discussed in the previous chapter. Another magnet has been abundant, cheap housing: "Texas metros have the ability to expand outward as far as the eye can see—and largely chose to let this expansion proceed rather than thwart it with restrictive zoning laws," Saving writes.

The key measure of home affordability anywhere is the share of any metropolitan area's housing that is affordable for the area's median-income household. In 2005, 61.9 percent of the Dallas area's houses were affordable to median-income households. In other Texas Triangle cities, the percentages were 62.6 percent in Houston, 70.7 percent in Fort Worth, 64.9 percent in San Antonio, and 61.5 percent in Austin, according to a public presentation prepared by Keith Phillips.

Phillips compared those percentages to the ones in New York City, where 8.6 percent of houses were affordable to median-income households—they were affordable to 3.6 percent in Los Angeles, 8.9 percent in San Francisco, 5.1 percent in San Diego, and 22 percent in Miami. This was near the height of the housing price bubble that began to burst in 2008. Texas therefore was better positioned to weather the housing price collapse when foreclosures zoomed.

In 2017, the housing affordability gap was narrower, but the Texas price advantage was still pronounced. That year, 46.9 percent of Dallas's houses were affordable. In other Texas Triangle cities, the percentages were 62 percent in Houston, 61.2 percent in Fort Worth, 59.3 percent in San Antonio, and 54.8 percent in Austin. The percent of affordable housing in San Francisco in 2017 was still low at 7.6 percent and in Los Angeles at 9.9 percent, but affordability had increased to 34.6 percent in New York City, 34.5 percent in Miami, and 20.1 percent in San Diego. In other words, Texas house prices rose only slightly relative to household income levels and maintained a significant positive edge over other US cities.

According to Phillips's presentation,

> Historically, Texas has been a very affordable place to live. For example, a worker moving from Silicon Valley to Austin with the same salary could afford a much larger home for less money. . . . While the relative strength in the Texas economy and our housing markets since the Great Recession [2007–9] has reduced affordability in Texas metros, Texas metros still generally remain affordable relative to the very large metros across the nation. However, if housing costs keep escalating at a rapid pace in the future, this may reduce the relative attractiveness of the state's economy and reduce its long-term growth.

Education

One answer to where people want to live is educational quality. People naturally want to live in neighborhoods with above-average public schools and opportunities for excellent higher education. Texas frankly is behind in education attainment and spending statistically, but the topic has been discussed widely and intensely for decades as a matter of top priority. Texas has made some strides in improving its public education system, if test scores are an indication. In 1992, eighth-grade math test scores in Texas public schools were slightly below the US average. By 2003, the scores were nearly identical, with Texas ranking thirty-third among the states. By 2015, however, eighth-grade math test scores had risen above the US average, lifting Texas to twenty-second among the states, according to Phillips's presentation that cited National Assessment of Educational Progress data.

"Texas achieves an unusually high level of performance for its education dollars. Looking solely at per capita K-12 education expenditures, Texas ranks forty-sixth out of the nation's 50 states," Saving writes in his "Why Texas Grows Faster" essay. "Despite this relatively low level of expenditure, Texas' high school graduation rate ranks around the national average. . . . Even more encouragingly, children of each ethnicity generally outperformed their ethnic peers, with Texas Blacks and Hispanics scoring above the national averages for Black and Hispanic students. This suggests that while there are very likely areas where more money could improve student performance, Texas teachers and administrators do remarkably well with the resources they are given."

That may be so, but the image of Texas as a state that underspends and underachieves in education has persisted because of a funding system that has not provided the means for the state to achieve what it could. In 2019, the Texas Legislature approved an education reform law called House Bill 3, also known as HB3, which raised public education funding and teacher salaries, reduced the amount property-rich school districts give up for poorer districts, and sought to reduce property taxes. But most observers agree that HB3 was only the first step toward bringing the state's public education spending up to national standards.

Average expenditures per student in Texas during the 2011–12 academic year were $10,541, lower than the US average of $12,201. The public high school graduation rate in Texas was 66.9 percent, below the US rate of 70.5 percent, according to "Texas' Education Challenge," an essay by Marta Tienda in the 2015 Dallas Fed book, *Ten-Gallon Economy*.[2]

Tienda writes, "Partly due to vigorous demographic growth, Texas has been producing outsized numbers of high school graduates—more than any other state in the union. Furthermore, the number of diploma recipients is expected to continue growing through 2025, providing a large pool of potential college students for the state to fuel economic productivity and long-term growth."

Texas still has ground to make up to reach average US education attainment levels. In 2010, only 26 percent of Texans aged twenty-five to thirty-four held a bachelor's degree or higher. The national average that year was 31.2 percent.

That said, the state's overall education attainment statistics are likely to improve, since net domestic migration since 2010 has included large numbers of skilled, working-age people.

Indeed, by 2015, the percentage of Texans aged twenty-five and older who held a bachelor's degree or higher had risen to 28.4 percent, according to the Texas Demographic Center.[3] But the increase did not necessarily mean the state was making strides in educating more Texans in colleges and universities.

"[The education attainment improvement] is consistent with the shift in demand for skilled labor," said Lloyd Potter during a 2018 Texas demographic conference in Austin. He continued,

> How much of this is happening because we are doing a better job of educating Texans and how much is this happening because people are moving here with college degrees or some postsecondary education? My guess is that a good proportion of this . . . has to do with people moving here. From an economic perspective, that's a pretty good deal because California is educating all of these people coming here and filling jobs in our economy. We're not having to pay for it. But when you talk to parents in Texas, they are like, "I want my kid to get the educational attainment. If low-skilled labor comes from California, that's okay, as long as my kid is getting the high-skilled, high-paying job." From an objective and financial perspective, it's great that other states are educating our labor force, but from a humanistic and family and values perspective, we want to be educating ourselves.

That is one way of expressing the goal of boosting education attainment in a state with a large, young Hispanic population growing into their employment years. However, Texas may not be able to forever offset its below-average education attainment levels by luring better-educated people from elsewhere to move to the Lone Star State and its large cities.

Taxes

People understandably prefer to live where taxes are relatively low.

Texas' tax burden is generally low, an average of 82.5 percent of the national average for state governments, which includes adjustments to account for city and local school taxes. In 2011, average state taxes per capita in Texas amounted to $3,536 compared to the national average of $4,295, according to the Dallas Fed. In California for that year, average state taxes per capita were $4,914. In New York, they amounted to $7,436.

Below-average tax burdens in Texas largely reflect a limited state government that administers fewer public services and whose elected leaders have restricted powers.

The Texas governor's powers are limited mainly to vetoing state legislative acts, calling legislative special sessions to address specific topics, and making certain appointments, such as to university boards of regents. Rick Perry, who served as governor of Texas from 2000 to 2015, enlarged the governor's constitutionally limited powers somewhat by winning passage of legislation in 2003, which created the Texas Enterprise Fund. The fund has given the governor's office, with approval of the speaker of the Texas House of Representatives and the lieutenant governor, the ability to award cash incentives to companies investing in Texas.

Many people regard the position of lieutenant governor as the most powerful in Texas because the lieutenant governor presides over the Texas Senate, a role that controls the flow of legislation.

Although many states have legislative bodies that convene every year, the Texas Legislature, with 150 House members and 31 senators, meets only 140 days every two years, except for special sessions called by the governor, as stipulated by the Texas Constitution. The regular biennial sessions start in mid-January and conclude by the end of May. Even with those limitations, many Texans continue to believe that a biennial session of 140 days is too long. Everyone who has worked at the state capitol building in Austin—lawmakers, staffers, lobbyists, and the media alike—has heard the joke that the Texas Constitution contains a typographical error, that its initial authors instead had intended a legislature that meets for two days every 140 years.

The distrust of government reflected in parts of the Texas Constitution can be tied directly to the state's history. The bloody struggle to separate from Mexico's antislavery government was followed by Texas' own difficult existence as an independent nation from 1836 to 1845, wedged between a still-hostile Mexico and the growing United States. As a US state, Texas resisted efforts to restrict the westward spread of slavery and ultimately seceded to join the Confederacy. After the Civil War and finally but reluctantly shorn of slavery, some white Texans were further alienated from the government by the activities of so-called carpetbaggers from the North, whom they resented for exploiting the chaos of the postwar Reconstruction era and for placing Blacks in public office. The 1876 Texas Constitution, which severely limits the size of the state government and its governmental powers, remains the basic law of the state. A 1974 convention of elected lawmakers to write a new, streamlined, and modern state constitution failed to produce a new document for a statewide vote.

Many business leaders and conservative public officials in Texas draw a strong connection between limited government and economic growth. For instance, Jason Saving's research suggests that government spending on infrastructure, public safety, and public education are the forms that most directly foster economic growth.

According to Saving, Texas "offers one of the smallest safety nets in the nation. . . . Its income cutoff for Medicaid benefits is one-sixth the national average, for example, and it generally does not extend coverage to able-bodied adults without children. A small safety net enables the state to offer a relatively low tax burden on individuals and businesses, fostering entrepreneurial activity and attracting high-skilled residents of other states to Texas."

In other words, when it comes to low-income people needing assistance often available in other states, in Texas they must rely on charities, churches, family members, friends, and neighbors more than on state government. This is not without irony. Many of the federal government's social and welfare programs stemmed from the "Great Society" programs that date back to the 1960s and the administration of then president Lyndon B. Johnson, a Texan.

Nevertheless, Texas' low-tax, low-regulation reputation remains attractive to business investments, which, in turn, lead to steady employment growth.

Texas famously does not levy a state income tax. Opposition to a state income tax remains steadfast in the state. It would take a constitutional amendment approved by voters to introduce a state income tax. A state constitutional amendment in 2019 approved by Texas voters doubled that ban. The state levies a 6.25 percent retail sales tax, on which local governments can add up to an additional 2 percent for general revenue purposes. Critics of the state's reliance on sales taxes argue that sales taxes are the most regressive form of taxation widely used in the United States, since they make lower-income households spend more of their income on basic needs. The state also imposes a variety of user fees, such as the gasoline tax, an energy severance tax, a motor vehicle sales tax, "sin taxes" on alcohol and cigarettes, and a business tax, called the margin tax, as well as a state lottery. Otherwise, the Texas state government largely pushes off other tax-levying responsibilities to local governments, such as property taxes to finance municipalities, county governments, public school districts, community college districts, and hospital districts, among others. These property taxes combine for some of the highest total property tax rates among the states. But with the absence of a state income tax, the overall tax burden remains below the national average.

The Texas business tax, called the margin tax, is probably the most disliked state tax. The margin tax was instituted in 2006 to replace the previous state business tax, called the franchise tax. The franchise tax, levied on corporations, was based on "earned surplus," which was the combination of federal taxable income plus executive and director compensation. Many Texas companies used loopholes to escape the tax.[4] But in 2005, the Texas Supreme Court declared the state's public-school financing system unconstitutional, leaving state government the task of restructuring some of its tax system. The franchise tax was abandoned in favor of the margin tax, which is a tax on revenues, not profits, minus a complex set of deductions, depending on the type of company. Retailers and wholesalers, for example, can deduct the cost of goods sold.

The margin tax has never produced the revenues for state government that had been projected, raising only 9.3 percent of total state tax collections in 2014 compared to nearly 54 percent from the state sales tax. But the margin tax has been unpopular because of its complexity and the fact that companies that lose money are still taxed on revenues. Fortunately for Texas, 2005 was also about the same time that the revolutionary technologies of horizontal drilling and hydraulic fracturing (or "fracking") started to produce a surge in oil and gas output in the state, dramatically increasing the energy severance tax collections. Each legislative session, bills are filed to eliminate the margin tax, but only reductions in tax rates and increases in revenue exemptions have whittled down the burden of the business tax. A simple solution would be a tax rate based on each company's federal income tax burden to raise a certain amount of state revenue, which would reduce the margin tax's complexity, since companies must calculate their federal income taxes anyway. But that solution is widely opposed because it would put an income tax on the books in Texas, possibly leading to an individual income tax. Again, for better or worse, income taxes are just not allowed in Texas. According to Saving's essay, "Studies have found Texas to be among the most regressive states in the nation in both the taxes it imposes and the services it provides, which may exacerbate income inequality. The state has the highest (medical) uninsured rate in the nation and a relatively high poverty rate. Other studies have found issues with pollution, infrastructure and health that cannot be easily addressed within current policy parameters. . . . It can certainly be said that Texas has chosen to prioritize economic growth over these concerns, with all the costs and benefits such a choice entails."

Profits

Can companies maximize profits in Texas, given its low-tax, low-regulation regime?

The large number of corporations, including Fortune 500 companies, with headquarters in the Texas Triangle seems to confirm that. Texas regularly has been number one on the list of best states for business in the Connecticut-based *Chief Executive* magazine. In its 2018 list, Texas was number one partly because it had the "fastest-growing metropolis," referring to the Texas Triangle's San Antonio–Austin corridor: "While the Lone Star state's growth cooled with the collapse of oil prices, Texas still boasts one of the fastest-growing regions in the country. According to data from the U.S. Bureau of Economic Analysis, Austin-Round Rock and San Antonio-New Braunfels each had the highest GDP growth of any metropolitan area in the nation in 2016, 5 percent and 5.9 percent respectively. That's more than double the 2.5 percent average of U.S. metropolitan areas."[5]

In another 2018 article, *Chief Executive* listed Texas as number one among "Five States to Watch":

> Texas has lots of advantages, and one of the biggest reasons it may stay No. 1 perpetually in the Chief Executive survey is something that will never change: its location. "That's not talked about much, but from D/FW airport, you can fly almost anywhere non-stop, and that's a terrific advantage for a national company like us," says Don Daseke, CEO of Daseke, which owns flatbed trucking companies across the US. Plus, notes economic development consultant Dennis Cuneo, Texas "borders Mexico, so it gets all that NAFTA [North American Free Trade Agreement] trade. Florida is becoming the [trade] gateway to South America, but the biggest trade flows are in NAFTA—and Texas is right in the middle of that."[6]

In 2018, Texas ranked second on the Small Business & Entrepreneurship Council's Small Business Policy Index, which ranks states on policies and costs.

According to the council's rankings, "Among key positives, the state imposes no personal, individual capital gains, corporate income, corporate capital gains and death taxes. In addition, Texas has fairly low unemployment taxes, workers' compensation costs, low gas and diesel taxes, ties for the lowest energy regulation burden, imposes no annual fee on LLCs [limited liability companies], is a right-to-work state and imposes no added minimum wage mandate."[7]

Texas' business climate has done well not just in magazine rankings. Investors are voting for Texas too. One small example is investment bank Piper Jaffray, based in Minneapolis. Jaffray announced in October 2018 that it had raised a $130 million private-equity fund to help companies expand in Texas, up to $15 million per company that had reached commercial stage and had room to grow. "The firm's targets in Texas show how the state is becoming a hotbed for global investors looking for these kinds of opportunities," a *San Antonio Business Journal* article reported.[8]

Just as Texas has also outperformed the nation in job creation, the state has seen strong growth in the number of new business establishments, according to the Dallas Fed, citing US Bureau of Labor Statistics data going back to 1990. Texas had a slightly higher percentage than the United States in the annualized percent change in the number of new companies during the 1990s and between 2000 and 2010. But the gap widened in favor of Texas between 2010 and 2016, when Texas saw a net increase in business establishments of 2.4 percent annually compared to the nation's 1.4 percent.

The Texas image of being business-friendly and the above-average rise in the number of companies helped mitigate losses during the Great Recession of 2007–9, when Texas lost a far smaller share of its jobs than most other US regions: "While the United States took over four years to recover all the jobs lost in the recession, Texas did so in half the time. This is in large part due to the more prominent role taken up by energy and exports over this period," according to Phillips's presentation on Texas economic growth.

Energy

Indeed, the picture of Texas as a fast-rising economy is not complete without a look at the effect of the state's energy sector. Energy—its

In August 2018, a consumer finance website called Magnify Money ranked the one hundred largest MSAs in the country to determine "the biggest boomtowns in America." The rankings were based on population, housing, workforce, and business growth statistics using US government data between 2012 and 2016. The Texas Triangle dominated the top fifteen boomtowns with all four metros. Austin topped the list at number one. The Dallas–Fort Worth area was number seven. San Antonio was number nine, and Houston was number eleven.[12] Each corner of the Texas Triangle was covered. A fifth Texas city, outside of the Triangle, also ranked. McAllen, in the Rio Grande Valley, was ranked number ten, giving Texas five of the top eleven rankings. Utah and North Carolina each had two cities in the top fifteen. No other region came close to the Texas Triangle.

Anyone who wants to know why a state grows faster than the others should ask two questions, according to Keith Phillips: (1) Where do people want to live? and (2) Can companies maximize profits there? The answers are clear. Although challenges—especially in education—exist, many people want to live in Texas more than anywhere else, and company executives say they thrive better in Texas than anywhere else.

What Texas Triangle Growth Means for Politics

The rapid population growth in the Texas Triangle has profoundly changed the entire state in one critical way: Texas has gained national political clout in leaps like no other state.

Texas gained four seats in the US House of Representatives following the 2010 US Census count of 25.15 million Texans after a 20.6 percent population gain between 2000 and 2010. It was the largest gain of any state in the nation.[1] The seat gain was also the largest for Texas since the 1880 US Census, after which Texas had garnered five seats to a total of eleven.

The four new seats added after 2010 gave Texas thirty-six members in the House, second only to California's fifty-three House representatives. Florida and New York each had twenty-seven House members.

The growth in the size of the Texas delegation to Washington, DC, has been impressive. After the Civil War, Texas had four seats in the House. As late as 1930, Texas had eighteen seats. That means Texas has doubled its House membership since 1930. As new congressional district lines are drawn each decade, the addition of new congressional districts in Texas over the decades have been concentrated in the Texas Triangle metropolitan areas. The Dallas–Fort Worth metro has gained four congressional seats, to twelve from eight, since 1975. Houston added three more seats, to eleven from eight, also since 1975. The Austin–San Antonio area's congressional seats rose to nine from five in the same period.

The more seats Texas controls in the US House, the greater chances the state possesses to grab top positions in key committees in the House, such as the budget writing committee or the armed forces committee, which directs funding to US Department of Defense installations, for example.

During the 2017–19 congressional session, Texas Republican members of the US House of Representatives were chairmen of seven of the twenty House standing committees. Five of them represented districts in the Texas Triangle metro areas. Foremost among them was US Rep. Kevin Brady, R-The Woodlands, who chaired the powerful Ways and Means Committee. Other Texas chairmen were Jeb Hensarling of Financial Services; Michael McCaul of Homeland Security; Pete Sessions of Rules; Lamar Smith of Science, Space, and Technology; Mike Conaway of Agriculture; and Mac Thornberry of Armed Services. In the US Senate, Republican John Cornyn of San Antonio was the Senate Majority Whip during the 2017–19 session. The other Texas senator is Ted Cruz of Houston.

With the projected growth in population between 2010 and 2020, Texas is expected to gain three or four new seats in the US House after the 2020 Census, the largest anticipated gain in the nation and in time for the 2024 congressional elections.[2] Florida would likely gain two seats after the 2020 Census count. States expected to gain one new seat each are Arizona, Colorado, North Carolina, and Oregon.[3] California is expected to retain its same number of seats.

Along with growing power within the US Capitol, Texas will have a larger say in US presidential elections. Texas had thirty-eight Electoral College votes in the 2020 election, calculated by the number of its House members plus the two US senators. California had fifty-five electoral votes, and Florida had twenty-nine.

Those three states along the US southern tier with the most electoral votes are often seen as critical to any US presidential candidate's campaign. Winning two of those three states usually results in victory. Since 1960, the presidential election winner carried two of the three states in thirteen of the fifteen elections. In 1960, John F.

Kennedy carried Texas but not California or Florida. In 1992, Bill Clinton carried California but not Texas and Florida. The presidential victors from 1996 to 2016 have all carried two of the states but not all three.[4]

In 2016, Republican nominee Donald Trump carried Texas and Florida and won the election. Democratic nominee Hillary Clinton carried California. But in 2020, Trump carried both Texas and Florida but lost the election to Democrat Joe Biden.

In the 2020 presidential election, Trump carried Texas by six percentage points after winning by nine points in 2016 over Clinton.[5] In 2012, Republican nominee Mitt Romney had carried Texas by sixteen points. The political party trend has narrowed as Texas grows in population. Of the thirty-five counties in the Texas Triangle, eight voted Democrat in the 2020 presidential election, including all five core counties in each metropolitan area—Dallas, Tarrant, Harris, Travis, and Bexar. Also voting Democrat were Fort Bend County in the Houston metro area and Hays and Williamson County in the Austin metro area.

Texas has had steadily increasing national political clout for the last century. Texan John Nance Garner was vice president under Franklin Roosevelt from 1933 to 1941 after being US House speaker. Garner additionally ran for president in the 1932 and 1940 races.

Since 1952, four Texans have occupied the White House as president. Dwight D. Eisenhower was born in Denison, Texas, in 1890. He was raised in Kansas but spent time in Texas, stationed at Fort Sam Houston from 1915 to 1917. Having been a varsity football player for the army while at West Point, Eisenhower coached football in San Antonio, first a youth football team and then the football team at St. Louis University, which in 1923 changed its name to St. Mary's University. Eisenhower and his wife, Mamie, moved back to San Antonio into a Fort Sam Houston house in the summer of 1941. He was taking a nap on December 7, 1941, when he was awakened by Mamie with the news of the Pearl Harbor attack. A week later, Eisenhower was working at the War Department in Washington, DC. He was elected president in 1952, reflecting national respect for his military leadership in World War II, especially the D-Day invasion of Normandy.

Texan Lyndon B. Johnson, from Stonewall near Johnson City in the Texas Hill Country, changed US history in a series of events. The 1960 Democratic presidential nominee, John F. Kennedy, chose US Senate Majority Leader Johnson as his vice-presidential candidate in the hopes that Johnson could win Texas' twenty-four electoral votes that year, which happened by a slim margin. Carrying Texas was critical for Kennedy to win the 1960 election over Richard Nixon.

By 1963, a liberal-conservative split in the Texas Democratic Party worried President Kennedy about the chances of winning Texas' electoral vote again in the 1964 election. Kennedy therefore planned a trip to Texas for November 1963 to try to mend the badly divided Texas Democratic Party. Bitterness separated the conservative faction led by Texas Gov. John Connally and the liberals led by US Sen. Ralph Yarborough. Kennedy's five-city trip, logically enough, covered the Texas Triangle exclusively. Kennedy began the trip on November 21, 1963, in San Antonio and then traveled to Houston and then later that day to Fort Worth. After a breakfast speech in Fort Worth on November 22, Kennedy flew the short distance to Dallas, where he was assassinated by Lee Harvey Oswald. Kennedy had been scheduled to travel to Austin later that day.

Instead, Johnson was sworn in as president that afternoon at Dallas's Love Field, putting Texas in the political spotlight in a way it had never been. Johnson was president until 1969.

Since Johnson, Texans, or people with solid Texas roots, have been active in pursuing the presidency. In the twelve presidential election cycles between 1976 and 2020, Texans were candidates in eleven of the races.

In 1976, US Sen. Lloyd Bentsen ran. In 1980, former US Rep. and Central Intelligence Agency Director George H. W. Bush tried for the White House but was chosen as Ronald Reagan's vice-presidential running mate. The Reagan-Bush team won, and Bush was vice president for eight years. Bush then won the 1988 race for president, serving one term. Bush was born in Massachusetts but had started his business career in Texas and represented a Houston district in the US House of Representatives. Another Texas candidate in 1980 was former Texas Gov. John Connally. His run was unsuccessful, but Connally, who as Texas governor had been injured in the Kennedy assassination, almost had a chance at the presidency before 1980 because of Nixon's Watergate scandal. When Spiro Agnew had to resign in 1973 as Nixon's vice president for accepting cash bribes, Nixon had to appoint a new vice president with Senate confirmation. Nixon's own presidency already faced early termination in 1973 because of Watergate. Senate Democrats warned Nixon against appointing someone who would be both a likely successor and a solid presidential candidate in 1976. Nixon had his own list of four names for vice president. He scratched his number-three choice Ronald Reagan, his number-two choice Nelson Rockefeller, and finally his number-one choice, his political advisor, Connally. Nixon settled instead for his number-four choice, Gerald Ford.[6] Ford was confirmed by the Senate and became president upon Nixon's 1974 resignation. Ford lost his reelection bid in 1976 to Democrat Jimmy Carter.

In 1988, former US Rep. Ron Paul of Texas was a presidential candidate. In 1992, Dallas businessman H. Ross Perot was a presidential candidate along with Paul. Perot ran again in 1996, as did US Sen. Phil Gramm of Texas.

George H. W. Bush's son George W. Bush, born in Connecticut, won the US presidential election in the 2000 election after six years as Texas governor, serving as president for two terms.

Paul was again a candidate in 2008 and 2012. In 2012, Texas Gov. Rick Perry entered the presidential race. Perry tried again in 2016 but became President Donald Trump's energy secretary. The 2016 presidential field was crowded with two additional candidates with Texas roots, US Sen. Ted Cruz and Texas-born Jeb Bush, the former Florida governor who grew up in Midland, Texas, as another son of George H. W. Bush.

In 2019, two Texans entered the 2020 presidential race, former US Rep. Beto O'Rourke from El Paso and ex–San Antonio Mayor Julián Castro. Both Democrats dropped out of the crowded field before the 2020 Iowa caucuses were held.

Texas clearly has been a launching pad for politicians with national ambitions. With thirty-eight electoral votes and at least forty-one by 2024, Texas likely will continue to be a base for future candidacies. The launching pads could be the Texas governorship, the state's US Senate and House seats, and even mayors' offices. Failed presidential candidates from Texas likely often get second looks as vice-presidential running mates because of Texas' large number of electoral votes. In fact, Texans were selected as vice-presidential candidates in 1960, with Lyndon Johnson selected by Kennedy, and 1980, with George H. W. Bush picked by Ronald Reagan, and yet again in 1988, when Democratic presidential nominee Michael Dukakis selected Bentsen as his running mate.

Another political shift is readily noticeable—leadership once came at random across the state, as steadily from rural Texas as from the Texas Triangle metros, in elections for statewide and national office.

In an earlier era, state leadership came from rural Texas. Garner, the vice president, came from Uvalde, in rural southwestern Texas, as did Gov. Dolph Briscoe later. Lyndon B. Johnson grew up in the rural Hill Country town of Stonewall near Johnson City in Blanco County, just north of the San Antonio metropolitan area. Gov. Rick Perry was raised in the tiny town of Haskell in North Central Texas. The late US Sen. John Tower, the first Republican senator from Texas since 1870, originally entered politics while living in Wichita Falls.

But in recent decades, political success seems to concentrate mainly on Texas Triangle residents. Gov. Greg Abbott is from Houston, as is Lt. Gov. Dan Patrick. US Sens. John Cornyn (San Antonio) and Ted Cruz (Houston), elected at-large on the statewide ballot, also hail from the Triangle. Wendy Davis, a Democrat who gained a spotlight in 2013 with a Texas Senate filibuster against a restrictive abortion bill and who ran unsuccessfully for governor in 2014, is from Fort Worth. Davis later moved to the Austin–San Antonio area, where she entered, and lost, a race for the US House of Representatives in 2020. And George W. Bush made his home in Dallas, both before entering politics and since retiring from the presidency.

While it is always possible that candidates for statewide and national offices may arise from people living in the rural and non-Triangle communities of Texas, many more candidates are likely to come from the Triangle metros for one simple reason: population density makes it possible for widespread name recognition and a better voter turnout to be achieved in the large cities, where most of the voters live, than in the rural and outlying metro areas.

Politics within Texas

The urbanization of Texas has also gradually changed the politics within Texas, especially within the Texas Legislature. The legislature has remained the same size, with 150 members of the Texas House of Representatives and 31 members of the Texas Senate. As more people live in urban areas, more lawmakers represent urban areas, especially since Texas' twenty-five metropolitan areas have 84.7 percent of the state's population, according to the 2010 US Census.

Nevertheless, Texas' rural population was the largest in the nation numerically in 2010 at 3,847,522.[7] By itself, the Texas rural population would be larger than the entire populations of each of twenty-one other states, just below the total population of Oklahoma (number twenty-eight) at 3.93 million and just above Connecticut (number twenty-nine) at 3.59 million.

The mix of rural and urban state lawmakers "makes for interesting bedfellows. It goes in cycles. From a political standpoint, there's an ebb and flow of influence. The rural representatives are on the same wavelength (among themselves) more than the urban representatives, who are so fractured there is not the concentration of power" that would be expected, according to Jim Gaines, chief economist for the Real Estate Center at Texas A&M University at College Station. "There are twenty-five or thirty House members from Houston, but they cannot agree on the time of day." Gaines explains that different loyalties and rivalries have skewed the voting patterns of urban legislators, especially as the legislature debated measures opposed by large city mayors during the 2017 legislative session. These bills included limiting powers of annexation and capping local government property-tax rates.

An urban-rural issue continues to arise in ongoing debates over school funding, according to Gaines: "The question is how much in resources should be dedicated to rural school districts that may have one hundred students versus the urban areas where the school districts have tens of thousands of students. It's the number-one issue before the Texas Legislature. Schooling is the future. The politics of school funding right now is being held together by chewing gum and bailing wire. . . . You can't have one size fits all."

A flexible funding mechanism recognizing the different needs of rural and urban school districts may provide part of the answer, Gaines explains: "Policies have to be flexible because, for example, rural school districts have to pay more for school bus routes that are longer in distance than in the urban school districts where routes may be only one or two miles. But what is flexible? People will argue about that. The question is how to manage school districts, not regulate. . . . If there was a statewide property tax for public schools, money could be distributed based on need, but there would not be local control anymore" by school district boards of trustees.

Then there is the level of state involvement through statewide standards. "The state sets the curriculums, the teacher standards, selects the textbooks, and sets the building standards," Gaines says, adding that the elected local school boards only have partial control over the hiring of teachers.

"Many of the top employers in cities outside of the Triangle are public school districts. They know schools are important," says Carlton Schwab, CEO and president of the Texas Economic Development Council.

Public school financing is only part of the broader issue of supporting Texas' rural economy at a time when more than ninety rural counties have been losing population. The problem, as Lloyd Potter has pointed out, is the lack of job opportunities in rural Texas counties.

"To be cold-blooded about it, for the counties that are losing population there has to be an economic basis to live there," Gaines says, citing ghost towns that have formed after being abandoned by residents. "Towns have disappeared because there is nothing to do. There's no reason to be there. There has to be a fundamental reason to exist. It must be a market or distribution center, or a transportation linkage. You have to be able to earn a living." Gaines suggests that highway and transportations systems could evolve to extend the economic reach of the Texas Triangle into rural Texas: "We need balanced state programs that recognize the different needs. It cannot be everything going one way or the other."

Overall, Texas political power is ascendant. A state that will soon have four of the ten largest cities in the nation will inevitably be in the forefront of congressional leadership and presidential consideration. National candidates understand the need to have Texas on their side. Rising political stars in Texas know they have the foundation to be taken seriously nationally. In the corridors of political power, Texans will have a presence like never before, thanks to the rapid population growth of the Texas Triangle metros.

Dallas

To understand the forces shaping the Texas Triangle today, one needs to dig more deeply into the evolution of each of the Triangle's five largest cities. In this and the next four chapters, we explore the distinctive and changing roles of Dallas, Fort Worth, Houston, San Antonio, and Austin within the Triangle megaregion and how they complement each other to form an increasingly integrated, cohesive, and powerful regional economic system.

The emergence of five distinct, large cities in Texas, spread relatively far apart from one another and operating more or less independently for much of their history, reflects the peculiar history and geography of the state. After all, a number of the US states that came into being before Texas grew up around a single dominant metropolis—think Massachusetts, Connecticut, New York, Pennsylvania, Maryland, Georgia, Tennessee, Indiana, and Illinois.

But Texas emerged from its independence struggle with Mexico and its accession as the twenty-eighth state in the Union as a far larger land mass than any previously existing state, with no obvious natural location for a dominant urban center. The absence of rivers that are navigable over long distances meant that different regions of the state were economically remote from one another in the circumstances of the nineteenth and early twentieth centuries, as economists from the Federal Reserve Bank of Dallas explain in a 2004 study.[1] Inland locations were inaccessible from the Gulf of Mexico. Locations directly on the Gulf Coast, it turned out, were highly vulnerable to hurricanes. Texans learned this lesson the hard way in 1900, when a devastating hurricane leveled Galveston—until then the largest city in the state, rivaling New Orleans as a Gulf Coast port. Galveston recovered slowly, ceding its leadership in Southeast Texas to Houston, which was somewhat better protected from the elements.

Texas arguably was destined to become a very big economy. Its vast physical extent pointed toward this destiny, but so did its strategic geographic position. Texas stood at the crossroads of interregional commerce along both North-South and East-West axes and on the front line of international trade with Mexico and the rest of Latin America. Its long coastline also guaranteed an important role in the United States' ocean-borne trade. So geography dictated that Texas would give rise to significant urban centers, but geographic imperatives demanded them in more than one location around the state.

As the state's history unfolded, numerous cities emerged, with distinctive personalities and serving very different economic functions. Houston emerged as a dominant port city, looking south—and across the oceans to trading partners around the world. Dallas emerged as a regional center for business and finance, looking east and north to larger commercial centers in the Midwest and Northeast. Fort Worth looked west as a trading and supply town for the great western cattle drives. San Antonio, by far the oldest city in Texas and the only one of the top five cities existing when Texas was under Spanish and then Mexican rule, looked southwest as the capital of Hispanic culture in the state. Austin emerged as the state capital because of its central location, relatively accessible from all corners of the state.

Other cities showed early promise as regional centers but lost out in the end. For instance, the Gulf Coast town of Indianola reached a population of five thousand by the 1870s, impressive by the standards of Texas cities at the time. But the fledgling port was itself obliterated by hurricanes in 1875 and 1886, leaving Indianola as a ghost town today at Matagorda Bay.

During the twentieth century, the state's big five cities grew along very different paths, but each shared the state's distinctive progrowth, open-for-business culture and public policy orientation. And each took its place among the United States' premiere cities. Houston far eclipsed New Orleans as the leading port city on the Gulf Coast, becoming the oil and gas capital of the world. Dallas left behind leading cities in all surrounding states to become the dominant finance and distribution hub of the south-central region of the country. Austin outgrew its position as a small, quirky city focused on politics and higher education to become the leading technology center between the West Coast and New York. San Antonio and Fort Worth, considerably poorer and less glamorous than the other three as recently as the 1970s, experienced explosive growth in the last quarter of the century to become diverse, dynamic economies with rich portfolios of manufacturing and service-sector activities.

As the state's leading cities grew over the last century, they inevitably became rivals for economic, cultural, and political position in the state. Often they bumped into each other in competing for corporate facilities or state infrastructure funds. But by the early twenty-first century, it was clear that the relationships among Dallas, Fort Worth, Houston, San Antonio, and Austin had evolved from outright competition to increasingly close "coopetition"— friendly competition alongside cooperation and increasing economic integration.

Three big trends help account for this evolution. First, the last several decades have seen growing geographic concentration of high-value-added activities and increasing specialization of individual cities in particular economic niches. Like other US cities, each of the big cities of the Texas Triangle grew more specialized in its areas of comparative advantage within the megaregion. Second, as all five cities became extremely large relative to other US cities, they inevitably became bigger trading partners with one another. And third, complementary strengths plus revolutionary improvements in transportation and information technology made it possible for the Triangle cities to create integrated business processes and supply chains across the megaregion.

As economist Robert W. Gilmer writes in a study of the Texas economy, the industry structures of the five Triangle cities "fit together neatly, like pieces of a puzzle." Close integration, he argues, means growth in one part of the Triangle has generally been a stimulus to growth elsewhere in the megaregion, rather than detracting from it.[2]

Because of growing integration, the Texas Triangle cities collectively enjoy a set of strengths that no one of them would have by itself: the leading technology center between the coasts; the leading ground transportation and distribution hub in the central part of the country; one of the nation's leading ports; one of the two dominant financial centers between the coasts (along with Chicago); the dominant centers for oil and gas, space, and business services; and a manufacturing base rivaling that of any other megaregion besides the Upper Midwest.

Just as each of the five big cities of the Texas Triangle has come to fulfill specialized economic functions within the megaregion, each has developed its own style and personality. At the risk of oversimplifying a complex reality, one can say that Dallas is the most glitzy, style-conscious, and buttoned-down of the five cities. Fort Worth is the most easygoing and "Western." Houston is the most global and diverse. San Antonio is the most culturally unique, and Austin scores highest for being techie, cool, and "weird."

We now take a look at each of the big five cities in the Texas Triangle—their stories, their distinct personalities, and how they contribute to a fast-growing megaregion whose collective weight in the world economy is greater than the sum of its parts. We start with Dallas.

• • •

Dallas is the most northeastern of the five big Triangle cities, both in its geographic position and in its social and economic similarities to the northeastern United States. Like New York, Boston, and Philadelphia, Dallas is above all a financial and service-sector metropolis. Elsewhere in the Triangle, people often think of Dallas as aspirational and money conscious. Like New York, Dallas is widely

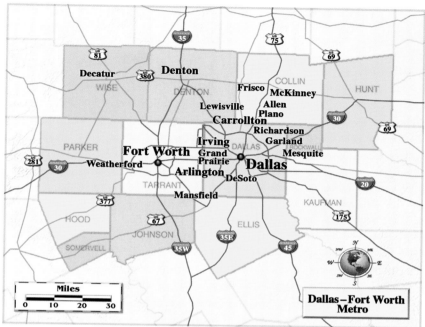

The Dallas–Fort Worth MSA covers thirteen counties. It is the state's largest urban area in population and economic size.

known for high fashion, as it is the birthplace of Neiman Marcus and the home of several of the most famous shopping meccas in the south-central region of the United States. The world also knows Dallas for its top-tier visual arts scene and for one of the most glamorous sports franchises in the United States, the Dallas Cowboys.

Dallas likes to think of itself as a bustling city of no-nonsense, bottom-line-oriented, entrepreneurial men and women. It devotes less attention to its own history than any of the other Triangle cities do. Its most respected citizens have long been business builders, not politicians, artists, or intellectuals. More than almost any large US city, it stands out for small government, big business, and its generous, can-do philanthropy.

Dallas, under Mayor Eric Johnson, is increasingly challenging Chicago as the third most important financial center in the United States, after New York and Los Angeles. It's the Triangle's principal base for investment banking, insurance, real estate, wealth management, private equity, and hedge funds, other than in specialized niches focused on the energy sector, in which Houston dominates.

As a logistics and distribution hub, Dallas is the Texas Triangle's most important link to the rest of the United States. It has the Triangle's busiest airport as well as its largest ground-transportation crossroads in the "Inland Port" of South Dallas.

While the Texas Triangle has the most diverse industry base of the United States' eight megaregions, based on an index published by Moody's, Dallas—along with San Antonio—has the most diverse portfolio of employers among the Triangle cities.

People who've moved to Dallas from elsewhere in the Triangle or from smaller places in the south-central United States will usually acknowledge that they've come to Dallas to pursue work opportunities—it's a great place to make money. They'll usually tell you that Dallas has a far higher energy level and a faster pace than where they came from. They'll point out how welcoming it is to newcomers who are ready to work hard and get involved in the community. When people move away from Dallas for other destinations in the region, they usually do so to enjoy a more relaxed lifestyle or to retire.

The greater Dallas area is, by some measures, the richest corner of the Texas Triangle. What the US Census Bureau calls the "Dallas-Plano-Irving metropolitan division," comprising the eastern half of the Dallas–Fort Worth metro area and roughly two-thirds of the metro area's population, has the highest GDP per person of the big Texas metros. On this measure, the Dallas area is indeed among the richest places in the urban United States, outside the Northeast Corridor and the San Francisco Bay Area. Within the Urban Midwest, Urban Southeast, South Florida, Southern California, Pacific Northwest, and Texas Triangle megaregions, only Los Angeles, Seattle, and much smaller Durham rank higher in wealth.

The Dallas area has enjoyed a remarkably good twenty-first century so far. The Dallas–Fort Worth metro has consistently ranked as one of the United States' biggest winners in corporate site-selection competitions, with most companies settling on the eastern side of the metro area. The Dallas–Fort Worth metro has experienced greater population growth since 2000 than any other US metro area in absolute terms. The city of Dallas itself has added world-class arts facilities, sports stadiums, urban parks, and signature bridges, plus stunning luxury apartments and office towers. The metro's northern suburbs are among the fastest-growing cities in the world. The Dallas area proved to be one of the most resilient local economies in the United States during the 2008 financial crisis. In the years since then, the area's ongoing economic boom has gone from strength to strength. In 2020, Dallas showed more resilience than most US cities during the early months of the COVID-19 crisis. Early signs during the pandemic pointed to an accelerating movement of people from the largest, most dense cities of the Northeast and California to the Dallas area, particularly to its high-growth northern suburbs.

Like Houston, Dallas in many ways grew large and rich before it fully grew up as a mature US megacity, and now it's working to catch up. Surging prosperity has fueled demand for new housing near the urban core and in wealthy North Dallas, but supply has struggled to keep up the pace. The city consequently faces a growing affordability challenge. Traffic congestion is steadily worsening. The urban core needs greater density, but the city hasn't fully figured out how to deliver it.

Dallas ranks alongside Houston and other large Triangle cities as among the most segregated cities in the United States along economic lines, with gleaming "have" neighborhoods but a vast expanse of "have-not" neighborhoods, mostly in Southern Dallas.[3] City leaders have devoted growing attention to the challenge of bringing more economic vitality to the southern part of the city. They've achieved some early wins, but this overdue effort is still in its early days. More and more, the city faces the same big-city problems of more mature places—crime, struggling inner-city schools, stark health-care inequities, shaky public-sector finances—but its small-government tradition limits its tools for addressing them.

And yet the booming Dallas metro area, like the other Texas Triangle metros, has powerful advantages over cities elsewhere in the United States as it addresses its challenges. People and businesses want to be in the Dallas area, and they keep coming. Both the city and the wider metro area have enormous stocks of undeveloped or underutilized land that can play a large role in tackling housing problems and creating a more inclusive pattern of development. The city's get-it-done spirit is as strong as ever, and the continuing boom in the wider metro area creates resources that most other US cities can only dream of.

Dallas History

John Neely Bryan founded Dallas in 1841, when he claimed a plot of land on an eastern bluff overlooking the Trinity River. The place where he and his family settled was part of the Republic of Texas, which had won its independence from Mexico five years before and would enter the United States four years later.[4] Dallas became incorporated in 1856, shortly before Texas seceded from the Union to become part of the Confederacy. Bryan himself served as a Confederate soldier.

Dallas established itself as an economic player in the early decades after the Civil War when it became a significant junction in the nation's growing railway network. Railroads connected Dallas to manufacturing centers in the North, fueling the city's emergence as a cotton trading and transportation hub. With the arrival of the Texas oil boom in the early twentieth century, Dallas bankers raised the city's financial prominence by playing a leading role in financing the nascent energy industry.[5]

Again and again, local boosters seized opportunities to attract people to Dallas and raise the city's profile. In 1886, Dallas launched what came to be known as the "State Fair of Texas." The fair, a quintessentially Texan mix of theme park and showcase for the North Texas region's commerce and culture, brought millions of visitors to Dallas during the early twentieth century and after. Early in the new century, promoters built a horse-racing track at the new Fair Park.[6]

Before long, however, Dallas boosters discovered a more potent attraction that would come to define the city: football. In 1930, the city demolished the racetrack to build the Cotton Bowl and soon after started to host one of the most prominent end-of-season

"Big Tex" greets hordes of visitors at the Texas State Fair in Dallas each fall. Shutterstock/RaksyBH.

college games in the country there. The Cotton Bowl also became the "neutral" site of the annual clash between the University of Texas Longhorns and the Oklahoma University Sooners, a ritual event full of pageantry held every October, during the twenty-four-day State Fair of Texas.

In 1960, Clint Murchison Jr., the son of one of the city's wealthiest oil men, convinced National Football League (NFL) owners to allow an expansion franchise in Dallas—the Cowboys. The team capitalized on its gridiron successes in the 1960s and 1970s to proclaim itself "America's Team," bringing further attention to the city. Under the ownership of another oilman, Jerry Jones, further shrewd marketing made the Cowboys one of the most valuable professional sports franchises in the world. Another Dallas oil heir, Lamar Hunt—son of the legendary oil magnate H. L. Hunt—played a central role in expanding the NFL and building it into the marketing juggernaut that it's become in the twenty-first century. Together, the Cowboys and Hunt's team, the Kansas City Chiefs, have won seven Super Bowl championships.

As much as the fair, football, and enthusiastic boosterism helped capture the public's attention, the pivotal events that cemented the city's rise to national prominence took place in the more mundane realm of transportation. Most important of these were the passage of the National Interstate and Defense Highways Act of 1956 and the development of D/FW Airport in 1974. The nation's new highway network placed Dallas at the crossroads of one north-south artery, Interstate 35, and two east-west routes, Interstates 20 and 30. Reinforcing the city's established position as a railway entrepôt, the highways ensured that Dallas would occupy a central place in the trade and logistics networks connecting Texas to the rest of the United States. D/FW Airport had equally transformational consequences. Located between Dallas and Fort Worth and replacing Dallas Love Field as the metro area's principal airport, D/FW capitalized on Dallas's central location on the North American continent to become a key hub in the nation's air transportation network and one of the busiest airports in the world.

In subsequent years, the city doubled down on these vital investments in transportation. Key moves included reopening and modernizing Love Field as the principal hub of the new Southwest Airlines in the 1970s, building out a massive hub-and-spoke system of highways connecting the central city to all corners of the far-flung metro area over subsequent decades, and developing the International Inland Port in South Dallas in the 2000s.

A crucial but little discussed aspect of the city's development was its progress in moving past the more painful features of its own history. Dallas experienced significant episodes of organized violence against its African American population during the Civil War and Reconstruction periods and into the twentieth century, including an infamous lynching in downtown Dallas in 1910. In 1916, Dallas became the first Texas city to impose racial housing segregation by law. For a time in the 1920s, Dallas was the national headquarters of the Ku Klux Klan (KKK), whose local membership numbered in the tens of thousands.[7]

In the 1960s and 1970s, the city, state, and federal governments obliterated numerous historic Black neighborhoods to pursue "urban renewal" schemes and to make way for the Central Expressway, Woodall Rogers Freeway, and other highways connecting outlying white neighborhoods with downtown. Shamefully, the city government seized more than fifty acres of private real estate near Fair Park by eminent domain at the behest of the State Fair in 1966, wiping out many Black-owned businesses. The city's stated objectives were to build a huge parking lot used three weeks of the year and to relieve white fair visitors of what the State Fair called the "intense emotional discomfort" of seeing "poor Negroes in their shacks."[8]

Dallas also became known in the 1950s and early 1960s for a strain of ultraconservative politics that sat uneasily alongside the city's self-image as an open, bustling city at the forefront of US economic growth. Leaders of this ultraconservative movement included H. L. Hunt as well as Rev. W. A. Criswell, US Rep. Bruce Alger, and *Dallas Morning News* Publisher Ted Dealey. Venomous politics erupted in violence on several occasions, such as two instances when angry crowds jeered and spat on visiting vice-presidential candidate Lyndon Johnson and his wife in 1960 and US Ambassador to the United Nations Adlai Stevenson in 1963. These incidents earned Dallas an unwanted reputation as a "city of hate" in the immediate aftermath of President John F. Kennedy's assassination on November 22, 1963.

But Dallas gradually transformed itself into the kind of place where business considerations would inevitably trump ideological or religious fanaticism. Top media and business leaders forced the KKK out of town by the end of the 1920s because the Klan's activities were bad for local business.

In the years after the trauma of November 1963, Dallas moved toward a decidedly pragmatic style of politics. The Dallas Citizens Council, speaking for the business establishment, largely chose mayors and city council people, while technocratic city managers supervised the city's modest administrative functions—invariably with an eye on what was good for commerce and economic growth.

The white business establishment reached out to the Black community to arrive at what Dallas journalist Jim Schutze termed "the accommodation" in a 1987 book: a series of implicit deals in which the city's white leadership increasingly included African American leaders in politics and other local institutions and recognized the African American community's interests, while Black leaders—especially South Dallas pastors—ensured that Dallas would not experience the race riots that struck other US cities in the late 1960s and 1970s.[9] Unlike most cities in the Southeast, Dallas lost interest in perpetuating nostalgia for the Antebellum South and the Confederacy.

Economic Diversification

The 1960s and 1970s also saw the emergence of a more modern, diversified economy in Dallas. Two homegrown companies in particular had a decisive influence on the development of the Dallas metro area. One of them, Texas Instruments, started life as an oil-field technology company in the 1930s but transformed itself into one of the nation's leading technology equipment companies after Jack Kilby, a Texas Instruments engineer, invented the integrated circuit in 1958. Historians generally credit Kilby and Robert Noyce of California's Fairchild Semiconductor for arriving at the integrated circuit simultaneously.

Texas Instruments went on to create the first electronic calculator and to dominate the markets for digital signal processors for mobile phones and, later, for analog chips powering the "internet of things." It spawned an array of Dallas-area electronics companies founded by Texas Instruments alumni. But the founders of the company also remade Dallas through their civic leadership and philanthropy. Cofounder Erik Jonsson became the most consequential mayor in the city's history, serving from 1964 to 1971. Jonsson launched the process that resulted in D/FW Airport, built a new marquee city hall and convention center, and led the city's first long-range planning exercise, called "Goals for Dallas." He and Texas Instruments cofounders Cecil Green and Eugene McDermott led the effort to create what became the University of Texas at Dallas (UT Dallas) in 1969—an institution that in turn played a tremendous role in creating the technical workforce making the technology and business-services sector of the Dallas–Fort Worth metro area possible.[10] The three cofounders and their families played leading philanthropic roles in building out the city's renowned private schools, universities, arts facilities, and medical institutions.

Just as significant was the emergence of Electronic Data Systems, or EDS, founded by Dallas businessman H. Ross Perot in 1962. EDS created the business process outsourcing industry, laying the foundation for a vast business-services sector in Dallas–Fort Worth, arguably the metro area's most important economic sector today. Like the Texas Instruments founders, Perot and his family powered the rise of the city's leading education, culture, and health-care institutions through their philanthropy and engaged leadership.

Culture

The decades after the early 1960s also saw the emergence of one of the United States' premiere arts communities in Dallas. While Dallas ultraconservatives generated a furor in the late 1950s over the showing of paintings by communist-sympathizer artists like Pablo Picasso in the city's museums, by the 1970s Dallas had become internationally known for its highly respected Dallas Museum of Art and for several of the world's greatest modern art collections in private hands. By the early 2000s, downtown Dallas had developed the United States' largest contiguous arts district, featuring a world-renowned symphony hall, three more architecturally distinguished performing arts facilities, and one of the nation's leading magnet high schools for the arts.

Dallas also attracted global attention through the television show *Dallas*, which aired from 1978 to 1991. *Dallas* centered on the shenanigans of an oil-tycoon family and reinforced the city's reputation for lavish glamour and outsized bravado—even if it amounted to a soap opera concocted by Hollywood screenwriters.

In the 1990s, the city's politics shifted again, to a more inclusive but less business-minded model. After a move to a city council consisting of a mayor and fourteen council members elected from single-member districts, individual city council members became more empowered within their districts, while Dallas's mayors and city managers saw an erosion in their ability to get things done. The city's leadership became more diverse in every respect. Starting in the 1980s, Dallas has elected two Black mayors and two female ones, as well as several gay city council members. While local elections are nonpartisan, four of the city's last five mayors have been widely known Democrats. Through these changes, however, all of Dallas's modern mayors have continued to embody a political style of moderate pragmatism, even as many other big US cities have become more partisan and ideologically charged in their politics.

Population Measures

As of 2019, the Dallas–Fort Worth metro had a population of just over 7.4 million, making it the fourth largest in the United States. The Dallas-Plano-Irving metropolitan division, the east side of the metro, had just over 5 million people, up 45.1 percent since 2000. In percentage terms, the Dallas area has grown slightly slower than each of the other four Texas Triangle metros, counting the Fort Worth area separately, but faster than any metro in the other seven leading US megaregions aside from a handful of far smaller places in the Southeast. If the Census Bureau chose to count the Dallas and Fort Worth areas as separate metros, the Dallas metro

Dallas is the nation's ninth-largest city in population. Shutterstock/dibrova.

area would be the ninth largest in the country and the second largest in Texas, after Houston.

As we noted in chapter 2, the Dallas–Fort Worth metro is the third most ethnically diverse metro in the United States after Houston and New York, based on a calculation by WalletHub using a statistical measure called the Herfindahl-Hirschman Index.[11] Dallas–Fort Worth and Houston together have absorbed the lion's share of the immigrants who've come into Texas over the last twenty years. At 18.7 percent as of 2017, Dallas–Fort Worth has a smaller foreign-born population share than Houston but a much higher share than San Antonio or Austin. Dallas–Fort Worth's surging Hispanic population represents 28.9 percent of the total population, a smaller share than in each of the other three metros. But since 2010, new immigrant arrivals to Dallas–Fort Worth from Asian countries have almost caught up with arrivals from Latin America, further changing the area's demographic complexion.

The core city of Dallas has grown since 2000, but at a far slower rate than the metro area as a whole. The city's population stood at 1,345,047 as of 2019, ninth among US cities.

The real demographic action has been in the Dallas area's booming suburbs. Four of Dallas's older inner-ring suburbs—Arlington, Irving, Garland, and Grand Prairie—have populations of more than 200,000. But the fastest-growing cities are further north, in the newer communities of Collin and Denton counties. The combined population of the five largest cities in these counties—Plano, McKinney, Frisco, Denton, and Allen—passed 900,000 in 2019, roughly doubling since 2000 (see table 7.1). Together, these five cities are larger than San Francisco and larger than Minneapolis and St. Paul combined.

Table 7.1

Large Dallas–Fort Worth area suburbs, 2019 populations

Arlington	398,854
Plano	287,677
Garland	239,928
Irving	239,798
Frisco	200,490
McKinney	199,177
Grand Prairie	194,543
Denton	141,541
Mesquite	140,937
Carrollton	139,248
Richardson	121,323
Lewisville	109,212
Allen	105,623

Source: US Census Bureau QuickFacts 2019 estimates.

These northern cities are growing more and more diverse, defying the outdated stereotype that they're ethnically homogeneous bedroom communities. In aggregate, their foreign-born population share is as high as that of the city of Dallas. Their Hispanic and Black populations—now amounting to more than 20 percent of total population—are rapidly growing as well. Their Asian and Asian American population share, at 14.2 percent, far exceeds that of the city of Dallas at 3.4 percent. The northern suburbs now feature a wide array of Asian restaurants, Chinese New Year festivals, cricket fields, and other signs of the area's rapidly changing demographic makeup.

These suburbs also constitute an increasingly self-contained economic system, with diverse employers from a wide range of industries. In Plano, Frisco, and Allen, the number of people working within the city limits each day is fast approaching the number of working people who go to bed there each night. The northern cities dominate the metro area's employment in technology, telecommunications, and back-office processing industries. Even industries that traditionally operate in the central city rather than the suburbs, like media and other creative fields, have become almost as big in these cities as they are in Dallas, measured in industry jobs per capita.

Demographers project that the Dallas–Fort Worth metro will reach ten million people by the 2030s, passing Chicago to become the United States' third-largest metro area. The majority of this growth is likely to take place in Collin and Denton counties and in a still-farther-out ring of fast-rising counties alongside the Oklahoma border.

Advantages

The Dallas area owes its economic success over recent decades to three advantages it enjoys over most other US cities: first, its central location and position as one of the United States' principal transportation hubs; second, the vast diversity of its economy; and third, its relatively low costs of living and doing business.

Dallas's location in the middle of the North American continent, coupled with its first-tier transportation network, has made all the difference to the city's growth and success—in this century as well as long before. D/FW Airport reinforces the city's position, built through the railroads and then the interstate highways, as a national crossroads. Thanks to the airport, traveling businesspeople can reach every major city in the United States within four hours, plus sixty-six nonstop destinations outside the US continent. D/FW is the twelfth-largest airport in the world in passenger numbers.[12] It's also one of the United States' leading cargo airports. Directly or indirectly, D/FW accounts for 228,000 jobs in the metro area.

This advantage has given Dallas a tremendous edge over many of its competitors in attracting corporate relocations and expansions. According to Mario Hernandez, a longtime Texas authority on economic development, Dallas is about "the servicing of the American economy, the linking of the two coasts. When the country thinks about the middle of the country, they think about the Dallas–Fort Worth area. It is further north than Houston or San Antonio. It's a checkmark on the list of factors when it comes to proximity to the two major coasts and of being able to serve the Midwest and, at the same time, all the way down into Mexico."

What's more, D/FW has continued to expand capacity in the twenty-first century, unlike overstretched airports in most other big US metros but similar to airports in the other Texas Triangle metros. The airport has added new terminals, modernized its runways, and increased routes and departures. The Dallas area has also continued to augment its ground transportation infrastructure to keep up with growing population and trade flows through the region, through the Inland Port and the highway system.

The diversity of the Dallas area's economy has also been a significant driver of its success. The largest private-sector employers in Dallas and its surrounding suburbs span a wide range of industries, including banking (JPMorgan Chase, Bank of America, Comerica), insurance (Blue Cross and Blue Shield of Texas, Liberty Mutual), defense and aerospace (Raytheon), air travel (Southwest Airlines), automobiles (Toyota), chemicals (Celanese), consumer goods (Kimberly-Clark, Frito-Lay, Dean Foods), retail (J. C. Penney), health care (Tenet Healthcare, McKesson), technology (Texas Instruments, Alliance Data Systems, NTT Data, Fujitsu), and telecommunications (AT&T). The Dallas side of the Dallas–Fort Worth metro is the site of the headquarters of twenty Fortune 500 firms, including ExxonMobil, AT&T, Energy Transfer, Fluor, Kimberly-Clark, Dr Pepper Snapple, and Texas Instruments.

D/FW Airport is one of the nation's largest airline hubs. Shutterstock / Casey Martin.

Economic diversity strengthens a metro area's economy in part by providing a hedge against decline in any one industry. The modest dependence of the Dallas economy on the energy sector, for example, has buffered the effects of declines in oil and gas prices in 2014–15 and again in 2019–20. But diversity is not just a hedge against adverse shocks but a spur to creativity and innovation. The urbanist Jane Jacobs famously argued that large, industrially diverse cities promote cross-fertilization of ideas and make residents more productive on average.[13] Research by the urban economist Edward Glaeser of Harvard University and others has confirmed this relationship in US data in recent decades.[14]

Eds and Meds

The depth and diversity of Dallas's economy extend beyond the private sector as well. Like the other Texas Triangle metros, the Dallas area has built a robust portfolio of leading "anchor institutions" in higher education and health care, or "eds and meds" institutions. Dallas had a late start in developing major universities and hospitals, relative to many of its peer cities. But in recent decades, it's been catching up.

SMU, whose students once hailed primarily from North Texas, is now a talent magnet for the Dallas–Fort Worth area. Sixty percent of SMU's undergraduates now come from outside Texas, but they tend to stay after college. Two-thirds of new graduates get their first job in the Dallas–Fort Worth area, and almost half of all living alumni are in Dallas–Fort Worth today.

UT Dallas has been one of the fastest-growing universities in the United States since 2000 and now ranks in line with flagship campuses in Missouri, Kansas, and Alabama. One transformational moment was the establishment of the McDermott Scholars program, a full-ride merit scholarship founded by the family of Texas Instruments cofounder Eugene McDermott, which attracts top students from throughout the United States. UT Dallas is a research leader in biomedical engineering, nanotechnology, brain science, and communications disorders, spending $120 million a year on research. The University of North Texas (UNT) at Denton, another public institution, has grown from fewer than 10,000 students in the 1970s to 38,000 today. In 2009, the UNT system established a new campus in South Dallas, which has grown to four thousand students, almost entirely from disadvantaged families in urban Dallas.

At the public school level, Dallas County voters in November 2020 approved $3.47 billion in a large Dallas Independent School District bond election to add new buildings and campuses, upgrade existing buildings, and improve technology systems.[15]

On the "meds" side, the University of Texas Southwestern Medical Center, or UTSW, the premiere research-focused healthcare institution and medical school in North Texas, has become one of the highest-ranking medical institutions in the United States in terms of research impact. It ranks first in the world on *Nature* magazine's index for research in biomedical science. Recent spinout companies have made breakthroughs in rare neurodegenerative disorders and gene-editing technology. Today, UTSW employs 18,000 people and spends more than $470 million per year on research. Its newly opened 750-bed Clements Hospital will allow UTSW to become an "exporter" of clinical services—that is, treating patients from far beyond the immediate Dallas–Fort Worth area—on roughly the same scale as leading institutions like the medical centers at Vanderbilt and Emory Universities.

Lyda Hill, a granddaughter of H. L. Hunt and the leading Dallas philanthropist alive today, has in recent years made enormous investments to support Dallas-area bioscience, to promote the region's nascent biotechnology industry, and to advance the position of women and girls in science-oriented fields. She will soon open a major biotech complex near UTSW that will further advance the Dallas area's health-care sector.

Together, Dallas–Fort Worth's hospitals provide 126,000 jobs, up more than 25 percent since 2005. Including indirect effects on other industries, the region's hospitals account for more than 8 percent of total Dallas–Fort Worth employment. Government-ordered restrictions on some "elective" medical care dealt a significant blow to the Dallas area's hospitals in the early months of the COVID-19 pandemic, but as of October 2020, they had all weathered the storm successfully.

Numerous studies have shown that research-focused institutions generate technological "spillovers" benefiting hometown economies. For instance, localities with a rich portfolio of research-intensive institutions have typically experienced greater research and development activity, innovation, and business growth than other places. Research by the George W. Bush Institute shows that metro areas with a rich portfolio of "eds and meds" institutions tend to have relatively high education attainment levels.[16] As in the other Texas Triangle cities, the Dallas area's anchor institutions are likely to become even more important drivers of local growth as the US economy becomes more knowledge-centric and less focused on making physical things.

A third driver of economic growth in Dallas has been the region's relatively low costs—particularly housing costs, other costs of living, and costs of doing business. As of 2017, the median home price in the Dallas–Fort Worth area was more than 40 percent lower than the average comparable value for the fifty-one metros in the United States' top eight megaregions. This difference amounted to more than $130,000. Median home prices stood at 3.9 times median household income compared to an average ratio of 5.0 times in the eight megaregions.[17] Within the Texas Triangle, Dallas-area housing costs are well below those of Austin though higher than in Houston or San Antonio.

Surging growth in the northern suburbs has played a large role in maintaining the Dallas–Fort Worth metro's housing cost edge over metros in the other seven megaregions. For one thing, the average ratio of median home price to median household income in Plano, Frisco, Allen, and Denton stood at only 2.9 times as of 2017—far below the comparable ratio in the more supply-strapped city of Dallas, which was 5.3 times. New development has also acted as a shock absorber for the whole metro, creating a fresh competitive housing supply that has helped hold down prices in the core city relative to where they otherwise would be. Even so, the city of Dallas faces a rapidly growing home attainability challenge, and the overall metro area's cost advantage against big coastal cities has been declining since 2012 as booming demand outstrips supply.

The cost of doing business in Dallas–Fort Worth is 16 percent lower than the eight megaregion average, according to a 2014 Moody's study. Above all, this advantage reflects lower land costs and business taxes. Dallas–Fort Worth is again a middling player on this measure compared to its Triangle peers, with lower business costs than Austin or Houston but higher than even more affordable San Antonio. Dallas–Fort Worth also has 6 percent shorter mean commute times than the eight megaregion average, despite its large size—another significant advantage, though this is harder to quantify in dollar terms.

Dallas can, in part, thank its fortunate geography for these cost advantages. Its vast, flat topography has enabled it to grow outward more easily than many coastal cities can manage. Also, the Dallas area has grown up with an unusually polycentric economic geography, with a smaller share of its commercial real-estate space in the central business district than virtually any other large US metro area. This aspect of the area's geography, too, has helped hold down both real-estate prices and traffic congestion in and around the urban core in the city of Dallas.

Just as much, though, Dallas owes its cost advantages to public policy. Only five of the fifty-one metro areas in the United States' top eight megaregions—including Houston and San Antonio—have more permissive land-use rules, based on a University of Pennsylvania-Wharton School study.[18] Looser rules have allowed for faster growth in the housing supply, which has helped hold prices down as the metro area has grown. New building permits and growth in the housing stock have slightly lagged in the Triangle's other four big urban areas by some measures but still score far ahead of almost all other US metros.

Similarly, only three of the fifty-one metros in the eight megaregions—including Houston—outperform Dallas on a measure of "economic freedom" developed by economists at SMU's Bridwell Institute for Economic Freedom, measuring tax levels, government spending, and labor market rules.[19] The Dallas area's probusiness policy orientation has clearly contributed to the city's edge in business costs over most other big US cities.

Upward Mobility

Like all US cities, Dallas faces challenges in developing a more equitable model of growth.

As a whole, the Dallas–Fort Worth metro area ranks relatively high as an engine of upward mobility for its residents. Dallas–Fort Worth scores in the top third of the fifty-one metros in the top eight megaregions for upward mobility among people who've grown up there, based on a measure developed by Raj Chetty. On this measure, Dallas–Fort Worth performs slightly ahead of the other four Texas Triangle metros.[20] Median earnings for residents with an associate's degree or some college but no four-year degree are 24 percent higher in Dallas–Fort Worth than the megaregion average, again higher than the other Triangle metros. Relatively attainable housing also reduces the pressure on lower-income Dallasites compared to their peers in more expensive cities.

That said, the stark bifurcation between the booming northern section of the city of Dallas and struggling South Dallas poses a formidable challenge to the city. Southern Dallas, with a land area larger than the whole city of Atlanta and a population of more than 750,000, has seen extremely little business investment or real-estate development for decades—outside of a handful of small "gentrifying" enclaves. Housing costs have risen even faster in Southern Dallas than in the more prosperous northern part of the city in percentage terms, reflecting the extreme lack of new investment. From 2016 to 2019, production of new housing units went backward, despite an array of policies to encourage it, and the COVID-19 crisis set these efforts back further still in 2020. As a large majority of Southern Dallas families rent their homes, this intensifying housing shortage and the upward spiral in rents have imposed growing pressure on lower-income residents.

By one measure, total jobs within Southern Dallas have declined more than 15 percent since 2000, even as the area's population has grown 7 percent.[21] Dallas has one of the highest rates of children living below the federal poverty line of any US city, and most of these children live in Southern Dallas.[22]

Former Dallas Mayor Mike Rawlings, who served from 2011 to 2019, launched an initiative called "GrowSouth" to promote economic development in Southern Dallas. GrowSouth has achieved some early successes. One notable step forward is the redevelopment of Redbird, a once-moribund indoor mall in a mostly African American neighborhood in far South Dallas that has returned to life as a mixed-use center with offices, health-care facilities, and the first freestanding Starbucks in Southern Dallas. Developers will soon break ground on a modern mixed-income, multifamily residential complex as well as a business hotel. The GrowSouth initiative has also played a role in the rapid emergence of the UNT at Dallas, also in far South Dallas, and the ongoing growth of the Inland Port.

Dallas has made progress, moreover, in addressing educational challenges in the southern part of the city. The last two decades have seen the emergence of several high-performing public charter school networks, above all Uplift Education and KIPP Dallas, as well as several private schools serving mostly nearby Black and Hispanic students at affordable tuition rates, such as St. Philips and West Dallas Community School. More recently, the Dallas Independent School District (DISD) has made significant strides in turning around several South Dallas schools through its "Accelerating Campus Excellence" program. The DISD has also started to roll out innovative early-college and technology-focused academic programs in its high schools and has seen its ratings steadily improve in the Texas Education Agency's grading system.

Like the other big Texas Triangle metros, the Dallas area presents a complex picture when it comes to inclusive growth. On the one hand, the metro area has performed better than most other large US metros in offering rich opportunities and upward mobility both to the million-plus people who've moved in from elsewhere since 2000 and, on the whole, to people who've grown up there. On the other, Dallas resembles the other Triangle metros in its exceptionally segregated geographic pattern and its concentration of poverty in part of its urban core. The COVID-19 crisis has brought to the surface extreme racial disparities that were hiding in plain sight before the pandemic, as in most US cities. Dallas has started to pay more attention to these challenges than ever before, but, like the other Triangle cities, it has a lot of work to do in making its impressive growth more broadly inclusive.

Dallas's Future

In the decades ahead, the Dallas area is likely to face several significant challenges to its growth model.

First, the emerging geography of the vast North Texas region will create growing social and economic strains. The region is on a path to a future in which the core city of Dallas consists mostly of wealthy families who can afford to live in the most attractive neighborhoods of the city and low-income families who can't afford anyplace else, while both the middle class and the majority of employers continue to move ever further northward. Further increases in the already-vast distances separating most of the area's lower-income residents from areas experiencing almost all the metro's job growth are likely to pressure the region's social fabric.

Second, the Dallas area's ongoing demographic and territorial growth will pose increasing infrastructure challenges. Sustaining an integrated labor market with manageable commute times across such a vast area will grow more difficult and will require substantial investment in the road network. Growing density will demand innovative shared-ride services and other means of getting people around. Although the Dallas Area Rapid Transit's light-rail system has expanded to reach an average of about 82,000 riders per day, this represents a tiny fraction of the area's commuters, and it's unlikely that expensive twentieth-century technology like fixed-line rail can grow to handle the twenty-first-century challenges posed by Dallas and the other physically enormous metros of the Texas Triangle.

Growth will also impose increasing pressure on the area's water infrastructure. In a 2018 update, Dallas utility company experts projected that the area served by Dallas water utilities will experience population growth just over 70 percent by 2070; existing water sources will fail to keep up, and the area will face shortages amounting to more than 20 percent of projected demand.[23]

Third, both the city of Dallas and the high-growth suburbs to the north are likely to face growing issues of financial sustainability. For the city of Dallas and surrounding Dallas County, the main financial challenges are not unlike those facing big older cities elsewhere in the country. They revolve around paying for public-sector pensions, health care, and social services for the city's large lower-income population. Dallas got a taste of the pension difficulties plaguing cities in other parts of the United States when its Police and Fire Pension nearly went bankrupt in 2018 after decades of mismanagement. The Texas Legislature had to intervene to orchestrate a financial fix that may or may not stabilize the system over the long term, depending on how stock markets perform.

As for the booming northern suburbs, the rapidly expanding physical infrastructure underlying the growth of these cities will demand increasing maintenance investment. As the urbanist Charles Marohn argues in his 2020 book *Strong Towns*, these cities may well find their development model hasn't generated the density and real-estate values to cover these expenses through property taxes. Marohn points out that many of the most financially troubled municipalities of today are among what used to be the fastest-growing suburbs of the mid-twentieth century.[24]

Fourth, the Dallas area's booming service-sector economy will likely face a challenge from growing automation of lower- to mid-level activities. Just as automation and robotics have replaced millions of blue-collar manufacturing jobs in the "Rust Belt" Urban Midwest megaregion, artificial intelligence will threaten even larger numbers of white-collar service-sector jobs in coming decades—with significant implications for greater Dallas as well as for the services-heavy economies of the Fort Worth and San Antonio areas. Staying ahead of these trends will require significant up-skilling of the Dallas area's tremendous middle-skilled workforce.

The Dallas area's wealth, its economic and demographic diversity, its abundant land, its entrepreneurial culture, and its pragmatic political tradition all suggest that Dallas can work its way through these challenges and thrive in the decades to come. As the Texas Triangle continues to grow, Dallas's position as the megaregion's most important link to the rest of the US economy is likely to lend further economic ballast to the Dallas area. The city known as "Big D"—along with its booming Dallas–Fort Worth neighbors—is likely to grow even bigger as the twenty-first century progresses.

Fort Worth

Fort Worth has long billed itself as the city "where the West begins." On the west side of the Texas Triangle's northern apex, Fort Worth grew up with a geographic orientation and personality entirely different from Dallas and the other Triangle cities. If one thinks of Dallas as a "northeastern" city like New York or Boston, Fort Worth has more in common with other westward-looking cities of the plains, like Oklahoma City or Omaha. Even as the Triangle has grown more integrated in recent decades, Fort Worth continues to bring a distinctive economic and cultural mix to the emerging story of urban Texas.

Fort Worth prides itself on enjoying a decidedly slower, more easygoing pace than nearby Dallas, though the two downtowns are just forty-five miles apart. While Dallas is known for a fine-dining scene that sometimes feels like an import from the East Coast, Fort Worth is renowned for its beloved downscale Tex-Mex and barbecue eateries like Joe T. Garcia's and Angelo's. If Fort Worthians make the drive to Dallas, they're likely going there to shop or meet with bankers. If Dallasites travel in the opposite direction, they're probably headed to Fort Worth's legendary Stock Show and Rodeo or its world-class art museums.

In Fort Worth, real cowboys drive a herd of Longhorns—the "Fort Worth Herd"—through a city street every day, in the Stockyards National Historic District. Fort Worth offers one of the United

A parade of Longhorn cattle is a common sight at Fort Worth's Stockyards. Shutterstock / T photograph.

States' greatest collections of paintings of the Old West at the Sid Richardson Museum.

Fort Worth stands out from the other big Texas Triangle cities in numerous respects. The Fort Worth–Arlington metropolitan division—the western side of the Dallas–Fort Worth metro area as defined by the US Census—has a higher white population share (51 percent as of 2018) and a lower Hispanic share (27 percent) than any of the other four metro areas. It has a higher Baptist population share and a lower Roman Catholic share than the other four as well. The Fort Worth area has a considerably smaller population share with a bachelor's degree or higher, at 30.5 percent as of 2018, than the Dallas metro division (38.1 percent), the Houston metro (32.1 percent), or the Austin metro (46.6 percent), though it's somewhat ahead of the San Antonio metro (27.5 percent). Fort Worth is also the most politically and socially conservative of the big Triangle cities. The city of Fort Worth is currently the largest US city with a Republican mayor.

In economic terms, the Fort Worth area performs in the middle of the pack for the Texas Triangle. Its average income per capita is

13 percent below that of the Dallas side of the metro area but higher than comparable income levels in Houston or San Antonio. Some 11.6 percent of its population was living below the federal poverty line as of 2018, slightly higher than the Dallas area (11.0 percent) and the Austin metro (11.2 percent), but well below poverty rates in the San Antonio metro (15.4 percent) and the Houston metro (14.3 percent).

In some important ways, Fort Worth is more representative of the qualities that attract people to the Texas Triangle than Dallas or Austin. For one thing, it's far more affordable. The median house price in the Fort Worth area, at $205,000, stood at just 79 percent of the level prevailing on the Dallas side of the Dallas–Fort Worth metro as of 2018 and only 68 percent of the Austin level. Home prices were virtually identical to those of Houston, even though Fort Worth is a moderately richer place than Houston. Fort Worth suffers less traffic congestion than Dallas, Austin, or Houston. It invariably scores high in national rankings of "livable" places. Like San Antonio, it also stands out for low costs of doing business by the standards of US cities. Its economy is much more diverse than those of Austin or Houston, based on Moody's data from 2014. Fort Worth's advantages have made it a magnet for families leaving northeastern and western cities in search of a more affordable, less dense, higher quality-of-life location since the start of the COVID-19 crisis.

For much of the twentieth century, Fort Worth considered itself to be in a rivalry with what Fort Worthians have long thought of as their glitzier, more aspirational neighbor to the east. In the 1920s and again in the 1940s, local leaders rebuffed proposals to build a shared airport between Fort Worth and Dallas, preferring to operate their own separate facilities. When they grudgingly agreed to take up the idea again in the mid-1960s, legend has it that Fort Worth leaders brought sack lunches to joint meetings in Dallas since they didn't want to give their business to Dallas restaurants.

Fort Worth–Dallas rivalry, however, has receded a great deal in the decades since the opening of D/FW International Airport in 1974. Negotiators indeed buried the hatchet by placing the forward slash between the *D* and the *F* in the airport's name, which they felt would connote equal status between the two cities to a greater degree than a more conventional hyphen. The airport stimulated tremendous business and real-estate development for many miles in every direction, creating a vast, continuous urban expanse with virtually no remaining undeveloped space between the two core cities. From the point of view of national firms and media organizations, the Dallas–Fort Worth area has largely become a single, integrated market.

Bernard Weinstein says of Fort Worth and Dallas, "They are not rivals anymore. It's so integrated now. People in Dallas work in Fort Worth. People in Fort Worth work in Dallas. . . . We get along. We're a unified metropolitan economy."

But it would be wrong to think of Fort Worth as a supersized suburb of Dallas. On the contrary, Fort Worth embodies a ferocious sense of civic pride and independence. A small, tight-knit community of city leaders and ultrawealthy philanthropists has long acted with impressive common purpose to shape a distinctive urban identity and built environment. They've revitalized downtown, built up the cultural district to the west, and strengthened the city's educational institutions. They've also preserved markers of local history to a much greater degree than Dallas or Houston has. The city of Fort Worth, moreover, has arguably outperformed the city of Dallas in retaining and attracting businesses within its city limits.

The city's success is visible in the form of its remarkable growth record. The population of the city of Fort Worth stood at 46 percent of that of Dallas in 1970, just before D/FW Airport opened for business. In the decades since, Fort Worth has grown significantly faster than Dallas, rising to 67 percent of Dallas's population by 2018.

Despite the explosive growth of Collin County, the center of population gravity in the Dallas–Fort Worth metro is inexorably moving westward as well as northward. Projections cited by officials of the North Texas Council of Governments suggest that Roanoke, a town northwest of D/FW Airport and almost due north of downtown Fort Worth with a current population of fewer than ten thousand, will by 2050 become the population centroid of the Dallas–Fort Worth metro—that is, the point that has equal numbers to the west and east and equal numbers to the north and south. Roanoke, by the way, nicely embodies the attractions of the Texas Triangle. It has close access to booming job markets in several directions and also has affordable neighborhoods, good schools, a charming and walkable town center, an easygoing vibe, and one of the best-rated barbecue spots in North Texas: Hard Eight BBQ.

History

In January 1849, General Williams Jenkins Worth—a veteran of the Mexican–American War and the US Army's commander for the Texas Department—mapped out a chain of ten forts to defend the state's growing white population from Comanche raids. The forts would stretch from the Gulf Coast to the convergence of two forks of the Trinity River, west of the small settlement in Dallas. As it happened, General Worth died of cholera near the Gulf Coast a few months later. The US War Department proceeded with his plan, naming the northernmost of its Texas forts in Worth's honor.[1]

The US Army abandoned the post in 1853. Before long, there was no sign it had ever existed. The population of the surrounding settlement remained tiny for the next two decades.

But in the 1870s, a new social and economic force arose that put Fort Worth on the map: the great western cattle drives. Sitting astride the famous Chisholm Trail, Fort Worth was perfectly positioned to serve as a rest stop and trading center for the cattlemen and cowboys moving their herds northward for sale. Cattle buyers started to set up offices in the town, and Fort Worth adopted its nickname "Cowtown." The city began to grow, electing its first mayor in 1873. Ironically for a place that later came to stand out as the most devout and socially conservative of the big Texas Triangle cities, Fort Worth became notorious in the late 1800s for the saloons, gambling establishments, and other illicit diversions in the district known as "Hell's Half Acre." Doc Holliday, Wyatt Earp, Butch Cassidy, and other legendary figures of the Old West became regular visitors to Fort Worth as part of what was known as the "gamblers' circuit."

Railroads eventually ended the cattle drives, but by the turn of the century, Fort Worth had become an important node of the rail networks connecting Texas ranches with the meat-packing centers of Chicago, Omaha, and elsewhere. The Fort Worth Stockyards became one of the nation's leading cattle trading hubs. The city moved into downstream beef-related activities as well. In what may be the first economic development incentive scheme in the history of Texas, Fort Worth business leaders created a $100,000 incentive offer that convinced two meat-packing companies—Swift & Co. and Armour & Co.—to open plants in the city in 1903.

In the 1910s, a coalition of Baptist preachers, prohibitionists, business leaders, and US Army commanders from a nearby World War I base finally succeeded in shutting down Hell's Half Acre. The closing of Fort Worth's vice activities imposed a particular cost on the city's small African American community, since numerous African Americans—excluded from almost all other industries and having few other choices—worked in Hell's Half Acre.

Like all the other big Texas Triangle cities, Fort Worth maintained rigid racial segregation in housing and public facilities from the Reconstruction era to the Civil Rights era in the 1960s. Most of the city's Black population lived in shanties in the city's southern side or in the Trinity River bottoms.

Like other Texas cities that rose to prominence, Fort Worth became an important player in the oil industry in the first half of the twentieth century. The city became a regional oil refining center, with refineries operated by Sinclair Refining Co. and Humble Oil & Refining Co. In terms of the city's subsequent development, the most consequential figures in Fort Worth's mid-twentieth-century oil industry were Sid Richardson and his nephew and successor, Perry Richardson Bass. They created one of the great US fortunes of their time and became pivotal philanthropists in their home city and around Texas. Bass's four sons—multibillionaires with interests spanning business, investments, science, education, and the arts—have continued to stand at the center of Fort Worth philanthropy and civic leadership.

After the Second World War, Fort Worth achieved remarkable success in diversifying its economy. Advanced manufacturing came to play a much larger role than it ever did in Dallas, Houston, or Austin. The first breakthrough came in 1951, when New York's Bell Aircraft Corp. moved its helicopter division to Fort Worth. The selection of Fort Worth may have been due to the presence of Carswell Air Force Base, which had come into being in 1948. Now part of Textron Inc., a diversified conglomerate, Bell Helicopter remains one of the Fort Worth area's largest employers.[2]

In 1978, General Dynamics added to the city's aerospace and defense sector, establishing its main plant to build F-16 fighter jets for the US Air Force in Fort Worth. The defense giant now known as Lockheed Martin took over General Dynamics' aircraft manufacturing unit in 1993 and continued to build the F-16 in Fort Worth until the Department of Defense ended the program in 2017.[3]

The automotive industry also came to Fort Worth in the early postwar years. In 1954, General Motors (GM) opened an assembly plant in Arlington, then a small suburb east of downtown. The plant continues to produce vehicles today, focusing on GM's Yukon, Suburban, Tahoe, and Escalade models.[4]

Another pivotal moment in the development of Fort Worth's economy was the opening in 1957 of the Dallas–Fort Worth Turnpike, a modern east-west highway connecting the downtowns of Fort Worth and Dallas. The turnpike started as a toll road but eventually became part of Interstate 30. It sparked a boom in residential and business development along its path between Fort Worth and Dallas, especially in the suburbs of Arlington and Grand Prairie. Arlington in particular emerged as a center for recreation and professional sports. Six Flags Over Texas, a pioneering theme park and regional tourism magnet, opened in 1961. Eleven years later, the Major League Baseball team formerly known as the Washington Senators, rechristened as the Texas Rangers, moved to a new ballpark in Arlington. In 1971, the Dallas Cowboys moved from Dallas's Cotton Bowl to their new home in the Dallas suburb of Irving, also between Dallas and Fort Worth. The Cowboys played in Irving until 2009, when they moved further westward along I-30 to Arlington. Since the 1970s, the undeveloped land along Interstate 30 has filled up with water parks and other attractions.

A distinctive finance industry also emerged in downtown Fort Worth from the 1970s on. Unlike Dallas, Fort Worth never became a national center for banking, insurance, or real estate. Rather, capital from the Bass family and other ultrawealthy backers gave rise to an innovative community of investment managers, mostly in the hedge-fund and private-equity industries. Among the most successful and nationally prominent were investor Richard Rainwater, hedge-fund manager John Kleinheinz, and private equity manager David Bonderman.

Like Dallas, Fort Worth developed a pragmatic, moderate style of politics in the decades after the 1960s. The city elected prominent moderate Democrats to federal and state office, such as Jim Wright, who became speaker of the US House of Representatives in the 1990s. Another centrist Fort Worth Democrat, Pete Geren, served four terms in the House of Representatives and as secretary of the Army under the Republican administration of President George W. Bush and now leads the Sid Richardson Foundation. The city has also elected two pragmatic center-right Republican women as mayor: Kay Granger, who went on to serve in the US Congress, and the current mayor, Betsy Price. Wendy Davis, another prominent Fort Worth Democrat, became nationally famous for holding a thirteen-hour filibuster on the floor of the Texas Senate in 2013 in an unsuccessful effort to block a restrictive abortion bill. Davis went on to win the Democratic gubernatorial nomination in 2014 but lost to incumbent Gov. Rick Perry.

Like Dallas, Fort Worth operates a council-manager form of government, in which council members represent single-member districts and the mayor has relatively weak authority. More than Dallas, however, Fort Worth has succeeded in maintaining an impressive degree of political consensus around the city's main policy objectives. Tarrant County, which includes Fort Worth and fifteen other municipalities, also has a long tradition of effective, business-friendly, consensus-driven government.

One area in which Fort Worth has achieved exceptional success is its vibrant arts and culture scene. Over six decades, the city's leaders have worked closely with its tight community of leading philanthropists—above all, the Bass family, their business associates, and Walmart heiress Alice Walton of Fort Worth—to build out a portfolio of cultural assets that attracts visitors from throughout the world. The city has long punched above its weight in the visual arts, with three world-class art museums, each an architectural masterpiece, in the city's cultural district. The Amon Carter Museum of American Art, designed by Philip Johnson, opened in 1961. The Kimbell Museum of Art, designed by Louis Kahn and holding the leading collection of European Old Masters paintings in the south-central part of the United States, arrived on the scene in 1972. And in 2002, the Fort Worth Museum of Modern Art (MOMA) opened its new home, a sleek glass jewel box of a structure surrounded by a shimmering reflecting pond designed by the renowned Japanese architect Tadao Ando. *Architectural Digest* in 2019 named the Fort Worth MOMA the best building in Texas, while *Travel + Leisure* magazine cites Ando's building as one of the "World's Most Beautiful Art Museums."

Other important features of Fort Worth's cultural landscape include the Fort Worth Zoo, one of the world's most respected zoos; the Water Gardens built in 1974; and the Bass Performance Hall, opened in 1998. Since 1962, Fort Worth has held the world-renowned quadrennial Van Cliburn International Piano Competition, named for the musical prodigy who lived much of his life in the city. Cliburn became an international sensation when he unexpectedly won a premiere piano competition in Moscow at the height of the Cold War in 1958 at the age of twenty-three.

Beginning in the late 1970s, the Bass family led a long-term effort to revitalize a thirty-six-block area of Fort Worth's downtown around what came to be known as Sundance Square, after the "Sundance Kid," who joined partner Butch Cassidy for several visits to Hell's Half Acre in the 1890s. Sundance Square is widely celebrated as one of the United States' great downtown redevelopments of recent decades, respecting the historic integrity of the neighborhood while adding walkable street life, restaurants, retail, and other attractions to what had been a moribund downtown area.

In the last thirty years, three further developments have provided dramatic boosts to the Fort Worth–area economy. First,

Ross Perot Jr.'s firm Hillwood Properties in 1989 opened Alliance Airport, the world's first purely industrial airport. Built on the northern edge of Tarrant County, Alliance Airport ensured that the Fort Worth side of the Dallas–Fort Worth metro would play a large role in the area's activities as a national distribution hub. Tenants at the airport include Bell Helicopter, FedEx, Amazon, Walmart, and the US Drug Enforcement Agency. Facebook operates a major data center near the airport. These tenants have easy access to the BNSF Railway, truck and warehouse facilities, and a tax-advantaged foreign trade zone. Alliance Airport directly or indirectly accounts for more than sixty-one thousand jobs in the Fort Worth area. What's more, the success of the airport led Hillwood to surround the facility with residential developments comprising more than eight thousand units. According to Carlton Schwab, Alliance has been "an incredible game changer for Fort Worth" in terms of the businesses the Fort Worth area has since been able to attract.

Second, the Dallas Cowboys moved further west, opening what became known as AT&T Stadium in Arlington in 2009. Costing more than $1.5 billion in 2020 dollars, the stadium—also sometimes called "Jerry World" for the team's owner, Jerry Jones—quickly became recognized as one of the most luxurious, technologically advanced sports arenas in the world. The move to AT&T Stadium has contributed significantly to the position of the Cowboys as one of the most valuable professional sports franchises in the world. In 2020, the Texas Rangers moved to their own new "Globe Life Field," immediately adjacent to AT&T Stadium.

Third, energy companies developed the Barnett Shale natural gas field, mostly on the Fort Worth side of the Dallas–Fort Worth metro area. The Barnett Shale formation consists of "tight gas," or gas-rich but relatively impermeable rock. It was the first major tight-gas field that became economic to exploit because of the new techniques of horizontal drilling and hydraulic fracturing ("fracking"). The field started producing in 1999 but hit its stride by 2007 as companies like XTO Energy Inc. and Chief Oil and Gas perfected these new methods. For a time, it became one of the largest gas-producing areas in the world, bringing tremendous wealth into

AT&T Stadium is the home of the NFL's Dallas Cowboys. The stadium is in Arlington, in Tarrant County. Shutterstock / Philip Lange.

the Fort Worth area. Dallas-based ExxonMobil acquired XTO in 2010, making the Fort Worth area one of the main operating areas for the United States' largest energy company.

Population Growth

Between 2017 and 2019, Fort Worth passed Indianapolis, Columbus, and San Francisco to become the thirteenth-largest city in the United States, with a 2018 population of 898,919. Between 2012 and 2017, Fort Worth was the third fastest growing of the United States' top fifty cities, after Seattle and Austin.[5] Tarrant County reached a population of 2,057,468 in 2019, making it one of the United States' ten fastest-growing counties over the 2010 to 2019 period.

Meanwhile, the Fort Worth area—defined as the Fort Worth–Arlington metropolitan division—reached 2.5 million people in 2019, accounting for approximately one-third of the Dallas–Fort Worth metro's total population. Since 2000, the Fort

Fort Worth is the thirteenth-largest city in the nation in population.

Worth side of the metro area has grown slightly faster than the Dallas side—46 percent to the Dallas area's 45 percent.

Much more than on the Dallas side of the metro, growth in the Fort Worth area has been balanced between the core city and its suburban counties. The four counties surrounding Fort West on the north, west, and south—Wise, Parker, Johnson, and Hood—collectively grew 48 percent between 2000 and 2018, just ahead of the city of Fort Worth. Together, their population stood at 438,000 as of 2018.

The Fort Worth area's western suburbs are likely to grow enormously over the next several decades. The combined population of Wise, Parker, Johnson, and Hood counties amounts to only about one-quarter of the combined population of Collin and Denton counties, north of Dallas, but these counties have far more undeveloped rural land than Collin and Denton counties do. Their county seats—Decatur, Weatherford, Cleburne, and Granbury—still offer the charming vibe and laid-back lifestyle that many people look for in the Texas Triangle but are within easy reach of Fort Worth's booming job market.

The area's western counties, like other suburban counties in the Texas Triangle, are also rapidly growing more ethnically diverse.

As of 2018, approximately 18 percent of the four-county population was African American or Hispanic—well below Fort Worth's 44 percent share, but steadily growing.

Drivers of Economic Growth

The Dallas–Fort Worth metro economy is so tightly integrated that the main drivers of economic growth in the Fort Worth area are largely the same as the drivers for Dallas that we outline in chapter 7: central location and transportation infrastructure, diversity of industries, and low costs of living and doing business.

The development of D/FW Airport and its location midway between Fort Worth and Dallas have made all the difference in the growth of the Fort Worth area's economy. While employers looking for young, highly educated talent—particularly in finance or technology—are likely to choose Dallas or Collin County over Fort Worth, companies in more blue-collar industries, especially manufacturing and distribution, often find Fort Worth's location and value proposition compelling. Alliance Airport has reinforced the centrality of Fort Worth as an ideally located hub in the United States' south-central region.

Both D/FW and Alliance have ambitious plans under way to expand capacity. Fort Worth has also reinforced its connectivity to D/FW Airport and the whole metro area by investing in light-rail lines. The Trinity Rail Express, opened in 2019, connects downtown Fort Worth to D/FW. An extension will soon connect D/FW to downtown Dallas, enabling easy transit access between the two cities.

As in the other Texas Triangle metros, the diversity of Fort Worth's economy has also been an important strength. The Fort Worth area's major employers span most sectors of the US economy. American Airlines Group, the largest employer in the Dallas–Fort Worth metro, has its headquarters in Fort Worth. Other leading private-sector employers include Bell Helicopter and Lockheed Martin (aerospace), BNSF (railways), GM (automobiles), XTO (energy), Alcon (eye care), and D. R. Horton (home building). While

Lockheed Martin has discontinued the F-16 and now produces the new F-35 Lightning II joint strike fighter in Greenville, South Carolina, the company employs more than fourteen thousand people in Fort Worth in design, engineering, and modernization. BNSF is now part of Warren Buffett's Berkshire Hathaway conglomerate, while D. R. Horton is the nation's largest home builder.

Fort Worth also is home to large federal government employers—more than Dallas. One is the Naval Air Station Joint Reserve Base Fort Worth. Another, the US Bureau of Printing and Engraving, produces more than half the nation's paper currency at its Fort Worth facility.

Like the other big Texas Triangle economies, the Fort Worth area's economy has grown more diverse over recent decades, even as metros in other megaregions like the Northeast Corridor and along the West Coast have in many cases trended in the opposite direction. As we discuss in chapter 7 regarding Dallas, diversity has served not only as a hedge against economic downcycles in the Fort Worth area but also as a stimulus to creativity and entrepreneurship.

As in the other Texas Triangle metros, "eds and meds" institutions are becoming an ever-larger driver of the Fort Worth–area economy. Texas Christian University (TCU), founded in 1873, is the oldest coeducational university in Texas and one of the oldest west of the Mississippi River. Although its original location was in Hell's Half Acre, the university's founders soon moved the campus to what they considered a more wholesome site west of downtown. Today, TCU plays a leading role in the booming Fort Worth economy, operating a premier business program. It now attracts 45 percent of its 9,700 students from outside Texas and, like SMU in Dallas, retains a large proportion of them in North Texas after they graduate.

The Fort Worth area is also home to the largest university in the Dallas–Fort Worth metro, the University of Texas at Arlington (UTA). UTA became part of the University of Texas (UT) System in 1965 and has grown to forty-three thousand students. It operates the fifth-largest nursing program in the United States and produces a large share of Dallas–Fort Worth's architects and landscape designers. UTA currently spends approximately $117 million per year on research, second among Dallas–Fort Worth institutions after UT Dallas. UTA researchers have made significant contributions in civil engineering, transportation, environmental technologies, medical devices, and other fields.

In health care, Fort Worth is known for Cook Children's Medical Center, founded in 1918 and consistently ranked among the best pediatric hospitals in the United States. In 2019, TCU and the UNT Health Science Center opened a new, jointly run medical school in Fort Worth.

A third driver of the area's growth is its relatively affordable costs of living and doing business. According to a cost-of-living calculator from Sperling's Best Places, the overall cost of living in Fort Worth is modestly below the US average, while Dallas and Austin are slightly higher than average.[6] San Francisco–based Thumbtack ranked Fort Worth as the second-friendliest big city in the country for small business in 2019, ahead of Dallas, Houston, and San Antonio, though behind first-ranked Austin.[7] Office rents in downtown Fort Worth are far cheaper than rents in premier Dallas locations like Uptown and the Park Cities.

Like Dallas, Fort Worth benefits from its expansive topography and its polycentric economic geography. A number of the area's biggest employers have their main facilities far from downtown, in some cases near D/FW Airport or Alliance Airport. These geographic factors help hold down housing and commercial real-estate costs. As we discuss in chapter 7, the Dallas–Fort Worth metro as a whole also benefits from its progrowth policy orientation, as measured by indices of land-use rules and "economic freedom." The city of Fort Worth indeed takes a significantly more permissive approach to new real-estate development than the city of Dallas does, helping account for Fort Worth's faster housing supply growth and lower home prices.

In all these respects—transportation infrastructure, economic diversity, and affordability—Fort Worth is highly representative of the Texas Triangle region as a whole. Its impressive growth over the last two decades is, in some ways, even more remarkable than the growth of Dallas or Austin, which enjoyed powerful tailwinds from their leading positions in high-growth sectors like finance, technology, and business services. The industries that figure most prominently in the Fort Worth economy, such as defense, aerospace, automobiles, home building, and government, have been among the slower-growing sectors of the US economy. The fact that Fort Worth has grown so fast all the same is a testament to the power of the Texas Triangle's model of economic growth.

Long-Term Challenges

At the same time, Fort Worth shares challenges similar to the other big Texas Triangle metros. Like all US cities, Fort Worth faces the task of making its economic growth model more inclusive. But Fort Worth—again like its Triangle peers—has some especially daunting challenges in this respect. The city of Fort Worth, for one thing, has a particularly acute pattern of housing segregation on income lines. The most disadvantaged parts of the city—southeastern and northern Fort Worth—are among the poorest neighborhoods in the Triangle megaregion.

Fort Worth has recently made strides in addressing the problems of its most disadvantaged neighborhoods. Starting in 2015, the city and local philanthropists have partnered with the Atlanta-based nonprofit Purpose Built Communities to develop Renaissance Heights, a mixed-income complex with a variety of wraparound social services, in the Stop Six neighborhood in southeastern Fort Worth. Renaissance Heights sits adjacent to a new school operated by Uplift Education, the leading public charter school network in North Texas, as well as a new Walmart store and YMCA.[8]

Philanthropist Alice Walton and her associate Brent Beasley, a former Baptist minister, have played a leading role in convening donors and other stakeholders around efforts to improve Fort Worth's public schools. Mayor Betsy Price has recently partnered with Fort Worth hospitals to make Fort Worth the first Texas city to join "Blue Zone Communities," a movement to create places that promote comprehensive well-being. The city has also been success-ful in creating a wide variety of new housing units in an attractive, walkable area near the cultural district west of downtown.

Fort Worth faces a significant challenge in raising its higher education attainment levels. At 30.5 percent, the share of the Fort Worth metropolitan division population with a bachelor's degree or higher is far below the average for the United States' eight lead-ing urban megaregions (36.8 percent) as well as the Dallas divi-sion's level (38.1 percent). The city's shortage of highly educated young workers, particularly those with technology backgrounds, limits the kinds of employers the city can attract. Fort Worth, for instance, was not a serious contender for Amazon's "HQ2"—unlike Dallas, which by some accounts came in third in the competition.

Like Dallas and the other big Texas Triangle cities, Fort Worth has been successful in attracting the educated workforce it needs from elsewhere in the United States. But Fort Worth leaders rec-ognize that great cities must create a highly educated workforce from the young people who grow up there, in addition to importing talent from elsewhere, if they wish to create an economy that is both broadly inclusive and globally competitive in the increasingly knowledge-centric economy of the 2020s.

Even more than the Dallas area, the Fort Worth area will need to modernize its economy in every respect, from education and workforce development to the makeup of its industry base, to adapt to rapid evolution in the economy. It seems likely that competing federal priorities—particularly in the aftermath of the global coro-navirus crisis—are likely to pressure the federal defense budget, a key driver of the Fort Worth–area economy. The automotive indus-try is likely to shift toward electric vehicles and other new prod-ucts, potentially threatening traditional facilities like Arlington's sixty-six-year-old GM plant. Gas production from the Barnett Shale has been declining for years. Fort Worth will increasingly feel the effects of its relatively weak position in technology, biotechnology, and the kinds of technology-enabled service industries in which Dallas and Collin County excel.

The Fort Worth area has impressive highway and road infra-structure, with much better traffic conditions than Dallas, Houston, or Austin. But like the other big Triangle metros, Fort Worth has a great deal of work to do in building out its infrastructure to keep up with galloping population growth throughout the region and growing population density in the core city. It will need new highways connecting the western counties efficiently to the rest of the Dallas–Fort Worth metro area.[9] The city of Fort Worth and surrounding Tarrant County will also need to reckon with an inadequate public transit network. As the Fort Worth Transportation Authority acknowledged in a 2015 master plan, the city's transit system is among the least well-funded and least functional of a group of peer systems around the United States.[10]

All this said, Fort Worth's political, business, and philanthropic leaders are as unified and determined as ever, and they have a keen sense of what their city and the surrounding area must do to sustain the remarkable record of success they have enjoyed in recent decades. Demographers project that the Dallas–Fort Worth metro area's population will rise from 7.7 million today to twelve to thirteen million by 2050. By that time, the Fort Worth side of the metro area is likely to constitute nearly half of the total, which means it's likely to be one of the fastest growing urban areas in the United States for decades to come. The city "where the West begins" will play a larger and larger role in the unfolding story of the Texas Triangle.

Houston

I f Texas is big, Houston is a testament to its bigness.

With 2.3 million people, it's by far the biggest city in Texas—almost as big as Chicago. The metropolitan area as a whole has almost seven million people and a GDP of $479 billion—big enough to be the fifteenth-largest state in population and the twenty-fifth-largest economy in the world. As the indisputable energy capital of the world, it is usually awash in money and prides itself on a wide-open culture that allows developers to build without zoning, encourages businesses to grow as fast as they can, and welcomes newcomers who want to get things done.

Houston is a truly international city, due not only to its energy dominance but also to its status as one of the major world's leading medical centers. It's also an extremely diverse city demographically, with large populations from all over the world. For all these reasons, it's an outward-facing place—the Triangle's connection to the rest of the world.

Within the Triangle, Houston has extremely strong economic ties to the megaregion's other major cities. Whereas the Dallas–Fort Worth metro is the leading warehousing and distribution center in the central part of the United States, many of those goods flow through the Port of Houston on the way to North Texas warehouses. And there's scheduled airline service every half hour, meaning the Triangle's Houston-Dallas "shuttle" is twice as frequent as the Delta shuttle between New York and Washington.

Houston also has strong ties to San Antonio. Many regional companies, including the grocery giant H-E-B, serve both cities and regard those two markets as linked. And as Houston emerges as a tech center, its connections to Austin's tech scene are getting stronger as well. Finally, Houston is also a national and regional leader in medicine, space technology, and architecture and civil engineering, exporting these and other types of expertise to other parts of the Triangle.

Yet Houston today faces significant challenges. It has always been hostage to the boom-and-bust economic cycles of the energy industry and has experienced two energy downturns in the past few years. Even though it is now more economically diversified thanks to medicine, space, and other industries, Houston will face a major challenge in dealing with the coming energy transition—which could challenge the city's preeminence as energy capital of the world. Furthermore, despite the strength of its demographic diversity, Houston suffers from deep inequities across the urban landscape. And as Hurricane Harvey has shown—to say nothing of COVID-19—Houston is at risk for extreme events that could damage both its economy and its reputation as a great city in which to live. All these challenges must be confronted if Houston is going to remain the Triangle's "world city."

But Houston's welcoming approach and can-do spirit—along with the city's continued growth and overall prosperity—bode well for the future. Houston has the tools required to take on these challenges and play its part in cementing the Texas Triangle as one of the world's most powerful megaregions.

History of Houston

In 1836, Sam Houston won the Texas war of independence by defeating Santa Anna in the Battle of San Jacinto on Buffalo Bayou, a location now surrounded by oil refineries and petrochemical plants along the Houston Ship Channel. Later that year, two merchants from New York—the Allen brothers—bought land some twenty-five miles upstream at the intersection of Buffalo

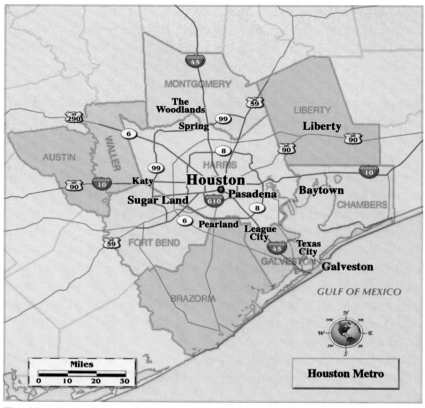

MONTGOMERY

The
Woodlands

Spring

LIBERTY

Liberty

AUSTIN

WALLER

Katy **Houston**

Sugar Land Pasadena Baytown

CHAMBERS

Pearland League
City

FORT BEND

Texas
City

GALVESTON

Galveston

GULF OF MEXICO

BRAZORIA

Miles
0 10 20 30

Houston Metro

The Houston metropolitan area covers nine counties.

and White Oak bayous and started a new settlement, which they named after the recent battle's hero. Houston grew slowly at first, but by the time of the Civil War, several railroads converged there. Partly for this reason, it became a bustling commercial center, providing transportation, banking, and trading services for the burgeoning cotton industry. Still, in the nineteenth century, it was overshadowed in shipping by Galveston, a nearby barrier island that had a port.

Then, around the turn of the twentieth century, two things happened that secured Houston's future as one of Texas' great cities. First came the devastating Galveston hurricane in 1900, which flattened the island and dramatically reduced confidence in the city as a shipping center. Then one year later, oil was discovered at Spindletop near Beaumont, less than one hundred miles from Houston. Thereafter, the rise of the oil industry and the development of Houston as a port city occurred hand in hand.

After the Galveston hurricane of 1900, an urgent need arose for an inland deepwater port in East Texas. This need led to an aggressive local-federal partnership to dredge the Houston Ship Channel along Buffalo Bayou. The ship channel was completed in 1914, laying the foundation for today's world-class port and energy and petrochemical facilities in the area.

Meanwhile, it didn't take Houston long after the discovery at Spindletop to become a global energy capital. The first large refinery in Houston was built in 1918 by Sinclair Oil Co. By 1929, Houston was home to more than forty oil companies, including Gulf and Texaco (both now part of Chevron) and Humble Oil (now part of ExxonMobil). Today it is headquarters to almost two dozen Fortune 500 companies, most of which are in the energy business, making it the second-largest headquarters city in the United States after New York. Other large energy companies, including Chevron and ExxonMobil, house a majority of their employees in the Houston area even though their headquarters are elsewhere. Although ExxonMobil is headquartered in Irving, near Dallas, some ten thousand employees from various locations were consolidated at its Houston campus near The Woodlands in 2014.

Today, the Houston Ship Channel alone accounts for a third of all refining and petrochemical capacity in the United States—the largest concentration anywhere in the world. It's also made Houston the world's most important city for engineers, especially petroleum and chemical engineers who work in these industries.

Primarily because of growth in the oil industry, the city's population grew from 44,000 in 1900 to almost 300,000 in 1930. During World War II, Houston surpassed New Orleans as the largest city in the South. By 1950, it had more than a half-million residents, making it the fourteenth-largest city in the country. Since then, metropolitan Houston has consistently grown by approximately one million residents per decade. Houston's population growth slows down when oil prices decline—as happened slightly between 2015 and 2017—but even during the last few years, Houston has

The Houston Ship Channel is a key component of Houston's world-leading energy industry. Shutterstock / Michael Reitz.

trailed only Dallas–Fort Worth in population growth. Today, seven million people live in metropolitan Houston. More than 4.5 million live in Harris County, ranking it third in the nation after Cook County (Chicago) and Los Angeles County—and more than two million live in the unincorporated areas, the most anywhere in the United States. Houston's suburbs sprawl into counties surrounding Harris County (see table 9.1).

The United States' Most Diverse City

Rice University Sociology Professor Stephen Klineberg, author of the 2020 book *Prophetic City*, often says Houston may be the most diverse city in the country. Once a predominantly white and Black town, Houston is now 40 percent Hispanic and almost 10 percent Asian.

Table 9.1

Greater Houston selected suburban populations

Pasadena	153,528
Sugar Land	129,423
The Woodlands	124,511
Pearland	124,018
League City	108,184
Baytown	81,859
Missouri City	79,390
Spring	68,371
Texas City	50,946
Galveston	49,638
La Porte	34,926
Deer Park	34,590
Katy	20,417
Stafford	19,260
Bellaire	18,425
South Houston	17,666
Humble	15,856
West University Place	15,851
Seabrook	14,150
Webster	11,982
Tomball	11,691
Galena Park	11,040
Jacinto City	10,483
Liberty	9,754
Jersey Village	8,073
Prairie View	6,560

Source: Texas Demographic Center, January 1, 2019, estimates.

Because of its proximity to the Gulf of Mexico and Louisiana, Houston has always been more of a southern town than Dallas, Austin, or San Antonio. Indeed, for most of the last century, it has been the largest city in the South. Houston was always one of the most important cities in the United States for African Americans, in large part because several of the largest freedman's communities were established there in the nineteenth century. By 1960, 25 percent of the city's population was African American—more than two hundred thousand people. During the 1960s and 1970s, both white and Black populations in the Houston area grew rapidly.

Since the early 1980s, however, the demographic profile of Houston has changed dramatically. Over the past thirty-five years, the number of white residents in Harris County has stayed about the same—at 1.5 million—while the African American population has risen in proportion to the overall population. However, the Hispanic and Asian populations have skyrocketed. Meanwhile, suburban Fort Bend County—centered around Sugar Land—is even more demographically diverse, with all four main racial and ethnic groups comprising at least 20 percent of the population. The mayor of Houston, Sylvester Turner, is African American. The Harris County judge (the county executive) is an immigrant from Colombia, and the Fort Bend County judge was born in a village in southern India that didn't have electricity.[1]

Demographic superlatives could continue all day long. The region's two biggest industries—energy and medicine—are highly international and draw people from all over the world. Almost one in every four Houston-area residents is foreign-born.[2] More Nigerians live in Houston than anywhere else outside of Nigeria, in part because Nigeria is oil-rich, thus having strong connections to Houston energy companies.[3] More Vietnamese live in Houston than anywhere else in the United States outside of California, in large part because Vietnamese refugees decades ago were drawn by the Gulf Coast shrimping industry. There are more refugees in Houston than in any other city in the United States, many of them from East Africa. The region probably has the biggest South Asian population anywhere in the United States outside of the New York region. Half the region's households speak a language other than English at home compared to a nationwide average of 35 percent.

This remarkable diversity is reflected in Houston's business community. Almost a third of business owners are foreign-born. More than five thousand Houston companies conducted foreign business in 2018, while more than one thousand Houston firms had foreign ownership.[4] More than ninety nations operate consular offices in Houston, the third-largest collection of diplomatic offices in the United States, and fifteen foreign governments maintained trade offices in Houston, along with thirty-five foreign chambers of commerce. Twenty foreign banks from ten nations conduct business in Houston.

Although Houston is demographically diverse—and growing fast—it has struggled with ensuring that all Houstonians share in its prosperity. For example, the Brookings Institution's "Metro Monitor" ranked Houston ninth in overall growth among fifty-three large metropolitan areas between 2008 and 2018—but forty-eighth in inclusiveness.[5] Similarly, another highly respected think tank, the Urban Institute, recently ranked Houston 273rd out of 274 major US metropolitan areas in inclusiveness, ahead only of Shreveport, Louisiana.[6] As will be described later, the recent extreme events Houston has grappled with—including both Hurricane Harvey and the COVID-19 crisis—have highlighted the cleavages in the city, with some populations and neighborhoods faring much better than others.

Even though it is likely to continue growing, Houston faces a great challenge in addressing inequity. But the city has always been remarkably welcoming of newcomers, and this wide-open approach—along with an emerging new generation of political leaders more attuned to inequity—means that the city is positioned well to address this challenge.

Energy Capital of the World

Through all the city's demographic changes, energy has remained Houston's most important industry. The oil business boomed unabated until 1986, when a dramatic and unexpected drop in the price of oil threw the town into the deepest recession it had ever seen. The region lost more than two hundred thousand jobs—one out of every twelve—and it took several years for Houston to dig itself out of the mess.[7] In many ways, Houston has never been the same. A lot of in-migration from other states stopped, and the region's white population has been flat in total numbers ever since.

In other ways, however, the 1980s recession was a wake-up call for both the city and its industries. Over time, the city strengthened both its economic infrastructure and its other economic sectors, such as medicine. But Houston also doubled down on petrochemicals—chemicals made from oil and natural gas—which are raw materials used to make a wide variety of products, including fuels, plastics, films, resins, fertilizers, waxes, and asphalt. That helped cushion the blow the next time a dramatic oil and gas price drop came along because the petrochemical raw materials dropped in price.

By 2015, fracking had led to a renaissance in oil production nationwide, and Houston was reaping the benefits. Then the price of oil dropped in half. Houstonians—especially those with long memories—held their breath, waiting for a repeat of the 1980s recession. But it didn't happen. As economist Robert Gilmer from the University of Houston points out, the region lost only about 4,300 jobs in 2015–16, partly because cheaper oil and natural gas prices allowed petrochemicals to thrive in the facilities along the ship channel.

Still, Houston's predominance in the oil industry is impressive. As Gilmer has written, Houston is to oil what Wall Street is to finance, Los Angeles is to entertainment, the Bay Area is to technology, and Detroit is to cars. The newest drilling technologies—horizontal drilling, deepwater offshore drilling, and hydraulic fracturing—all began or were advanced in Houston, which is home to several energy-related research institutions, usually affiliated with major oil or petrochemical companies. "The more difficult and complicated the drilling job, the more likely that a phone call for technical help will be placed to Houston from somewhere around the world," Gilmer writes in *Forbes*.

Today, Gilmer estimates that there are 175,000 Houston-based employees working directly in production, oil services, and machinery and fabricated metals, and tens of thousands more serve as suppliers or contractors. Half of the United States' oil-extraction payroll is based in Houston.[8]

The city is unquestionably still the energy capital of the world. But there's no doubt that Houston faces a major challenge on this front as well. Although worldwide usage of oil and gas remains high, even Houston's business leaders acknowledge there has been a loss of public confidence in the traditional energy industry and an alarming flow of capital away from oil and gas investments. In recent years, for the first time ever, Houston's business leaders have spoken publicly about the threat of climate change and the need to reduce greenhouse gas emissions.

As the world's "energy transition" unfolds and different sources of energy become more important, Houston must find a way to ensure that it is the energy capital of the world, not merely the oil and gas capital of the world. But Houston and its energy leaders are beginning to address this challenge in an aggressive way.

Ports and Airports

Fitting for such a large city, Houston has one of the largest ports in the United States and two major airports, both of which are vital to the local economy. Perhaps the most important piece of economic infrastructure in the region is the Port of Houston, which ranks number two in the United States overall and number one in foreign tonnage. Almost half the imports are from Asia, while exports are shipped all over the world.

Along with the Houston Ship Channel, the port gives Houston's blue-collar economy a truly international flavor. "Houston looks toward the world through the water," says Mario Hernandez, the former chairman of the Texas Economic Development Council. "It's very much an international city, more so than all the others [in the Texas Triangle]. You have Dallas connected in a big way to the country, and Houston connected in a big way to the world by the water." Most of the exports are energy-related, making Houston the most important port in the world for energy imports and exports. However, the recent expansion of the Panama Canal provides Houston with the opportunity to compete with West Coast ports for the import and export of other products as well.

Furthermore, port activity in Houston is intimately connected to the rest of the Texas Triangle. Houston sits along Interstate 10, which connects the port to New Orleans to the east, to San Antonio to the west, and to both coasts. It's connected to Dallas by Interstate 45—known in Houston as the Gulf Freeway, which was the first freeway in the region. (Along with I-35 between Dallas and San Antonio, I-45 and I-10 literally create the Texas Triangle.) Freight railroads also have a large presence in Houston, with Union Pacific Railroad, Kansas City Southern Railway, and Burlington Northern Santa Fe Railway all moving freight in and out of the Houston region.[9]

As the energy industry expanded in Houston, so did the need for global airline service. The main airport—now known as George Bush Intercontinental Airport—opened in 1969, a few years after a group of business leaders purchased land some twenty miles north of downtown and persuaded the city to build the airport. Bush Intercontinental handles more than forty million passengers per year and is United Airlines' second-biggest hub—almost as busy as Chicago O'Hare. After Intercontinental opened in 1969, commercial air service ended at Houston's original airport—William P. Hobby Airport, which dates back to 1937 and was named for Texas' former governor in 1967. Two years later, however, Southwest Airlines began service to the Texas Triangle from Hobby, and since then the airport has grown into a major air facility. Today Hobby carries about thirteen million passengers per year.

Eds and Meds

As the Houston economy has diversified beyond energy, educational and especially medical institutions have come to play an increasingly important role. Though the "eds and meds" sector in

Houston was seeded in large part by philanthropic contributions from donors in the energy industry, over time it has matured into a thriving independent sector.

With forty-five thousand students, the University of Houston—a state-supported institution—is the largest in the metro region and became a Tier One university in 2011, a designation from the Carnegie Foundation for the Advancement of Teaching. Elite Rice University, although it has only seven thousand students, is widely regarded as the best university in Texas. Rice is ranked seventeenth in the nation by *U.S. News & World Report* magazine, the highest of any Texas university for 2020.[10] Texas Southern University in Houston, with almost ten thousand students, ranks number two among historically Black colleges and universities in Texas.[11]

Meanwhile, health and medicine has become the second most important economic sector in the region. From modest beginnings in 1945, the Texas Medical Center (TMC) complex now covers 1,345 acres, equal to the eighth-largest US business district, and employs more than 106,000 people at more than sixty different medical institutions, all in a one-square-mile area, making it one of the densest employment centers in the country. The medical center reported ten million patient visits per year and more than 180,000 annual surgeries, or one starting almost every three minutes around the clock. More than 13,600 heart surgeries occur yearly, and 750,000 patients visit the medical center's emergency rooms each year. A baby is born every twenty minutes at the TMC.

Today, the TMC is the largest and most prestigious clinical medical district in the world—so significant that it is basically an "export" industry for Houston, attracting patients from around the world seeking care. "If you are wealthy in South America, and you need specialized health care, it's where you go," says Carlton Schwab. "Go to Houston."

Space and Technology

No less important to Houston is the space sector. Houston has been synonymous with manned space travel for more than half a

Houston's TMC, bounded by Hermann Park, is the world's largest medical center, serving patients from around the globe. Shutterstock / All Stock Photos.

century. In July 1969, Neil Armstrong spoke the first words by a human from the moon's surface: "Houston. Tranquility Base here. The Eagle has landed." Less than a year later, Apollo 13's astronauts uttered one of the most famous phrases in US history: "Houston, we've had a problem."

NASA established the Manned Spacecraft Center in 1961 on 1,700 acres near Galveston Bay some twenty-five miles southeast of downtown Houston. Shortly thereafter, President John Kennedy delivered his famous "moon speech" at Rice University, saying, "We seek to go to the moon not because it is easy, but because it is hard." Although the Houston location was selected after a rigorous site-selection process, then vice president Lyndon Johnson was chair of the National Aeronautics and Space Council at the time and undoubtedly exerted considerable political influence as well. The facility was renamed Johnson Space Center after Johnson's death in 1973.

Today, Johnson Space Center is a major economic driver in the Houston region. The space center itself employs some ten thousand people and is indirectly responsible for another forty thousand jobs. The space center has an overall budget of close to $5 billion, half of

A rocket display is part of Houston's Lyndon B. Johnson Space Center, a leading tourist destination and home of the NASA Manned Spacecraft Center. Shutterstock / John Silver.

which is spent in Texas.[12] In addition, the space center has spun off innumerable business startups involved in space exploration. Most recently, the Houston Airport System launched the Houston Spaceport at nearby Ellington Field in order to incubate and grow such businesses. Space Center Houston—a nonprofit education center at the Johnson Space Center—attracts more than one million visitors a year, making it one of the biggest tourist attractions in Houston.

Houston has also recently sought to strengthen its tech startup sector. Significant tech innovation already occurs inside the large energy companies and within the institutions at the TMC. With the creation of business incubators and accelerators such as The Cannon, with three locations, and The Ion, currently located in downtown Houston, venture capitalists have become interested in Houston's innovation economy. In 2021, The Ion will move into a renovated former Sears building in Midtown Houston owned by Rice University.

How Hurricane Harvey Changed Everything

Located near the Gulf Coast, Houston has always been prone to flooding and therefore has a long history of dealing with extreme weather events. But in 2017, Hurricane Harvey dumped forty to fifty inches of rain in the Houston area over five days and led to flooding that featured in the national news day after day.

Hurricane Harvey did not knock out Houston's economic infrastructure for long—primarily because Houston didn't experience the storm's high winds. But more than two hundred thousand houses were either damaged or destroyed, along with close to a half-million cars and trucks. Simply cleaning up all the debris from people's homes in Houston cost the city more than $250 million.

Devastating as it was as an individual event, Hurricane Harvey highlighted the fact that Houston is increasingly vulnerable to extreme events. Two years before Harvey, the Memorial Day Flood dumped twelve inches of rain on Houston in ten hours. One year before Harvey, the Tax Day Flood dumped almost twenty inches in one day and, among other things, washed away mailboxes containing people's tax returns. Thus, in three years, Houston experienced three extraordinary floods. Some neighborhoods flooded all three times. These floods came on top of the damage caused by Tropical Storm Allison in 2001, which dumped almost forty inches of rain on Houston, and Hurricane Ike in 2008, which threatened the Houston Ship Channel before it changed course at the last minute.

Although it was a worldwide event rather than a local event, the COVID-19 crisis of 2020–21 reinforced Houston's sense of vulnerability as well as concern about the city's growing reputation as a flood-prone city. Officials are entertaining a wide variety of proposals to create a structure in Galveston Bay that would protect the Houston Ship Channel from hurricanes. Meanwhile, the city is actively looking at alternative approaches to making Houston more resilient—more able to survive and bounce back from extreme weather events. In the wake of Harvey, for example, local officials discovered that one-third of multifamily units—165,000 in all—are in a flood plain, and risk could be reduced if these housing complexes are moved, raised, or shored up. In early 2020, Mayor Sylvester Turner released a wide-ranging resiliency plan that called for not only additional improvements to flood mitigation but strengthening nonprofit charities and social networks of neighborhoods around the city, especially in underserved neighborhoods.

Houston's Future

After a century as the undisputed energy capital of the world, Houston—like many other cities—faces increasing competition from other cities for educated and talented young people. For most of the last century, Houston's growth has come largely because outsiders have moved to the city in search of opportunity. Houston's climate was warm, if humid. Jobs were plentiful, and housing was inexpensive. As Rice's Stephen Klineberg likes to say, the attitude used to be "Houston's ugly, and it smells, but it's the smell of money, so come on down."

Now, however, Houston is facing increasing housing costs, especially in the center of the city, while at the same time, traffic congestion is getting worse, and some 40 percent of the workforce is stuck in low-wage jobs. Civic and business leaders realize Houston must focus more on quality-of-life concerns to remain competitive, especially as the energy industry becomes more technology-based and therefore must compete for talent with the likes of San Francisco, Seattle, and New York.

In response, the city has led the nation in parks planning, especially with the Bayou Greenways 2020 plan—the most ambitious linear parks effort in the nation, which is spending more than $200 million to renovate and make accessible more than one hundred miles of trails along the region's bayous. Houston is also trying, with some success, to improve its public transit system so that residents have alternatives to driving.

But Houston still struggles with overcoming the deficiencies of its car-oriented culture, especially as low-wage residents are displaced from the center of the city and forced to live in low-amenity, auto-oriented suburbs. And as is the case elsewhere in Texas, Houston struggles to provide successful education for many of its youth, especially those who grow up in underserved neighborhoods—a problem that may underlie the city's struggle with inequity. Local youth often do not have the opportunity to become upwardly mobile, and companies often must import skilled workers from elsewhere.

Despite ongoing concerns about inequity, the future of the energy industry, and extreme weather events, Houston has always been a resilient and resourceful city. For more than a century, it has been known as a place that is always on the lookout for new people with new ideas. It is this quality that has always provided Houston with a critical role in the Texas Triangle: the welcoming and wide-open city on the eastern edge of the Triangle, connecting the region's other cities to the rest of the world.

Austin

Austin once had a memorable motto (more memorable than mottos from other cities of the Texas Triangle): "Keep Austin Weird." The phrase is fading in popularity like a worn-out T-shirt, but Austin's distinctive "weirdness" is still visible in the casual hipster vibe of Central Austin street life, in its nationally renowned live-music scene, in the youthful energy that comes from being the state's premier college town and, most recently, in the pervasive presence of its booming technology sector. If Dallas is the Texas version of a northeastern financial metropolis and Fort Worth is a western city of the Plains, Austin is the closest thing there is in Texas to a West Coast technology and culture mecca—a Silicon Valley or Seattle, but with cowboy boots and great barbecue. No city away from the West Coast can match Austin's "cool" factor. And virtually no other metro area in the United States has matched Austin's spectacular record in recent decades for demographic and economic growth.

Austin's unique recipe for growth has had four unmistakable ingredients. First, it dominates Texas politics and policymaking as the state's capital. Second, it's home to UT Austin, the state's leading public university. Third, its cultural scene is a powerful magnet, both for visitors and for people moving for good from elsewhere in the United States. And fourth, it is one of the nation's leading technology centers.

These assets are closely interconnected. Unlike most states, Texas decided early in its history to locate its capital in the geographic heart of the state and its flagship public university close by in the same city. Together with the state's vast size, these decisions ensured that Austin would become both a nationally significant political center and a cool, youthful college town. Austin got lucky with live music, catching lightning in a bottle thanks to Willie Nelson and a handful of other artists, but—like any great city—it capitalized on its early good luck to create a cultural landscape unlike any other in the United States. Austin's educational and cultural assets have made all the difference in attracting the young, creative, highly educated workforce that in turn has brought so many technology companies to the area.

Austinites often like to think of their city as separate from the rest of urban Texas, especially from faraway Houston and Dallas–Fort Worth. It's easy to view Austin this way, in light of the obvious cultural differences between, say, business-minded Dallas and Houston and relaxed, "weird" Austin. But Austin is intimately connected to the rest of the Texas Triangle through dense webs of economic interdependence and shared political interests. And even though Austin and San Antonio still feel quite different from one another, the truth is that the two metros are increasingly growing into each other and becoming a single, intertwined economic unit at the southwest corner of the Triangle.

Although the Austin metro is the smallest of the four Texas Triangle metros in population terms, it brings its own distinctive contributions to the Triangle megaregion and plays an outsized role today in shaping the Triangle's future. Austin's technology prowess is a key asset in helping make the Texas Triangle one of the United States' four leading megaregions for cutting-edge technology, along with Northern California, the Pacific Northwest, and the Northeast Corridor. Austin's "cool" factor gives the Triangle an edge in attracting young creative types that the Urban Midwest, the Urban Southeast, South Florida, and smaller urban regions can't match. As the political nerve center of the Texas Triangle, Austin reinforces the Triangle's capacity to act as a unified, powerful force in national politics.

Starting from the capitol building, one doesn't have to go far in any direction in Central Austin to discover some of the places that give the city its distinctive vibe. Just to the north is the Bob Bullock Texas State History Museum, named for a revered lieutenant governor who served in the 1990s, which makes clear that Austin takes the state's history much more seriously than Dallas or Houston do. (San Antonio, of course, has the Alamo and a rich history all its own.) A little further north is the vast 150-building campus of the University of Texas, centered on its iconic UT Tower. Near the Capitol are numerous quirky, beloved eateries, like Fonda San Miguel, Texas Chili Parlor, and Stubb's BBQ—plus a variety of live-music venues, many with casual outdoor seating. Head south on Congress Avenue and one reaches Lady Bird Lake, really the dammed Colorado River, named for the former First Lady of the United States Lady Bird Johnson. Stop at the Ann Richards Congress Avenue Bridge at dusk, and one can see more than a million bats fly out from under the bridge. Cross to the South Side and one soon comes to the thoroughly "weird" but charming stores, boutique hotels, and coffee shops along South Congress as well as unique Austinite tourist attractions like the Cathedral of Garbage and the South Austin Museum of Popular Culture, celebrating artists who've helped make Austin weird. A little to the west is Zilker Park, where Austinites like to fight the summer heat by jumping into the spring-fed Barton Springs Pool—in water that is always about sixty-eight degrees.

Perhaps paradoxically, Austin has benefited from the state's small-government tradition—and particularly from the fact that the Texas Legislature is only in session for five months every two years. In contrast to capital cities in states with a more conspicuous public-sector presence—places like Albany or Sacramento—Central Austin doesn't seem overrun with state agencies or lobbying firms, which would perhaps detract from the city's cool factor. Other than in the beehive of activity around the Capitol when the legislature is in session, the city's education, music, and tourism scenes feel like a larger presence in Central Austin than its small political community does.

Longtime Austinites will tell you that their hometown felt like a small, quirky community as recently as the 1990s. Since then, its transformation into a top-tier technology center and the hub of an enormous metropolitan area has been breathtaking. While Central Austin is more vibrant than ever, the center of gravity has shifted northward, where the most important technology companies have office campuses and manufacturing facilities. Williamson County to the north of Austin as well as Hays County to the southwest have been among the fastest-growing counties in the United States since 2000.

A Distinctive Place within the Texas Triangle

The Austin metro area stands out among the large metros of the Texas Triangle in a number of ways. To start with the most visible, it has grown extraordinarily fast even by the standards of the fast-growing Texas Triangle. From 2000 to 2017, the Austin metro area population grew 69.3 percent—far ahead of Houston at 46.2 percent, San Antonio at 44.5 percent, and Dallas–Fort Worth at 43.4 percent. In terms of ethnic makeup, the Austin area's population leans more white—52.0 percent of the population compared to 41.6 percent for the Triangle as a whole. African Americans, meanwhile, constitute 6.8 percent of the Austin metro's population compared to 13.8 percent for the Triangle as a whole. Hispanics make up 32.5 percent for Austin compared to 35.8 percent overall.

The Austin metro has considerably higher education attainment levels than any of the other Texas Triangle metros. For instance, 44.8 percent of the population has a bachelor's degree or higher, while 15.7 percent has a graduate or professional degree. In the Triangle as a whole, 34.1 percent have at least a bachelor's degree, and 12.1 percent have a graduate or professional degree. Austin ranks eighth among the fifty-one metro areas in the United States' top eight megaregions in bachelor's degree attainment rates, just behind San Francisco, San Jose, New York, Boston, and three much smaller metros.

In economic terms, Austin ranks just behind Dallas–Fort Worth in GDP per worker as of 2017. But the Austin area has grown faster on this metric since 2000 than any of the other Triangle metros,

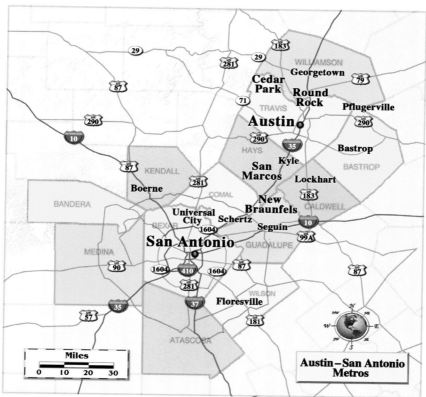

The Austin–San Antonio MSAs cover thirteen counties.

reflecting high incomes in its burgeoning technology sector. Including inflation, Austin's GDP per worker has grown 83.2 percent over this period, well ahead of the overall Triangle growth rate of 67.6 percent and the average for the United States' eight largest megaregions at 70.9 percent.

The Austin metro also performs ahead of the other Texas Triangle metros in terms of the absolute number of businesses per capita as of 2017 as well as in the growth rate in businesses per capita since 2000. Indeed, based on the 2015 Kauffmann Foundation Startup Activity Index, Austin ranked first among the United States' forty largest metros for the absolute number of startups that year. By comparison, Houston ranked eighth, San Antonio tenth, and Fort Worth fifteenth.

The Austin area's workforce looks very different from the rest of the Triangle in the composition of occupations it pursues. Based on US Department of Labor occupational data, a far higher share of the Austin metro area workforce works in computer and mathematics occupations than do those in the Triangle as a whole, and a somewhat higher share works in life, physical, and social science occupations.

As of 2017, the Austin area had a lower share of its population living under the federal poverty line compared to those in the Texas Triangle as a whole: 10.4 percent compared to 12.6 percent for the Triangle metros overall. It also had a larger share of its population in the middle class, according to a 2016 Pew Research study. The Austin middle-class share was 53 percent compared to 52 percent for San Antonio, 51 percent for Dallas–Fort Worth, and 48 percent for Houston.

Austin generally earns better scores than the other Triangle metros in quality-of-life rankings. Austin, for instance, easily outperforms the other major cities on the Trust for Public Land's "ParkScore," measuring the quality and quantity of public greenspace. In 2018, Austin earned a ParkScore of 57.5 out of a possible 100 compared to Dallas–Fort Worth at 47.1, Houston at 43.5, and San Antonio at 42.5.[1]

At the same time, Austin's remarkably rapid growth has increasingly created even more severe side effects than in the other Triangle metros—above all, skyrocketing housing costs and insufferable congestion—which we'll discuss in the last part of this chapter. But the tremendous influx of people and businesses has had another important consequence just as troubling to many long-term Austinites: it's making the city less weird. The growing presence of large corporations and the surge in high-income businesspeople working in technology and other sectors are powerful forces remaking the Austin area in sometimes unwelcome ways. Spiraling housing costs are forcing out musicians, writers, bartenders, and others who've always added so much color to Central Austin. In a larger sense, Austin's position as the Texas metro most similar to the major cities of the West Coast raises the possibility that Austin might follow in the footsteps of San Francisco and Seattle and become deeply unaffordable, ideologically charged in its politics, and unwelcoming to middle-class families.

Even the motto "Keep Austin Weird" has experienced this jarring transformation. The phrase originally came from local author Red Wassenich, who touched a chord when he called for maintaining the colorful quirkiness that had made Austin special on a radio show in 2000. Wassenich went on to publish *Keep Austin Weird: A Guide to the Odd Side of Town*. But various companies quickly seized the opportunity, over Wassenich's objections, to commercialize the phrase on T-shirts, coffee mugs, and other products. Before long, nearly identical T-shirts arose in Portland, Louisville, and elsewhere—proving how hard it is to keep things weird in the face of transformative growth and prosperity.

History

Settlers first established the tiny hamlet of Waterloo on the banks of the Colorado River in the early 1830s, more than one hundred years after the founding of the San Antonio de Béxar Presidio. Waterloo was a dangerous place, coming under attack from both native tribes and the Mexican army in its first few years of existence.

After Texas independence in 1836, the leaders of the new Republic of Texas had many competing ideas on where to locate the republic's capital, and Waterloo was hardly a unanimous choice. The republic's first president, Sam Houston, described it as "the most unfortunate site upon earth for the seat of Government." But the next president, Mirabeau B. Lamar, selected Waterloo as the capital in 1838, recognizing its natural beauty as well as its central location in Texas. The Texas Congress renamed the city Austin in honor of Stephen F. Austin, an early colonizer and leader of the Anglo "Texians" whom the state now remembers as "the father of Texas." Lamar asked his friend, Edwin Waller, to develop plans for a fourteen-square-block area that would feature Congress Avenue as its main street. After the Texas Congress convened there in 1839, Waller became Austin's first mayor.

When Sam Houston became president for the second time in 1841, residents of Austin feared he would move the capital to Houston, newly renamed in his honor, and formed a vigilante committee to preserve their city's status. In September 1842, Mexican forces—still fighting the Republic of Texas for control over the disputed territory between the Rio Grande and Nueces rivers—briefly captured San Antonio. President Houston, worried that the Mexicans would reach Austin as well, moved the Texas government to Washington-on-the-Brazos, near Houston. When he sent a company of Texas Rangers to collect state papers stored in Austin, local residents resisted. Only a few shots were fired in the Texas Archive War, but the Rangers gave up the documents to avoid bloodshed, and the archives remained in Austin until it became the republic's capital again in 1844.

After the United States annexed Texas in 1845, Austin became the official state capital. Builders completed the state's first capitol building in 1853 and added a governor's mansion in 1856.

During the Civil War, goods shortages and price inflation ravaged Austin. But the city's role as a trade center recovered rapidly with the arrival of the Houston and Texas Central Railway in 1871. Austin's population doubled over the next five years thanks to an influx of immigrants, in particular from Germany, Mexico, Ireland, and Sweden. Streetcars, a bridge across the Colorado River, and another railroad connection stimulated growing activity in the city.

In 1875, a statewide election confirmed Austin as the state capital once and for all. Construction of a new state capitol building began that same year. In 1888, the state dedicated its iconic pink granite capitol building and, proving even then that "everything is bigger in Texas," made sure that it was taller, by 14.64 feet, than the US Capitol.[2]

Education became an important force in the city at about the same time. In 1883, the University of Texas opened its doors, answering the state constitution's call for "a university of the first class." In its first year, the university consisted of one building with eight professors and 221 students.

Austinites invested aggressively in infrastructure as well. In 1893, the city built the Tom Miller Dam, named in honor of a

The Texas State Capitol in Austin is slightly taller than the US Capitol building in Washington, DC. Shutterstock/amadeustx.

previous mayor, on the Colorado River to provide electricity to Austin residents. Floods caused its collapse in 1900, and it took until 1940 to replace it. The newer dam provides hydroelectric power and flood control and forms Lake Austin, one of the six beautiful Texas Highland Lakes along the Colorado River.

During the Great Depression of the 1930s, the city suffered, as all cities did, but an aggressive building program at the University of Texas alleviated some of Austin's misery. A number of projects funded by Roosevelt's Works Progress Administration (WPA)—arranged largely by then US Rep. Lyndon B. Johnson—also helped mitigate unemployment while adding lasting improvements to the city's buildings. Another important boost to Austin's economy occurred in 1942 with the establishment of the Del Valle Army Base, which later became Bergstrom Air Force Base.

The modern high-technology sector first arrived in Austin in 1955 with the foundation of Associated Consultants and Engineers. The company got started conducting science research for federal government agencies and private industries. Renaming itself Tracor in 1962, the firm built a substantial business manufacturing electronic components unit for both defense and commercial applications. On the defense side, Tracor's technology figured prominently in the Aegis air defense system on US Navy cruisers and destroyers for three decades. Tracor components also played a significant role in the development of the radio, television, stereo, home appliance, automobile, aircraft, and computer industries. At its peak, Tracor employed eleven thousand people worldwide. In 1998, it became part of Marconi Electric Systems, which the next year in turn became a subsidiary of UK-based BAE Systems, a multinational defense, security, and aerospace conglomerate.

Tracor was an early example of the close relationships between higher education and industry that have since become ubiquitous in the United States' economy, particularly in thriving college towns. Tracor hired numerous graduates of UT Austin and worked closely with University of Texas researchers on commercializing university research.

In 1967, International Business Machines (IBM) opened a typewriter manufacturing plant in Austin. Mario Hernandez cites IBM's selection of Austin as a turning point for the city: "That was the first major coup." Dallas-based Texas Instruments followed with a new Austin facility in 1969, attracted by the expanding research programs at UT Austin. The communications technology giant Motorola opened a facility in the city in 1974.

During the 1980s, the federal government, alarmed by what it saw as a growing challenge by Japanese electronics companies to US dominance in semiconductor technology, established two publicly funded research consortiums: Microelectronics and Computer Technology Corp., known as MCC, and SEMATECH. In both cases, authorities chose Austin as headquarters, based in part on a sponsorship by retired US Navy Admiral Bobby Inman, a former head of the National Security Agency. These pivotal decisions cemented the Austin area's role as a leading electronics center.

An even more transformational moment came in 1984, when a UT Austin student named Michael Dell dropped out of college to launch a new company specializing in made-to-order personal computers. With just $1,000 of capital, Dell founded PC's Limited. Three years later, he changed the company's name to Dell

Computer. Before taking the company public in 1988, Dell invited two respected local technology leaders to serve on his board: Admiral Inman and Dr. George Kozmetsky, the founder of technology-focused IC2 Institute at UT Austin and a professor widely known as "the father of Austin's tech industry."

Dell Computer's public offering was a coup for Austin. Dell, based in the Austin suburb of Round Rock, became a long-standing Fortune 500 company, until Dell took the company private again in 2013. The company produced numerous "Dellionaires," as early employees who become wealthy on Dell stock options became known in Austin. Today, Dell employs more than thirteen thousand people in the Austin area and more than one hundred thousand worldwide. Its founder's net worth was $27 billion as of 2019, according to the Bloomberg Billionaires Index.

Austin's world-famous live-music scene started from humble beginnings. In 1972, Willie Nelson returned to his home state of Texas after building a successful career as a country and western singer-songwriter for Nashville's Grand Ole Opry, settling in the Austin area. Back in Texas, he developed an entirely new sound and "outlaw" persona, releasing huge hit albums like *Red Headed Stranger* and *Wanted! The Outlaws*. (The latter was a collaboration with Texas artists Waylon Jennings, Jesse Colter, and Tompall Glaser.) In 1974, Willie recorded a pilot television show for a series called *Austin City Limits*, using a small studio in the Communications Building complex at UT Austin. The "ACL" show became the longest-running music television series in US history.

From this start, the Austin music community grew as the city became a leading destination for musicians and music fans from all parts of the country and beyond. In 2002, promoters launched the Austin City Limits (ACL) Music Festival, based on the television show and presenting live performances on multiple stages in Zilker Park over two consecutive three-day weekends. More than 450,000 people now attend the ACL Music Festival each year.

Austin's live-music scene also gave rise to the South by Southwest festival, established in 1987. SXSW, or "South By," as locals call it, started life as a local music festival but over time came to become one of the world's leading multimedia events, including live music, film, interactive media, and technology content. SXSW now runs for ten days each March—although it had to cancel for the first time in 2020 because of the COVID-19 crisis—and attracts more than twenty thousand paying participants and more than 250,000 people overall from around the world. SXSW routinely attracts top-tier speakers and performers to Austin, in recent years including former President Barack Obama, Lady Gaga, Garth Brooks, Steven Spielberg, Elon Musk, and, of course, Willie Nelson. Today, SXSW generates a local economic impact of more than $350 million each year.

Another important moment in Austin's recent history was the repurposing of Bergstrom Air Force Base and its reopening as Austin-Bergstrom International Airport in 1999. While the city had operated a municipal airport, Mueller Airport, since 1930, it was too small for the city Austin had become, and travelers typically had to change planes in Houston or Dallas–Fort Worth on the way to destinations outside the Southwest. Austin-Bergstrom gave rise to connections throughout the United States and numerous other countries, helping put Austin on the map as a major business center and destination in its own right.

In its politics, Austin has long been a deeper shade of blue than the rest of the Triangle. While the Austin metro is a progressive Democratic bastion, the city of Austin and its surrounding counties and suburban cities have broadly shared the pragmatic tradition common throughout the Triangle metros. Under current mayor Steve Adler, the city of Austin has pursued increasingly progressive policies to address Austin's growing housing challenges, but it's also remained one of the more business-friendly big cities in the United States.

Population

As of 2019, the city of Austin had a population of 974,580, making it the eleventh-largest city in the United States.[3] It's likely to overtake the number-ten city—San Jose, California—after the 2020 Census count, which would give the Texas Triangle four of the nation's

Austin is the nation's eleventh-largest city in population. Shutterstock / Roschetzky Photography.

top ten cities. The Austin metro area, meanwhile, had a population of just under 2.2 million as of 2019, ranking thirtieth in the United States.

Austin's tremendous pace of population growth is primarily due to an ongoing influx of people moving from elsewhere in the United States. Domestic net in-migration contributed 36.8 percent toward the Austin metro's total growth of 69.3 percent between 2000 and 2017. Of the fifty-one metros in the United States' top eight megaregions, only Raleigh, North Carolina, and the two Florida retirement destinations of North Port–Sarasota and Cape Coral–Fort Myers experienced a larger percentage contribution from domestic in-migration. Immigration from abroad, on the other hand, has been a much smaller driver of Austin's population growth. The contribution of immigration to the Austin metro's growth between 2000 and 2017, at 9.7 percent, was roughly in line with the eight-megaregion average and below the contributions to growth in Houston (12.7 percent) and Dallas–Fort Worth (10.4 percent).

Within the metro area, Travis County—home to the city of Austin—is growing fast, by 55 percent from 2000 to 2019. But the most remarkable growth rates in the area—or in the Texas Triangle, for that matter—are in neighboring Williamson and Hays counties. Both saw population growth of 132 percent over the same period. Williamson County, which includes the booming smaller cities of Round Rock and Georgetown, has benefited enormously from the rapid growth of technology-sector employment in the northern part of Travis County as well as in Round Rock itself. Hays County includes the fast-growing smaller city of San Marcos, sitting alongside I-35 to the southwest of Austin, on the way to San Antonio.

As the Austin and San Antonio metros continue to grow, the picturesque countryside between the two cities—including the colorful historic towns of Fredericksburg and New Braunfels—has turned almost entirely suburban. It has become routine for people to work in Austin and live in New Braunfels or even San Antonio itself. On the current trajectory of urban growth, it might make sense before long to think of the greater Austin–San Antonio area as a single metropolitan area. If the US Census Bureau treated the area this way today, it would have a population of approximately 4.7 million as of 2019, ranking it thirteenth in the nation, just behind the San Francisco metro.

Unique Drivers of Economic Growth

The Austin metro area's GDP totaled $146.8 billion in 2018. This figure exceeds that of the San Antonio metro at $133.63 billion, despite the Alamo City's larger population. After two decades of exceptional income growth on a per-capita basis, Austin was a significantly richer place, with a GDP per worker of $144,305 compared with $124,493 in San Antonio. In January 2018, the Austin metro surpassed the San Antonio metro in total number of jobs as well, even though San Antonio's population is larger by about 350,000 people. San Antonio has a higher population share of minors and older people, while more of the booming Austin area's population consists of working-age people, between sixteen and sixty-four.

UT Austin is the flagship campus of the UT System. Shutterstock/ Blanscape.

A key driver of Austin's growth has been its great success in attracting and retaining a young, highly educated workforce. The city owes this success in turn to two powerful assets: its position as the higher education capital not only of Texas but of the south-central region of the United States and the lifestyle edge it has over most other US cities, including those in the Texas Triangle.

UT Austin is an enormous talent magnet and economic engine for the Austin area. Enrollment is at more than fifty thousand. The university's campus, once nicknamed the "Forty Acres" for its original footprint in 1883, now covers 433 acres and includes 150 buildings. UT Austin is the flagship campus of the huge UT System, comprising more than 240,000 students across fourteen campuses. As of 2019, the UT System had a total endowment of $31 billion, second after Harvard University among US universities.

UT Austin consistently ranks among the leading public universities in the southern United States. It produces more than ten thousand career-ready graduates each year and retains a substantial share of them in the Austin area after they graduate. It also provides a powerful economic boost to Austin through its massive research spending, amounting to more than $600 million per year.

The university also contributes to the city's economy through its beloved sports programs, above all UT Longhorns football. The Longhorns play in the university's renowned Darrell K Royal–Texas Memorial Stadium, which can hold one hundred thousand fans—and often does. The legendary late coach Darrell Royal's long-standing joke was that, in view of UT Austin's 482,000 alumni, incoming Longhorn coaches needed to remember that the team actually has more than four hundred thousand coaches.[4]

Despite UT Austin's high profile as a Tier One research university, Austin was for decades one of the largest cities in the United States without a medical school. When the legislature established the university in 1883, it decided to build its flagship campus in the capital city and to place the UT "medical branch" in the then booming city of Galveston. In more recent decades, the question of whether to bring a medical school to Austin was a constant part of the city's dialogue.

In 2011, State Sen. Kirk Watson led the charge in a new effort to make the vision a reality. Watson and his colleagues succeeded in convincing the University of Texas Board of Regents to commit buildings and seed money to hire faculty. They created a public-private partnership with the Travis County Health Care District, and they won over Travis County voters in a 2011 property tax vote. And crucially, the plan won the support of Michael and Susan Dell, who pledged $50 million over ten years. The Dell Medical Center welcomed its first students in 2016. According to Dr. Clay Johnston, the inaugural dean of the medical school, "Dell Med" is creating "an entirely new model of academic medicine to drive innovation, improve health and do it all efficiently." Dell Med's model has included the 2017 establishment of Capital City Innovation, a nonprofit entity focused on using the new medical school as a catalyst to attract life-science and health-care businesses to Austin. The recent announcement by pharmaceutical giant Merck of a new Austin facility is an early indication that the plan is working.

In addition to its highly visible University of Texas, the Austin area has a number of other higher education institutions contributing to the city's skilled workforce. St. Edward's University is a private Catholic college founded in 1877 by Rev. Edward Sorin, who also established Notre Dame University in South Bend, Indiana. Named for King Edward "the Confessor" of England, St. Edward's University has an enrollment of about 4,400 students. Huston-Tillotson University, Austin's historically African American university, grew out of a merger in 1952 between Samuel Huston College, founded in 1900, and Tillotson College, dating back to 1877. In 2018, Huston-Tillotson had an enrollment of 1,160. The eleven-campus Austin Community College started classes in 1973 and grew to an enrollment of 41,500 credit students by 2015.

Texas State University in nearby San Marcos has a current enrollment of almost forty thousand. Lyndon B. Johnson, thirty-sixth president of the United States, graduated in 1930, when the institution was still known as the Southwest Texas State Teachers College. Southwestern University, a Methodist institution founded in 1840 and located in Georgetown, twenty-eight miles up I-35 to the north, has an enrollment of almost 1,500 students.

Together, the Austin metro's four-year institutions enroll more students than the comparable university portfolios of any of the other Texas Triangle metros, despite the larger populations of Dallas–Fort Worth, Houston, and San Antonio. Austin's vast student population adds immeasurably to the city's youthful vibe and—since Austin does such a good job of retaining them in the area—contributes significantly to the Austin population's exceptionally high education attainment levels.

The availability of a young, highly educated pool of graduates has been pivotal to site-selection decisions by leading technology companies. According to Carlton Schwab, UT Austin in particular has been "the ticket to the dance, once folks realized that UT, and especially its engineering and business schools, were great reservoirs of talent."

Austin's other great asset in attracting an educated, creative workforce—including young individuals and families moving from all over the country—is its leading position as a star performer among US metros in terms of lifestyle. As much as any large city in the United States, Austin demonstrates that, in the hypercompetitive labor market of the twenty-first century, talented people go where they want to live, and companies go where they can find sufficient numbers of talented people. According to Schwab, Austin's "cultural openness" and cool factor have strongly attracted young people to the city, which in turn attracts employers—especially in the technology sector. "There was an emphasis on place," Schwab says. "You had thousands and thousands of graduates who always wanted to stay in Austin if they could find a job. Once the microelectronics industry started taking off, there was a way to stay and not have to move to Dallas or Houston for their careers." Mario Hernandez agrees that "quality of life" considerations have made a decisive difference in attracting technology firms to the Austin area ever since the 1980s.

With its large and growing technology community, Austin's economy is more concentrated in industry terms than the more diverse metro-area economies of Dallas–Fort Worth and Houston. But its success in technology, particularly in recent years, is irrefutable. Locals increasingly refer to the Austin area as "Silicon Hills." Leading companies with significant Austin-area facilities include Amazon, Google, Facebook, Oracle, Advanced Micro Devices, Tokyo Electron, and Samsung Electronics as well as Dell and IBM. Perhaps most important, Apple has made Austin a major hub for the company since coming to town in 1992. In 2016, Apple opened a 1.1-million-square-foot campus in northern Austin that employs 6,200 workers. In November 2019, Apple broke ground on a new facility that will produce the Mac Pro and will have the capacity for 15,000 workers. This expansion is likely to make Apple the city's largest employer.

Challenges

Like other leading technology-oriented cities, Austin faces an intensifying challenge from high and rising home prices. Since 2000, the median house price in the Austin metro has more than doubled, reaching $299,900 by November 2018. Austin is significantly more expensive than the other Triangle metros, with median house prices

12 percent higher than in Dallas–Fort Worth, 26 percent higher than in Houston, and 31 percent higher than in San Antonio.[5]

According to Jon Hockenyos, an economist who is president of Austin-based TXP, a person making the median wage in Austin—$18 an hour—can't afford the median one-bedroom Austin apartment. Middle-skilled workers increasingly find themselves priced out of the market, as do the musicians, coffee baristas, and shop employees who do so much to keep Austin "weird."

Like the even more expensive West Coast metros of Los Angeles, San Francisco, and Seattle, Austin's skyrocketing home prices and rents are driving a surge in homelessness.

Austin has done a better job than the West Coast metros of allowing the housing supply to grow. But over the last decade, supply hasn't kept up with demand as much as it has in the other Texas Triangle metros. Looking ahead, inadequate housing supply and rising prices may start to impede inbound migration. San Francisco, San Jose, and Los Angeles have seen net outflows of native-born people since 2000 in large part due to unaffordable costs of living. If Austin continues to follow in their footsteps, the area's growth could start to slow down. And if the city of Austin becomes too expensive for anyone but tech workers, financiers, lawyers, and lobbyists, it may start to lose the distinctive cultural vibe that has done so much to make the city attractive.

Another challenge, as in the other Texas Triangle metros, is building out sufficient physical infrastructure to accommodate the area's growing population and business community. Austin-Bergstrom, which currently serves more than seventeen million passengers a year, continues to invest in new facilities—a strong point in Austin's favor. The airport will need to move fast, as analysts project it will need to serve more than thirty-one million passengers per year by 2040.

On the other hand, Austin's road network is wholly inadequate for the current size of the city. Unlike the other Texas Triangle cities, which have multiple interstate highways, Austin has only one, the north-south Interstate 35, although US Highway 290 connects Austin to Houston. Frustrating congestion along I-35 in Austin has long been a daily—and almost all-day—occurrence, partly because of the large number of freight trucks that carry cargo to and from the Mexico border at Laredo. Austin added a north-south expressway called MoPac parallel to I-35 to the west and a semi-circle loop thoroughfare called the "Capital of Texas Highway" in the 1970s, but in more recent years, traffic congestion in the fast-growing city has become a serious headache. The good news: a booming bicycle culture, inspired some years ago by local cycling star Lance Armstrong, has become popular as an alternative means of transportation.

Capital Metro, usually called CapMetro, is Austin's main public transit system, operating buses and light rail. CapMetro operates a form of Bus Rapid Transit, operating in dedicated lanes and serving eighty-nine stations. CapMetro has also operated its MetroRail light rail system since 2010, but ridership remains small relative to the metro area as a whole. Plans include redeveloping the downtown MetroRail station next to the Convention Center, adding new trains and expanding their frequency. CapMetro is also a partner in the Plaza Saltillo District—a ten-acre development project under construction east of downtown that will provide affordable apartments, retail and office space, plus an expanded bikeway along its bus and rail systems.

More good news came in November 2020, when Austin voters approved a $7.1 billion package of transit projects, including a light-rail tunnel under downtown Austin on a route to the airport, which will take until 2030 for construction completion. Much of the cost of the CapMetro projects will be paid by a property tax increase.[6]

Demands from a growing population and frequent drought conditions have put growing pressure on Austin Water, the city's water and sewage utility. For a week in October 2018, Austin Water suffered an image setback when it had to ask customers to boil water for drinking, cooking, and making ice. That month, rainfall flood waters from the Llano River and its lakes had pushed silt and dirt into Austin's Lake Travis drinking-water supply, damaging the city's ability to treat water. Looking ahead, Austin Water is studying numerous options to expand water supplies, including stormwater harvesting, desalination of brackish groundwater, or even importing desalinized water.

A key question facing Austin in the future is whether it will follow in the footsteps of West Coast cities like San Francisco, Los Angeles, and Seattle in other ways in addition to its tech-focused economy and increasingly unaffordable home prices. As the most unabashedly progressive metro area in the Texas Triangle, Austin is more likely than the other large Triangle cities to import West Coast policy experiments that many argue have made West Coast cities less livable and driven middle-class families away. Texans will watch closely to see whether Austin adopts West Coast ideas like laissez-faire approaches to homelessness, retreats from law enforcement in the face of social unrest, counterproductive housing policies like rent control, and economic policies that drive businesses away.

For now, Austin's largest challenges are the kind a city would prefer to have, as they arise not from stagnation but from rapid growth. Austin's housing and infrastructure challenges are even more acute than in the other Triangle metros, reflecting its exceptional successes of recent decades. A large part of Austin's future is likely to involve closer integration with the rest of the Triangle, especially with nearby San Antonio. Its distinctive challenge will be to manage this increasing integration while sustaining the unique characteristics that make it special—that is, by staying weird.

San Antonio

Over the last five decades, San Antonio has undergone a transformation as profound as any major US city. A city wracked by intense conflict, implacable exclusion, and unbridgeable divides in the mid-1960s is today respected for its diverse economy, rapid growth, and collaborative governance. In the 1960s, San Antonio had higher poverty rates than most metro regions and indices of inequality among the highest in the nation. Unequal public services and capital investments in Latino and African American neighborhoods meant, for example, the annual flooding of poor neighborhoods via inadequate drainage systems, resulting in destroyed homes and deaths. Schools in the Latino South Side and West Side and in the African American East Side were underfunded, understaffed, and underperforming.

Chris Brenner and Manuel Pastor, in a seminal study of equitable progress in *Equity, Growth, and Community*, describe conditions in that period in San Antonio: "Then, the city and the region were the site of one of the country's most intense struggles to challenge stark racism in the allocation of public resources and to confront a business elite who seemed committed to marketing the region based on cheap labor (indeed they had a plan prepared on this basis)." The public rancor and paralyzing contentions of that era mandated serious introspection and dialogue on the part of business, civic, community, and religious leaders. Confrontations were so severe and frightening that one of San Antonio's top business leaders lamented to the *Wall Street Journal* that sometimes in life things need to burn down before something can be built again.

Fortunately, it didn't have to come to that. New leaders, new ideas, and new efforts led to confidence-building successes and meaningful discussions. Several events—one in the late 1960s and another in the mid-1970s—helped San Antonio turn the corner.

One was the half-decade, multiethnic cooperation devoted to produce a world's fair, HemisFair '68, an idea first broached by US Rep. Henry B. Gonzalez, the first Latino to serve as a full member of the US House of Representatives. HemisFair chose as its theme "Confluence of Civilizations" and paid respectful attention to the city's diversity in a way that enlightened San Antonians about the value of the city's multicultural richness as an asset. The leaders of the city also gained confidence from HemisFair's success that the different sectors of the city could work together.

The other event was the transition that began in 1975 to a more representative form of city government, including a Latino and African American majority on the City Council for the first time in the city's modern history. Simultaneously, a major community-based organization, Communities Organized for Public Service (COPS), based on churches across the city and using direct-action tactics, created a counterbalance to the business leadership's power and voice. The result was frank dialogue, effective action on grievances, and unprecedented progress on jobs and wages.

From these two streams of community experience was born the modern "San Antonio Way." The city has now experienced more than four decades of a solid political consensus based on inclusive economic growth, fair public investments, collaborative governance, and racial and ethnic mutual respect. Today, San Antonio with 1.5 million residents is the seventh-largest city in the United States and is generally listed among the five fastest-growing cities in the nation by population.

More importantly, an analysis of employment growth in cities between 2007 and 2017 ranked San Antonio's job growth of 24 percent over that decade as third in the nation, behind only Austin and

Nashville. Over that span of years, wages have risen, residential segregation has declined, education attainment has increased, and leadership is more inclusive.

Brenner and Pastor write, "If you talk to civic leaders in San Antonio today, they proudly boast of an increasingly multifaceted economy that has been able to move beyond reliance on military spending and now boasts of vibrant tourism, medical, energy, manufacturing and professional services sectors. They attribute that success—evident in jobs, earnings and relative improvement in median household income and poverty—to a spirit of collaboration among government, business, universities and community groups that has become part of the regional DNA."

Modern San Antonio is profoundly different in attitude, outlook, and substantive achievements from the San Antonio of the early 1960s. Yet it maintains certain intangible attributes—one might say personality traits—that must be explored to understand this unique Texas place. Indeed, it is fair to say that San Antonio owes a good deal of its modern accomplishments to the many cultural features that set it apart from all other US cities. In an age when many cities look more and more like everyplace else, San Antonio is different. It has in that sense been shaped by its geography and its history.

Geography and History

Indigenous people—mainly the Payaya, a branch of the Coahuiltecan tribe—came to live along the riverbank of what we now call the San Antonio River. They called the place *Yanaguana*, which translates to "the place of restful waters." The Payaya were hunter-gatherers who ranged across the arid brush country of South Texas, where it has been said that every living thing either pricks, burns, stings, or bites. The names given to features of the land described the harshness of the territory: prickly pears, poison oak, horned toads, fire ants, and killer bees, all of which thrive amid the cactus, scorpions, and rattlesnakes. But a few miles to the north, the South Texas brush country transitions to a landscape of rocky cliffs, fresh water, springs, and massive trees along clear rivers. This ecological zone is the Balcones Escarpment, a massive limestone formation that includes underground caves and sub-terranean water reservoirs. Modern-day San Antonio straddles both topographies, the brush country to the south and the Edwards Plateau to the north. The Payaya found a verdant oasis on a spring-fed river, shaded by giant cypress, pecan, and poplar trees, and they settled into more permanent encampments.

Beginning in 1671, when New Spain mounted expeditions to the wild frontier that is now Texas, the restful waters attracted soldiers and missionaries as well. In 1718, Martín de Alarcón, governor of the Spanish colonial province of Texas, officially established the San Antonio de Béxar Presidio on the banks of what is now San Pedro Creek. With the help of indigenous artisans, the Spanish built five missions along the river: San Antonio de Valero (known as the Alamo today), Concepción, San José, San Juan Capistrano, and Espada. Inside their limestone walls, residents found protection, education, rudimentary health care, and, of course, Catholicism. In 2015, the missions became a UNESCO World Heritage site. The missions attract more than six hundred thousand visitors annually and are a unique component of the city's historical assets.

Established fifty-eight years before the US Declaration of Inde-pendence and more than one hundred years before any of the other Texas Triangle cities, San Antonio was already a bustling, vibrant settlement when Mexico won its own independence from Spain in 1810. But just twenty-five years later, its residents—including the ones born in Mexico and calling themselves "Tejanos"—thirsted for their own independence from Mexico. The ethnically diverse population of San Antonio largely sided with the Anglo "Texians" in the growing disputes that ended in the Texas war for indepen-dence in 1836. The bloody battles that took place that year are the stuff of legend and have provided endless subject matter for history books, popular literature, and movies. The most infamous moment of the war, and in all of Texas history, was of course the thirteen-day siege of the Alamo. On March 6, 1836, the Mexican army of more than 1,800 soldiers, under the command of Mexico's president, Gen. Antonio López de Santa Anna, overcame the

Alamo's defenses and killed all 186 Texian independence fighters. Although the fall of the Alamo was a devastating loss for the Texian side, the siege ultimately contributed to their victory in two ways. First, the March 6, 1836, battle bought time for Texian commander Gen. Sam Houston to expand his army and prepare for subsequent battles. And second, it gave the Texians a rallying cry that resounds to this day: "Remember the Alamo!" On April 21, 1836, Houston's army defeated Santa Anna at the Battle of San Jacinto, near present-day Houston. Santa Anna sued for peace, and the independent Republic of Texas was born.

Later in 1836, the city named for Sam Houston came into being, becoming the second city of the Texas Triangle. Sam Houston went on to become the first president of the new republic. Over the next thirteen years, Texans established the other three cities that comprise the Triangle—Austin in 1839, Dallas in 1841, and Fort Worth in 1849.

While Texas was still a republic, its largest county was Bexar, named for Spain's Duque de Béjar. Béjar is a small Spanish town near Salamanca. The word *béjar* is a pre–Roman Empire term meaning "place of the beehives." Miguel de Cervantes dedicated his classic 1615 novel *Don Quixote* to the Duque de Béjar—the Duke of Béjar.

Bexar, by 1845, included almost all of western Texas and parts of New Mexico, Colorado, and Wyoming. Its county seat was San Antonio, a busy center of agrarian and business growth and the republic's largest city. After Texas joined the United States in 1845, Bexar County was carved into 128 separate counties, eight of which now comprise what the US Census defines as the San Antonio metropolitan area.

Texas independence did not end the violent struggle with Mexico. The Republic of Texas and Santa Anna's government continued to squabble over disputed territory between the Rio Grande and Nueces River, leading to a Mexican invasion and, in 1842, a brief reconquest of San Antonio by Santa Anna. The annexation of Texas by the United States in 1845, followed by the US Army's decisive victory in the Mexican–American War of 1846–48, solidified the border and secured San Antonio as an integral part of the United States.

For much of the nineteenth century, San Antonio was the largest city in Texas. In the late nineteenth and early twentieth centuries, the city experienced rapid growth, thanks to successive waves of immigrants arriving in the area. An influx of German immigrants arrived in the 1860s, establishing breweries, flour mills, banks, and mercantile businesses. Large numbers of people moved to town from rural areas after the Southern Pacific Railroad added San Antonio to its route in 1877. Early in the twentieth century, the Mexican Revolution let loose a flood of immigrants fleeing the conflict across the southern border.

Five US military bases were established over time, resulting in the city's long-standing reputation as "Military City USA." The army constructed its first post in 1876, when Native American wars were still a threat. In 1890, it named this base Fort Sam Houston. The army held imprisoned Apache Chief Geronimo there in 1886 until he was moved to a reservation. In the early twentieth century, with the Mexican Revolution raging a few hundred miles to the south and World War I underway in Europe, the US government came to value San Antonio's important strategic military position. Its consistently clear weather also made it an ideal place for the emerging field of aviation. Consequently, the federal government established Kelly, Brooks, Randolph, and Lackland air bases.

The military has remained committed to the San Antonio area ever since. During and for some time after World War II, the Kelly facility was the largest employer in the city. San Antonians widely credit Kelly Air Force Base with creating and sustaining a Latino middle class in San Antonio. Brooks Air Force Base was known for its aerospace medicine breakthroughs and its early participation in the US "Space Race," described in a speech by President John F. Kennedy on November 21, 1963, the day before his assassination in Dallas. After all air force activities ended in 2011, it became a mixed-use development with manufacturing and retail tenants. Brooks City Base is home to the University of the Incarnate Word's School of Osteopathic Medicine.

In more recent times, the Pentagon has incorporated San Antonio's military installations into what it calls Joint Base San Antonio (JBSA). JBSA-Lackland, on the Southwest Side, remains the site for all air force basic training. In early 2020, Wilford Hall, an outpatient care center on Lackland's campus, was responsible for processing some of the cruise ship passengers quarantined because of the COVID-19 pandemic. JBSA-Randolph, on the city's Northeast Side, is the headquarters for the air force's Air Education and Training Command, providing a wide range of air force training. Camp Bullis, just northwest of San Antonio, handles US Army medical field training. As of 2018, the four JBSA units employed 55,760 active-duty personnel, supported by 31,624 civilians and contractors.

While San Antonio grew fast early in the twentieth century, it was clear by the 1930s that Dallas and Houston were outpacing San Antonio in both population and economic growth. They had developed prosperous banking and energy-related businesses, while San Antonio continued to rely on its military bases and tourism. The 1930 Census count confirmed that San Antonio had relinquished its position as the state's largest city, demoted to number three at that time.

The Great Depression, for all the misery it brought to San Antonio and cities throughout the United States, had at least one important unexpected benefit for San Antonio. Plans to develop what became the River Walk turned into a reality during the 1930s, thanks in large part to Roosevelt's WPA.

The Turn for the Better

In the 1950s and 1960s, San Antonio was among the poorest of large US cities. But in the 1960s, things began to change for the better. A catalyst for this new infusion of energy and capital occurred in 1968. As San Antonio business leaders watched the Triangle cities of Dallas and Houston boom in the 1950s and 1960s, they grew increasingly concerned about their city's lagging economy. When US Rep. Henry B. Gonzalez suggested a solution to the problem, they listened and took an imaginative leap of faith.

The San Antonio River Walk, with its river barges and riverside restaurants, is a leading Texas tourist destination. Shutterstock / f11 photo.

Gonzalez was born in San Antonio in 1916, the son of immigrants who had escaped the Mexican Revolution. He was the first Latino to be elected to the Texas Senate and US Congress. Gonzalez suggested that San Antonio organize a catalytic event—in the form of a world's fair—to celebrate the city's 250th birthday and to generate national and international visibility. Community leaders embraced the idea and chose the fair's theme, "Confluence of Civilizations," to recognize the diversity that has always been a defining characteristic of San Antonio. They named the undertaking HemisFair '68 and engaged every part of the city in its execution.

The city cleared ninety-seven acres in the center of downtown. The now iconic 750-foot Tower of the Americas, a new convention center, and a five-hundred-room Hilton Palacio del Rio Hotel came into being before the fair opened in 1968. The city transformed the River Walk with new landscaping, restaurants, and retail shops, making it the remarkable attraction millions visit today. HemisFair proved to be the catalyst the city needed. Along with nearly seven million visitors to the fair, citizens from every part of San Antonio

San Antonio's Tower of the Americas overlooks downtown's HemisFair Park, site of the 1968 world's fair. HemisFair '68 rejuvenated the San Antonio economy for more than fifty years, establishing the city as a large tourist and convention destination. Shutterstock / f11 photo.

celebrated the city's unique cultural diversity and recognized that San Antonio had successfully managed a community covering that in later years would be regarded as a point of inflection in the city's long trajectory.

In the years after 1968, the San Antonio business community developed a new sense of momentum. Under the leadership of new CEO Robert F. McDermott, USAA—with a long history as the United States' largest insurance company focused on military personnel and families—emerged as one of the country's leading insurance giants. USAA is today the city's second-largest employer with more than eighteen thousand local employees and more than thirty thousand worldwide. McDermott, a dynamic retired air force general who had arrived in San Antonio in 1968, became the city's leading business voice for economic progress and civic unity, establishing the San Antonio Development Foundation in 1974. From the start, the foundation reflected McDermott's conviction that the city needed to come together and do more to strengthen its workforce, increase wages, and attract new businesses.

While San Antonians of all races and national origins took pride in the substance and symbolism of HemisFair '68, residents of the city's marginalized neighborhoods saw inconsistencies in the celebration of cultural confluence and downtown progress compared to the unrelenting poverty and hardship in their daily lives. Meanwhile, the national civil rights movement aroused hopes for greater fairness and meaningful opportunities.

San Antonio became an incubator of national Mexican American advocacy for justice. The League of United Latin American Citizens, or LULAC, founded in Corpus Christi, set an example of how organized Latinos could give voice to united ambitions for inclusion. San Antonio–bred leaders breathed life into organizations to serve national Latino constituencies from their offices in San Antonio. The Mexican American Legal Defense and Education Fund (MALDEF) was founded by a group of Latino lawyers and judges led by Mario Obledo in 1968 to serve as legal strategists for Latino litigation against unfair practices at all levels. The Southwest Voter Registration and Education Project (SVREP) was established by Willie Velasquez in 1974 to organize around its motto: "Su voto es su voz" (Your vote is your voice). Both organizations operate nationally today. San Antonio earned national significance in American Latino history, not unlike Atlanta's as a platform for African American civil rights.

From the barrios of San Antonio's South and West Sides, an original and effective mobilization that was to profoundly change the city began in 1974. Ernesto Cortes organized local church congregations to argue for public improvements in long-neglected neighborhoods. Under the banner of COPS, residents argued not for vague abstractions that could easily be deflected by powerful institutions; they demanded concrete and measurable progress on drainage and flood control, paved streets, sidewalks, parks, libraries, and public-school improvements. Using Saul Alinsky's methods of community organizing, COPS elicited responses from local officials in "accountability sessions" with thousands of residents in attendance. COPS tried to meet with business leaders to generate support, but when those executives refused to meet, COPS employed peaceful though disruptive and confrontational approaches, such as lining up at the bank-teller windows of the leading bank for an entire day to secure a meeting. COPS' insistence created white-hot emotions on all sides but raised awareness about the need for basic fairness in city expenditures, utility-rate hikes, bond issues, and capital programs. With the hindsight of decades of hard work on these agendas, many would argue that San Antonio today is immensely stronger, more unified, and infinitely fairer.

As these battles were being waged in the neighborhoods, in 1976, the US Justice Department objected to the San Antonio city government's electoral system, highlighting the lack of minority representation that resulted from the at-large election format. Despite a majority population composed of people of color, on a city council of nine members, only two were Latinos and one was African American. The difficulty of being elected citywide as a person of color with limited means against well-funded, business-backed candidates created the disparity. The Justice Department recommended a districting system with at least part of or the entire council elected from geographically based single-member districts. A "Ten-One Plan" with ten districts and a citywide elected mayor was offered to the voters and in an intensely fought election was passed by the equivalent of ten votes per precinct across the city. In the subsequent 1977 city election under the Ten-One Plan, San Antonio's first City Council majority of people of color was elected—five Latinos, one African American—on a council of eleven members. The ensuing years were challenging, and adjustments to political realities were awkward, but these changes along with the concrete evidence of COPS' advocacy in the poorer neighborhoods ushered in an era of growth and economic progress. It became clear that once issues of representation, fairness, and voice were addressed, the citywide conversation could begin in earnest concerning the content of policies and mutual commitments to progress.

In their evaluation of that era in San Antonio, Brenner and Pastor conclude, "Over the past four decades, San Antonio has moved from conflict to collaboration, from stark racism and poverty to incorporation and income mobility. . . . Over time—and facilitated through the deliberate efforts of a few bridge-building individuals—this continued engagement evolved to a growing sense of common destiny and the broad culture and social norms of collaboration that characterize the region today."

Population Growth

As of 2019, the city of San Antonio had a population of 1.53 million, making it the seventh-largest city in the United States. From 2000 to 2019, the city's population grew by 34.2 percent, among the fastest growth rates of any large US city. Between 2016 and 2017, San Antonio was the fastest-growing city in the United States with a numeric growth of 24,208 people, or sixty-six new residents per day.

The San Antonio metro, meanwhile, has a population of 2.27 million. Among US metros, the San Antonio area ranks twenty-fourth. The city of San Antonio represents a much larger share of its surrounding metro-area population than the core cities of Houston, Dallas, or Fort Worth within their metros, since San Antonio has long been more aggressive in annexing developing areas on the outskirts of the city. The city limits of Dallas and Fort Worth, by contrast, are largely fixed in perpetuity by large suburban cities. Houston—uniquely among large US cities—is surrounded by vast areas in Harris County that are heavily populated but unincorporated. Houston's city limits, however, do extend into an adjacent county, Fort Bend County. From 2000 to 2017, the San Antonio metro area's population surged by 44.5 percent, faster than Dallas–Fort Worth in percentage terms and just behind Houston. Within the metro as a whole, Hispanics make up 55.4 percent of the population, far above their 35.8 percent population share in the Texas Triangle as a whole. White residents constitute 33.6 percent of the metro population compared to their overall Texas Triangle share of 41.6 percent. African Americans account for 6.4 percent, well below the Triangle's 13.8 percent, while Asian Americans constitute just 2.2 percent compared to their Texas Triangle population share

San Antonio is the nation's seventh-largest city in terms of population. Shutterstock / Andrew Yoshiki.

of 6.4 percent. Net migration from elsewhere in the United States added 20.3 percent to San Antonio's population, or almost half its growth.

All the Texas Triangle metros have experienced large influxes of people in recent years. San Antonio, however, has seen a different pattern from those of Houston and Dallas–Fort Worth. In percentage terms, immigration from abroad has contributed much less to the San Antonio metro's growth since 2000 than it has in Houston and Dallas–Fort Worth. But net migration from elsewhere in the United States has contributed considerably more to San Antonio's growth than in the other Triangle cities, relative to the population in 2000. Net domestic migration has contributed 20.3 percent to San Antonio's growth, while it has contributed 13.2 percent to that of Dallas–Fort Worth and 9.6 percent to that of Houston. The San Antonio metro is increasingly attractive to Americans from all over the country.

Economic Growth in the Last Three Decades

In 1985, the private supermarket chain H-E-B moved its head-quarters from Corpus Christi to San Antonio. It was a transformative event for the company and for the city. With more than 350 stores throughout Texas and northern Mexico, H-E-B has since become the city's largest private employer, with more than twenty-three thousand workers in San Antonio and annual revenues of more than $21 billion. Established as a family-run country grocery store in 1905 in Kerrville, Texas, H-E-B ranks twelfth on *Forbes*'s list of the United States' largest private companies. Chairman and CEO Charles Butt, grandson of company founder Florence Butt, has directed corporate and personal contributions to San Antonio—especially in the realm of education—that have played a critical role in the city's development.

More recently, San Antonio achieved a critical breakthrough when Japan's Toyota Motor Corp. chose the city as the site for a new Tundra pickup truck plant in 2003. The assembly plant opened in 2006 and soon expanded to include production of Tacoma pickup trucks. The backstory behind Toyota's move illustrates much about San Antonio and the Texas Triangle as a whole. From the start, Toyota was interested in the South, like other US and international automakers that had been pulling away from Detroit since the 1980s. Toyota's US marketing department suggested Texas as a possibility because US automakers Ford and GM had a large volume of pickup truck sales there. But the only auto manufacturing presence in Texas of any significance was the GM assembly plant in Arlington. Auto industry supply chains were thin in Texas. Nevertheless, Toyota executives visited the Dallas area and were stunned as they walked through the parking lot of Texas Stadium in Irving during a Dallas Cowboys game. In the parking lot, they saw an overwhelming number of pickup trucks. The executives began to think about the value of building pickup trucks in the heart of a vast state market for their product.

The years after HemisFair also brought memorable changes to San Antonio in the areas of sports and culture. The San Antonio Spurs began playing in San Antonio, having played for several years in

Dallas as the "Chaparrals" in the American Basketball Association before San Antonio buyers, led by B. J. "Red" McCombs, purchased and moved the franchise to the Alamo City. McCombs renamed the team the Spurs after his hometown of Spur, Texas. The Spurs were the first top-tier professional sports franchise in San Antonio and have become the most dependable unifying force across the city. The team has won five National Basketball Association championships since 1999 and, in the three decades since 1990, achieved the highest game-winning percentage of any US professional sports franchise in history.

Like all the core cities of the Texas Triangle, San Antonio has maintained a pattern of moderate, pragmatic politics. Since 1975, for forty-five years, successive mayors have governed with an inclusive, socially progressive, business-minded approach that has contributed to the economic development of the city. San Antonio's pragmatic city leadership is reflected not only in the many physical improvements the city has added in recent decades but also in its pristine credit ratings. As of 2018, the city of San Antonio was the only US city of more than a million people that had preserved the highest possible AAA bond rating from all three of the United States' principal rating agencies for each of the eight previous years.

Drivers of Economic Growth

Like the other large metros of the Texas Triangle, San Antonio has benefited enormously from two powerful drivers: a broadly diverse economic base with numerous leading companies across many industries and relatively good housing affordability and high quality of life by the standards of large US cities.

Based on a 2014 Moody's study, San Antonio's metro-area economy was among the four that scored highest of the fifty-one metros in the United States' top eight megaregions for economic diversity. Using the Herfindahl-Hirschman Index, a standard statistical measure, the Moody's study assigned a high score to metros whose employment is spread widely across many industries and a comparatively low score to metros highly dependent on a single industry—such as Detroit's dependence on automobiles or Las Vegas's dependence on tourism.

San Antonio's leading private-sector employers represent a notable range of industries: food retail (H-E-B), media (iHeart-Media), technology (Rackspace), medical equipment (3M, originally known as Kinetic Concepts Inc. and later Acelity, which 3M acquired in 2019), automobiles (Toyota), banking (JPMorgan Chase, Citigroup, Cullen/Frost Bank), insurance (USAA), and oil and gas (Valero Energy, NuStar Energy), among many others.

Rackspace Technology, a pioneer in cloud computing, is San Antonio's greatest success story in technology. Graham Weston, the company's billionaire cofounder, is contributing to San Antonio's progress far beyond the technology sector. Weston established Weston Urban, a real-estate development company, focused on reinventing downtown San Antonio. Weston Urban's development includes a thriving new tech district, anchored by the technology coworking space Geekdom. The firm is also working with the University of Texas at San Antonio (UTSA) on a massive expansion of the university's downtown campus, with a new school of data science to attract more tech talent to the San Antonio area.

Like the other Triangle metros, San Antonio has seen powerful growth in its health-care sector. Health care in San Antonio blossomed in the last half of the twentieth century, beginning with the establishment of a UT System medical school in 1968. Now called UT Health San Antonio, the school partnered with the Bexar County Hospital, later renamed University Hospital, to form the centerpiece of today's nine-hundred-acre South Texas Medical Center. Altogether, the center's medical facilities treat more than five million patients a year. The South Texas Medical Center is aggressively adding hospital capacity and specialty institutes to accommodate the area's growing population as well as to play an increasingly prominent role in medical research. Bioscience employment in the San Antonio region exceeds 140,000 positions, the largest sector in the region's economy.

Military medicine adds another important component to San Antonio's biomedical concentration. San Antonio has emerged as the premier center for military medical training for the US Army,

Navy, and Air Force. The Pentagon consolidated numerous facilities to create the world's largest medical school, located at Fort Sam Houston and now called Joint Base San Antonio–Fort Sam Houston. The base houses the nation's leading burn center, famous for its invention of "artificial skin" used for wound treatment.

San Antonio has a world-class life sciences research asset in the Texas Biomedical Research Institute, known as Texas BioMed. Founded by oilman and philanthropist Tom Slick during the 1940s, Texas Biomed has the only private level-four biocontainment laboratory in the United States as well as the nation's largest primate research colony. Texas Biomed researchers have been actively engaged in the development of vaccines and therapeutic medications for COVID-19.

Another significant contributor to San Antonio's research sector is the Southwest Research Institute (SwRI), also founded by oilman Slick. SwRI's research breakthroughs have included automobile airbags, renewable power generation, space research for NASA, and rescue submarines for the US and Australian navies. With an annual budget of more than $584 million, SwRI employs more than 2,600 people on its 1,250-acre campus.

San Antonio has also experienced substantial growth in its higher education sector. The city's largest universities are UTSA and Texas A&M University–San Antonio. San Antonio is the only Texas city with a branch campus of both of the state's largest university systems. With more than thirty thousand students, UTSA is the third-largest institution within the UT System. Founded in 1969, UTSA operates one of the thirty largest business schools in the United States. It spends more than $80 million per year on research, including prominent work in space physics and energy efficiency in data centers. Texas A&M University–San Antonio, founded in 2009, now enrolls some 6,500 students. Notably, it's the first of the Texas A&M University System's eleven campuses to be located in a major urban center.

San Antonio also has a rich portfolio of smaller institutions, including Trinity University, the University of the Incarnate Word, St. Mary's University, and Our Lady of the Lake University. Alamo Colleges, comprising San Antonio College near downtown and other branch campuses, is a large, nationally respected community college district with an enrollment of more than ninety thousand students.

Challenges

Perhaps San Antonio's most important long-term challenges are in education. San Antonio lags behind national averages for both high school and college attainment. The city's high school graduation rate is 81.6 percent compared to the US average of 82.3 percent. Among San Antonians aged twenty-five or higher, 28.1 percent had a bachelor's degree or higher compared to 35.0 percent for the US population and 34.1 percent for the Texas Triangle as a whole. Lower education attainment rates translate to lower income levels for San Antonians. The median wage in the city of San Antonio as of 2018 was $49,024 compared to a national average of $61,937. The San Antonio metro's GDP per worker was $124,493 compared to $150,375 for the Texas Triangle as a whole.

San Antonio leaders recognize that their city's success in the twenty-first-century economy will require more effective invest-ment in the development of its human capital. In 2014, San Antonio voters approved a sales-tax increase to create innovative prekin-dergarten programs. The city has expanded access to its colleges and universities, including its fast-growing community college system. San Antonio's fifteen higher education institutions have also modernized their academic programs to improve their gradu-ates' workforce readiness. A number of them, for instance, have designed new degree programs in technology-related fields. The city has repurposed sections of the shuttered Kelly and Brooks Air Force bases to create programs focused on cybersecurity, making San Antonio an education hub of excellence in the United States for students in the burgeoning field. In 2020, after the stunning evidence of economic inequities laid bare by the pandemic, San Antonio voters renewed the sales tax to extend pre-K education and redirected another one-eighth of a cent of sales tax to augment worker training programs.

Austin–San Antonio Corridor

As in the other metros of the Texas Triangle, the suburban counties surrounding the core city are generally growing faster than the core city itself. In addition to Bexar County, home to the city of San Antonio, the San Antonio metro area includes Atascosa, Bandera, Comal, Guadalupe, Kendall, Medina, and Wilson counties. Two of these counties are growing particularly fast: Comal County, home to the city of New Braunfels and located northeast of San Antonio along I-35, and Kendall County to the north, with its county seat at Boerne. Both counties saw population growth of 98 percent between 2000 and 2019. Comal County reached about 156,000, while Kendall County grew to 47,000. Both have appeared frequently on lists of the fastest-growing counties in the United States.

It's also instructive to consider the rapid changes that are taking place in the combined San Antonio–Austin areas at the Texas Triangle's southwestern corner. The downtowns of San Antonio and Austin are only seventy-four miles apart. The two adjoining metropolitan areas had a combined population of about 4.72 million people as of 2019. If the two MSAs comprised a state, it would be the twenty-fifth largest in the nation, between Alabama at number twenty-four and Louisiana at number twenty-six. Taken together, the combined San Antonio–Austin area is the fastest-growing urban center in the Texas Triangle. Between 2000 and 2017, the combined area grew 55.0 percent, ahead of the Houston metro at 43.4 percent and the Dallas–Fort Worth metro at 46.2 percent. Amazon and Walmart have invested heavily in distribution facilities along the Austin–San Antonio corridor.

A challenge and an opportunity for San Antonio is how to collaborate with Austin to plan the future of a globally significant unified metropolitan center. The rapid growth of these two large, booming metro areas—now bumping into each other in Comal and Hays counties—raises important long-term questions for both of them and for the Triangle as a whole. The experience of other pairs of geographically proximate and closely connected large cities suggests that working together can create considerably more value than cities might generate on their own. Most immediately, Dallas and Fort Worth—thirty miles apart—have cooperated to build the powerful North Texas metro. Their cooperation includes D/FW Airport as well as closely interconnected supply chains and shared amenities such as professional sports stadiums between the two cities in Arlington. Washington and Baltimore share airports and employment centers along their corridor, including Defense Department installations, intelligence agencies, and National Institutes of Health facilities. San Francisco and Oakland are linked by their respective airports, shared public transit systems, and robust cross-bay commuting patterns. The whole San Francisco Bay Area, including the San Jose metro and all the small cities that comprise Silicon Valley, effectively function as a single economic unit. Outside the United States, pairs like Tokyo-Yokohama, Milan-Turin, and Hong Kong–Guangzhou provide other examples of successful collaboration between large, adjacent metro areas.

San Antonio and Austin have made preliminary efforts toward collaboration since the establishment of the Austin–San Antonio Corridor Council in 1986. Agenda items for leaders in the greater San Antonio–Austin region include regional economic development strategies, traffic congestion and mobility, coordination of air travel hubs, affordable housing development, access to higher education, advanced research, and even new professional sports teams. In time, integration of communities in the Austin–San Antonio region may lead the US Census Bureau to redesignate the San Antonio–Austin area as a single MSA, which would result in the United States' thirteenth-largest metro area and radically change the way the region thinks of itself and how the wider world views the Texas Triangle.

The Essence of the "San Antonio Way"

In attempting to pinpoint the most descriptive characteristics of San Antonio's modern era, one also uncovers the theme that San Antonio can most constructively share with the nation and its cities. These characteristics revolve around concepts of collaboration, conflict resolution, fair representation, ongoing communication, aligned goals, and pride in place.

According to the analysis of Brenner and Pastor,

> Collaboration has, in some ways, become so embedded in San Antonio that for many young leaders and organizations it is a modus operandi—they report that "it's just how we do things here . . ." But collaboration in San Antonio has come about only through the activities of social movements unafraid of sparking conflict and controversy, including highlighting the need for political representation of the region's significant and growing Latino community . . . there was also a sort of rootedness in the region—a "place pride"—that seems to have anchored communities, including the San Antonio Chamber of Commerce's more recent support for a sales tax to fund Pre-K.

Brenner and Pastor's emphasis on collaboration as a community ethic is real in San Antonio. It is based on a consensus on such long-term goals as generating economic growth to raise incomes, expand the middle class, and invest in human capital. That high degree of consensus is uniquely interwoven with what can be called a distinct culture. It is not Texas or Mexico. It is not cowboy or Tejano. It is not liberal or conservative in national terms; it is just San Antonio. San Antonio encapsulates a rich history, has learned the wastefulness of racial and ethnic conflict, strives to play fair, and may have something to teach the nation.

The Rest of the Texas Triangle

Dallas–Fort Worth, Houston, San Antonio, and Austin are the four giant metro areas that define the Texas Triangle. But three smaller metros are within the Triangle geographically when looking at the interstate highways that connect the four large metros. College Station–Bryan is tucked inside the Triangle boundaries northwest of Houston. Along Interstate 35 between Dallas–Fort Worth and Austin sit two other MSAs—Waco and Killeen-Temple. The US Census Bureau defines an MSA as having at least one central urban core area of fifty thousand people or more.[1] As of September 2018, the United States had 384 MSAs.

Of the three smaller metros along and inside the Texas Triangle's boundary, the largest is Killeen-Temple with a three-county population of 451,902 in 2019.[2] The population in the two-county Waco metro is 273,162, while College Station–Bryan, a three-county metro area, follows closely with a population of 264,610. These three metros total 989,674 people, far fewer than any of the four large Texas Triangle metros, each of which has a population of more than two million.

Moreover, in all three of the smaller metros, the populations are highly transitory, with many residents staying only a few years and being constantly replaced with new residents. Killeen-Temple includes Fort Hood, one the largest of the US Army's installations.

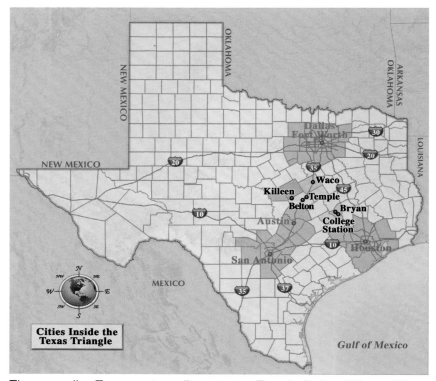

Three smaller Texas metropolitan areas—Temple-Belton-Killeen, Waco, and College Station–Bryan—are along or within the three interstate highways—I-35, I-10, and I-45—that form the Texas Triangle shape.

Waco is the home of Baylor University and its students. College Station–Bryan is anchored by the flagship Texas A&M University campus, where enrollment—at more than sixty-eight thousand—is in a virtual tie for the nation's largest campus with the University of Central Florida, not counting institutions that mainly operate through online courses or community college systems.

Although many residents are transitory, these three metros play vital roles in cementing the economic power of the Texas Triangle through the strengths of their largest sectors. The three smaller metros not only help connect the three corners of the urban Texas Triangle; they provide supporting roles that boost the rising fortunes of the Texas Triangle as a whole.

Killeen-Temple

The Killeen-Temple metro area comprises three main urban centers. Killeen has a population of 151,547. Temple's population is 77,295, and Belton adds 22,281. The metro covers three counties—Bell, Coryell, and Lampasas. Belton is sixty-one miles north of Austin, while Temple and Killeen are both sixty-eight miles from Austin. The 2018 GDP of the Killeen-Temple metro was $18.84 billion, according to the US Bureau of Economic Analysis.[3]

The Gulf, Colorado and Santa Fe Railway company founded Killeen in 1881, when it purchased 360 acres of land and outlined a seventy-block town on the site, naming it after the company's assistant general manager, Frank P. Killeen.[4] Killeen became a shipping point for cotton, wool, and grain produced in the area. Killeen remain a farm trading town until 1942, when Camp Hood, renamed Fort Hood in 1950, began operating as an armored military training base during World War II. Soldiers and their families, along with construction workers, moved to Killeen. The base significantly changed the town, especially as much of the farming activity went by the wayside as the 158,000-acre base took over many farms

The Bell County Courthouse is in Belton. Shutterstock / Tricia Daniel.

and ranches. New companies started to supply Fort Hood along with new schools and hospitals. In 1965, a community college, Central Texas College, was established. In 2015–16, Central Texas College had an enrollment of 15,355 at the Killeen campus and another 5,628 students at the Fort Hood campus.[5] In 2009, the Texas A&M University System added a campus in Killeen called Texas A&M University–Central Texas. It had an enrollment of 3,470 in 2018.

But Fort Hood itself, as one of the largest military installations in the world, was the development that transformed Killeen and Central Texas. It eventually grew to more than 210,000 acres. In 2017, Fort Hood had an on-post military-personnel population of 35,577.[6] On-post family members totaled 13,169, and off-post family members numbered 35,011. Fort Hood had an economic impact of $35.4 billion on the Texas economy in 2015, according to the Texas Comptroller of Public Accounts.

Nearby Temple was founded in 1880 by the Gulf, Colorado and Santa Fe Railway that established Killeen. The city was named for Bernard Moore Temple, the railway's chief engineer. After Temple was incorporated in 1882, the Santa Fe Hospital was established in 1904, later renamed Scott and White Hospital in 1922. This hospital has grown to become one of the top medical centers in the Southwest. Temple's economy diversified with American Desk Manufacturing Co., established in 1921, and a Coca-Cola bottling plant in 1925. Temple Junior College started in 1926 and is now called Temple College. The Texas Agricultural Experiment Station became the state offices for the US Soil Conservation Service. A Veterans Administration hospital expanded Temple's health-care industry in 1942.

Scott and White remains the main economic pillar in Temple, part of a hospital system that was widely known throughout the twentieth century with patients coming from across Texas and beyond. Doctors Arthur Carroll Scott and Raleigh R. White were the original partners at the railroad hospital.[7] The hospital pioneered group practice, or medical specialists working as teams. For decades, Scott and White enjoyed the highest reputation in rural and urban Texas for health care, especially for specialists, before the rise of Houston's medical center. Scott and White also conducted research projects. Eventually, numerous satellite clinics spread from the Temple hospital base across Central Texas and elsewhere in Texas. The 640-bed hospital in Temple is now part of Dallas-based Baylor Scott & White with fifty hospitals.

Belton is the county seat of Bell County, which also contains Temple and Killeen and part of Fort Hood. Belton started in 1850 under the name of Nolanville, after an adventurer named Philip Nolan.[8] The town incorporated in 1851, and the name changed to Belton, after Bell County. Belton was a stop on the mail route stretching from Little Rock, Arkansas, to San Antonio. A period of lawlessness occurred after the Civil War with a series of political murders and lynchings. The KKK had a presence in the late 1860s. Belton, like Killeen, became an agricultural trade post and provided services for cattle drives, since one of the Chisholm Trail routes ran along Belton's eastern fringe. Baylor Female College, later the University of Mary Hardin-Baylor, came to Belton in 1885. The university became coeducational in 1971 and now has an enrollment of 3,900 students on a 340-acre campus.[9] Belton city and Bell County local governments and the University of Mary Hardin-Baylor are Belton's top three employers. The Killeen-Temple metro area, once an agricultural stronghold, today functions as an urban center for military, health care, and higher education along the Interstate 35 corridor with numerous ties to the Texas Triangle.

Waco

Waco is another city that reinforces the highly urbanized Interstate 35 corridor in the Texas Triangle between Dallas–Fort Worth and San Antonio. The Waco metro area covers two counties—McLennan and Falls—but Waco is the only large municipality, with a population of 139,324.[10] The Waco-area economy was $14.29 billion in 2018.[11] Waco sits on the Brazos River about seventy miles south of Dallas and thirty-five miles north of Temple on I-35.

Waco's site was originally an indigenous people's village of the Waco nation.[12] The Waco tribe was driven from the site around

1830 by the Cherokee. An initial settlement in 1837 lasted only a few months. "Waco Village" was selected as the county seat when McLennan County was organized in 1850. Ranger and Native American fighter Shapley P. Ross started a ferry at the river and opened a hotel. In 1856, Waco Village was incorporated as Waco, and the city grew as a cotton trading center. Cattle drives along the Chisholm Trail helped broaden Waco's economy in the late 1860s and 1870s until railroads reached the city. The railroads reinforced Waco as a transportation center for cotton farmers and various manufacturing enterprises. Waco Classical School started in 1860, became Waco University in 1861, and merged with Baylor University in 1887. The merger moved Baylor to Waco from the Texas town of Independence. During World War I, Camp MacArthur opened in Waco as an infantry training post, training thirty-five thousand soldiers from 1917 to 1919. Rural Blacks moved to Waco from 1900 to 1930 seeking jobs and education. But like many other cities in Texas at the time, the KKK established a presence in the city, with two thousand members parading in the city in 1923.

On May 11, 1953, Waco was slammed by one of the deadliest tornadoes in Texas history. The storm killed 114 people and injured another 145. Almost two hundred Waco business buildings were destroyed, and about four hundred more were eventually torn down. The Dr Pepper bottling plant was damaged but survived and now is a soft-drink history museum. Over time, many of the storm-damaged businesses moved to the city's suburban fringe, leading to inner-city stagnation. The construction of a convention center and the establishment of the Texas Ranger Hall of Fame and Museum and the Texas Sports Hall of Fame helped revive the city's economic fortunes.

Waco is best known as the home of Baylor University. The university was established in 1845 by the Congress of the Republic of Texas after it was proposed in 1841 by the Union Baptist Association.[13] The suggestion for a Baptist university in Texas came from Rev. William Milton Tryon and District Judge R. E. B. Baylor. The university opened in 1847 in Independence, Texas, and moved to Waco in 1886 in the merger with Waco University. The university calls itself the oldest continuously operated university in the state.

Magnolia Market at the Silos, operated by Chip and Joanna Gaines of the *Fixer Upper* television show, has revitalized downtown Waco and is a popular tourist attraction. Shutterstock / Lunasee Studios.

Baylor University grew to a one-thousand-acre campus that, in 2018, had an enrollment of 14,188 undergraduate students and 3,029 graduate students. A member of the Big 12 Conference, Baylor is widely known, too, for its nineteen varsity sports teams.

In 2013, the HGTV cable television network began broadcasting *Fixer Upper*, featuring an enterprising Waco couple, Chip and Joanna Gaines, who restore houses in impressive style. Over its five years, the TV series has rebranded Waco as a city that is investing in itself. The effect gathered momentum, with Waco visitors zooming to 2.7 million per year from 650,000 in 2014, partially because out-of-state visitors to Dallas, Houston, Austin, and San Antonio took side trips to Waco.[14] They come mainly to visit the Gaines couple's Magnolia Market at the Silos, a complex of stores and restaurants. Downtown residency in the form of lofts and condominiums has risen in Waco along with the number of high-end restaurants.

College Station–Bryan

The College Station–Bryan metro area revolves around the large Texas A&M University flagship campus. Texas A&M University at College Station is a Tier One research university along with UT Austin and Houston's Rice University, as designated by the American Association of Universities. College Station is eighty-three miles northwest of Houston, ninety-five miles by highway, and about forty miles west of Interstate 45 connecting Houston with Dallas, putting the metro within the Texas Triangle boundary.

In 2019, College Station had a population of 116,998, and Bryan's population was 85,224.[15] The metro area covers three counties—Brazos, Burleson, and Robertson. College Station–Bryan's economy in 2018 was $13.25 billion.

In 1860, construction on the Houston and Texas Central Railway crossed through Brazos County. Eleven years later, Brazos County was selected as the site for the proposed Texas A&M College, which opened in 1876. A year later, a post office opened near the railroad tracks. The post office was called College Station, and the community that was stimulated by the university took that name, although the city was not incorporated until 1938. An electric rail route between College Station and Bryan began operations in 1910, replaced by buses during the 1920s.

The seat of Brazos County, however, is Bryan, which adjoins College Station. Members of Stephen F. Austin's Mexico-era colony first settled Bryan in the 1820s and 1830s. An Austin nephew, William Joel Bryan, donated land in 1859 for the railroad, which did not arrive until 1867 because of the delay caused by the Civil War. Town leaders named the town for Bryan, and it was incorporated in 1872.

In the early 1900s, Bryan, like Waco, became a large rail shipping point for area cotton production. In 1943, the Bryan Army Air Field opened as a school for flight instructors with an additional assignment for developing instrument flight training, a new element of pilot training. The field was renamed Bryan Air Force Base in 1947. A phase-out of the installation started in 1959, and the site was added to the Texas A&M campus. Today, it serves as

Texas A&M University in College Station is the flagship campus in the Texas A&M University System. Shutterstock / Grindstone Media Group.

the RELLIS Campus of Texas A&M University, which is also the home of the Texas Transportation Institute. Nearer the main Texas A&M campus is Easterwood Airport, owned and operated by the university and served by United and American Airlines.

Texas A&M is the heart of the College Station–Bryan metro area. At its founding, Texas A&M became the state's first public university. The Texas Legislature approved an "agricultural and mechanical" college in 1871, based on the US Congress's 1866 Morrill Act, allowing for land donations for universities teaching certain disciplines, including military tactics.[16] Brazos County citizens made the land donation, and classes began in 1876, with all students required to receive military training. Fundamental change came in the 1960s, when participation in the Corps of Cadets became voluntary. Female and African American students were admitted, ushering in an era of rapid growth and new research programs. The George Bush Presidential Library and Museum open in 1997 on the campus.

In 2018, the 5,200-acre campus had an enrollment of 69,367, of which undergraduates numbered 54,369, making Texas A&M one two largest universities in the nation.[17] The alumni count has surpassed 480,000. The university's Corps of Cadets commisons more officers than any institution other than the US military service academies. In 2018, there were more than 2,400 cadets. The university's athletics teams are members of the Southeastern Conference.

The flagship campus in College Station is one of eleven campuses in the Texas A&M University System with a combined enrollment of about 153,000 students.[18] Two A&M System campuses operate in Texas Triangle metros: Texas A&M–San Antonio and Prairie View A&M University in the Houston suburban county of Waller. Other A&M System campuses are in Commerce, Stephenville, Canyon, Kingsville, Corpus Christi, Laredo, Texarkana, and, as mentioned earlier, Killeen.

Culture Clash

Not all was peaceful in Central Texas as these three smaller metropolitan areas developed. College sports rivalries almost became real wars, especially along the Brazos River, which runs through both Waco and College Station about ninety miles apart. A bitter Baylor–Texas A&M rivalry called the "Battle of the Brazos" developed and reached a hostile and fatal stage in 1926.[19] Tensions rose between the then all-male university, Texas A&M, and Baylor, where male students did not like to see Baylor coeds dating Aggie cadets. At halftime of the 1926 football game in Waco, Baylor men dressed in clownish cadet uniforms to mock Aggie calisthenics drills. Then a red car entered the field carrying Baylor female students holding placards showing scores of past Baylor victories over Texas A&M. Two Aggie cadets at the stadium, from about four hundred of them, dashed onto the field toward the car. One woman fell off the car, igniting a riot that involved many people from both schools. Baylor male students, including freshman football players and other reserve players wearing football gear, rushed to the field ostensibly to defend the Baylor women. Weapons included wooden folding chairs used as sideline seating for the Baylor freshmen football team. Signals to the Aggie Band to play a piece called "Taps" and then the national anthem eventually calmed the violent free-for-all. A Texas A&M cadet named Charles M. Sessums had received a bloody head wound and initially seemed to recover. But Sessums died the next day at a Waco hospital. That was not the end of the episode. After the Texas A&M cadets returned by passenger train back to College Station, legend has it that some of them loaded a rail car with a cannon and munitions, intending to return to Waco and shell the Baylor campus. According to one version of Aggie lore, Texas Rangers learned of the planned attack and halted the assault train by chopping down trees to block the tracks. Another version of events states that cooler-headed Texas A&M cadets stopped the train before it started. Despite a probe by a Dallas-based private investigator, no one was ever arrested for the fatal halftime blow to Sessums. Athletic contests between the schools were suspended until 1931.

The incident reflects how Texas towns grew from their agri-cultural roots into urban areas in different ways and with vary-ing cultures. The emerging urban areas competed and clashed with each other for economic opportunities. They established their own identities and senses of pride but still became interdependent despite rivalries.

Other Triangle Gems

Dotting the land inside the Texas Triangle's three boundary inter-state highways are small, urban-like treasures that enrich the region even though they are far too small in population and economic size to rank as metropolitan areas. Two of the numerous examples are Brenham and Round Top. Brenham is widely known among the residents of the large Texas Triangle metros because it is the home of Blue Bell Ice Cream. Brenham sits halfway between Austin and Houston along US Highway 290 and dates back to the 1840s. In 1907, the Brenham Creamery Co. started making butter and, a few years later, ice cream.[20] In 1930, the company was renamed Blue Bell Creameries. Its ice cream became legendary in Texas before expanding outside the state during the 1980s. Its products are now sold in twenty-two states. Brenham's 2019 population was 17,752.[21] Round Top has a population of only eighty-eight people as of 2019 and is barely more than a restaurant, antique shops, and several bed-and-breakfast establishments. Round Top is twenty-eight miles from Brenham. But the tiny town is where the Round Top Festival Institute operates on a 210-acre campus called "Festival Hill."[22] Founded in 1971 by concert pianist James Dick, the year-round classical music / performing arts training program draws students internationally. The annual highlight is a summer festival of instrumental, chamber, and orchestral concerts, drawing audiences mainly from San Antonio, Austin, and Houston. The campus is an idyllic nature preserve with a large concert hall, historic houses, gardens, and libraries of manuscripts and rare books. A few miles outside of Round Top is a historic center called Winedale, basically a house and converted barn/theater, where UT Austin operates a program called "Shakespeare at Winedale," which stages Shakespearean and similar plays, mainly in the summer.[23] Another large attraction in the area is Santa's Wonderland at College Station, which operates in November and December, presenting rides on carriages, hay wagons, ponies, and a train, plus live music, a gingerbread village, and a petting zoo, all in a snowscape of Christmas decorations and lights.

Growth

The Belton-Temple, Waco, and College Station metro areas are slowly strengthening and melding commercially into the nearby Texas Triangle urban giants, according to Jim Gaines, chief economist of the Real Estate Center at Texas A&M University in College Station. Austin's success as a high-technology center is spreading along the Interstate 35 corridor, especially north toward Belton-Temple.

Gaines explains that "growth is slow getting to Waco. Waco hasn't had the magnet in it. Baylor is a fraction of the size of College Station." College Station is another matter, Gaines continues:

"I joke in my speeches that the good news for College Station is that it is right in the middle of the urban triangle. The bad news is that it is right in the middle of the triangle." In other words, College Station is not along one of the connector interstate highways that would better tie the College Station–Bryan metro to Dallas or Houston. "But the university has sixty thousand students," Gaines says, adding that the Texas A&M University System continues to make large investments in College Station to expand its academic degrees and programs.

While College Station is not exactly isolated, its ability to establish relationships with the Dallas–Fort Worth and Houston metro areas will strengthen enormously by as early as 2024 with the Texas Central high-speed passenger rail project. Texas Central plans to connect Dallas and Houston with only one stop in between, near College Station. That would position College Station only forty-five minutes away by train to stations near the Dallas and Houston central business districts.

Overall, more people are looking into the secondary and tertiary metro areas, like Temple-Belton and College Station–Bryan, to reside in "as bedroom communities" while holding jobs in the Texas Triangle metro areas. "There are people in College Station and Bryan who drive to work in Houston's suburbs. It's an hour to The Woodlands," Gaines says. "It allows people the benefit both of living in a less crowded metro area and of having jobs in the big-city suburbs."

In all, much of the area between the three corners of the Texas Triangle and along the Triangle boundaries are hotbeds of skill development through higher education and military training, which enlarges worker pipelines to employers in Texas' large cities. The three metros—Killeen-Temple, Waco, and College Station–Bryan—also provide increased availability of health-care services to Texas Triangle residents and rural Texans. Without the three smaller, supporting metros, growth would have been slower in the Texas Triangle, and the large Texas metros would be less cohesive economically.

Texas Metros outside of the Triangle

The Texas Triangle's four giant metros dominate the state in population and economy. But the Triangle only partly defines urban Texas. Outside of the Triangle, Texas is dotted with cities that have risen well above rural or small-town status. They pulled themselves up by their own bootstraps, established their own economic roles and foundations, and continue down the path of urbanization. These cities have economic connections to the Texas Triangle giants. They also have their own independent bearings and growth trends.

In all, Texas contains 25 of the 384 MSAs in the United States, ranking Texas second to California, which has 26 MSAs.

Of the twenty-five Texas MSAs, the four largest are composed of the metros at the corners of the Texas Triangle: Dallas–Fort Worth, Houston, San Antonio, and Austin. Three others—Killeen-Temple, Waco, and College Station–Bryan—are within the Texas Triangle boundaries delineated by Interstate Highways 35, 45, and 10.

That leaves eighteen Texas urban areas outside of the Triangle, each contributing to the momentum of the Texas economy. See table 13.1 for an account of the twenty-five Texas MSAs ranked by population.

As middle-sized urban areas outside of the Texas Triangle, these cities play a critical supporting role in Texas, including their

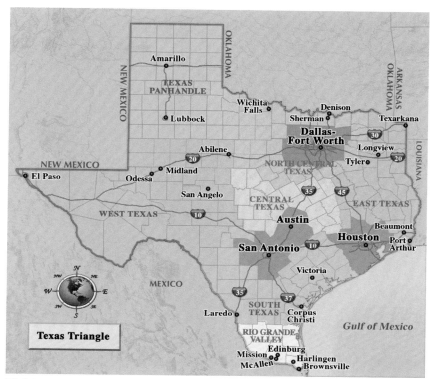

Eighteen smaller Texas metropolitan areas dot the Texas map outside of the Texas Triangle boundary.

proximity to the agricultural industries of rural Texas. These mid-sized cities provide supplies to farms and ranches and assist in distributing agricultural commodities to food production and processing firms across the state. They also offer higher education, both four-year universities and two-year community colleges, providing skills and knowledge to their residents and serving dispersed counties in every part of Texas.

Rio Grande Valley

The McAllen-Edinburg-Mission metropolitan area at the southern tip of Texas ranks as the fifth-largest urban area in the state with

Table 13.1

Texas' twenty-five MSAs

Cities	2019 population estimate
1. Dallas–Fort Worth–Arlington	7,481,664
2. Houston–The Woodlands–Sugar Land	7,051,556
3. San Antonio–New Braunfels	2,531,095
4. Austin–Round Rock	2,190,335
5. McAllen-Edinburg-Mission	890,414
6. El Paso	859,278
7. Corpus Christi	427,347
8. Killeen-Temple	451,902
9. Brownsville-Harlingen	425,849
10. Beaumont–Port Arthur	396,282
11. Lubbock	319,581
12. Longview	289,854
13. Laredo	281,964
14. Waco	273,162
15. Amarillo	269,397
16. College Station–Bryan	264,610
17. Tyler	230,086
18. Midland	181,505
19. Abilene	172,655
20. Odessa	165,230
21. Wichita Falls	153,867
22. Sherman-Denison	137,479
23. San Angelo	120,224
24. Victoria	99,928
25. Texarkana	97,488

Source: Texas Demographic Center at the University of Texas at San Antonio. The center's population-estimate program is a refinement of US Census Bureau figures.

a population of 890,414. The three largest cities in the metro area all exist within Hidalgo County along the Rio Grande. McAllen is the largest, with a population of 144,379. Edinburg's population is 98,160, while Mission's is 86,309. The 2018 GDP of the McAllen-Edinburg-Mission metro is $23.35 billion.[1] Sitting alongside the McAllen-Edinburg-Mission metro area is the Brownsville-Harlingen metro area within Cameron County. Cameron County sits at the confluence of the Rio Grande with the Gulf of Mexico. The Brownsville-Harlingen metro area, the ninth-largest metro area in Texas, has a population of 425,849. Brownsville has a population of 185,625, while Harlingen's population is 68,328. The GDP for Brownsville-Harlingen is $11.34 billion.

Together, the two adjoining areas would be a metro area with a population of 1.31 million. The McAllen and Brownsville metros are part of a broader population cluster at the southern tip of Texas known as the Rio Grande Valley, or just "the Valley," a region consisting of Hidalgo, Cameron, Willacy, and Starr counties. The distance across the palm-tree-filled counties is about 120 miles. The four-county Valley population is 1.4 million. Typical of Texas border cities, a large Mexican urban area sprawls across the Rio Grande from the Valley. The main Mexican cities are Reynosa (estimated population 733,974[2]), across from McAllen, and Matamoros (estimated population 520,351), across from Brownsville, along with a cluster of smaller cities in the Mexican state of Tamaulipas. In total, on both sides of the border, the "borderplex" adds up to a massive urban area along the last stretch of the Rio Grande before the river empties into the Gulf of Mexico. This binational urban area, functioning as one unit, has been threatened with disruption because of a national discussion, driven by the Trump administration, of a border wall. As of 2020, little work toward such a wall has occurred, but the discussion continues.

On the US side, the cities of McAllen and Brownsville are among the most impoverished US cities. The US poverty rate is 12.3 percent of the population, but in McAllen it is 25.2 percent and in Brownsville 31.4 percent. While the availability of Mexican labor keeps a lid on wages, the abundant supply of labor also makes the McAllen-Brownsville area competitive by restraining business costs and local costs of living.

Most employment in the Valley, moreover, is in low-pay categories, such as retail and food service. Health care employs a high concentration, almost 40 percent, of workers in McAllen and is a sector that normally pays doctors, nurses, and hospital workers high wages.[3] But in McAllen, most of the health-care workers are in home health-care services, which are unlicensed positions that compensate well below typical health-care jobs. The low wage levels in McAllen—$45,057 versus the US average of $57,652—also reflect a low cost of living in the Valley. The median house in McAllen is valued at $120,500 versus the US average of $193,500.

New developments point to a better future for the Rio Grande Valley. The UT System in 2013 merged its two small Valley campuses—UT Pan American in Edinburg and UT Brownsville—into a unit named UT Rio Grande Valley, with branches in the two cities. The UT System also added to the campus the first medical school in South Texas, the UT Rio Grande Valley School of Medicine, in 2016. Total enrollment at UT Rio Grande Valley is 28,644, making it the largest public university in the Texas border region.[4]

The Rio Grande Valley for decades has benefited economically from an annual influx of seasonal residents known as "snowbirds" and "winter Texans," mainly retirees who travel from the US upper Midwest and Canada to enjoy the balmy winters in a low-cost location. In 2017–18, about 106,000 snowbirds spent approximately $528 million in the Valley. The spending keeps retail employment in McAllen at a high level. But the Valley's retail sector is more highly dependent on the US dollar-peso exchange rate because many purchases are made by Mexicans. When the Mexican peso weakens against the US dollar, sales on the US side of the borderplex suffer, while a strong peso boosts sales. For several years, uncertainty in US-Mexico trade policies tended to weaken the peso.

El Paso

Of the approximate two-thousand-mile US-Mexico border, Texas accounts for one thousand miles. El Paso, at the westernmost tip of the Texas-Mexico border, is the sixth-largest Texas urban area with a metro area population of 859,278. The metropolitan area covers two border counties, El Paso and Hudspeth, along the Rio Grande. Both El Paso and Hudspeth sit amid a picturesque mountain range. The city of El Paso population is 681,877. The GDP of the El Paso metro is $35.57 billion. El Paso's companion Mexican city across the Rio Grande is much larger in population. Ciudad Juárez's population is an estimated 1.5 million. El Paso is along Interstate 10, which runs from Florida through Houston and San Antonio before reaching El Paso and eventually California.

The 1854 establishment of the US Army's Fort Bliss led to El Paso's formal founding in 1859, and the city grew along with the fort. Fort Bliss remains El Paso's largest employer, with thirteen thousand civilian workers along with 38,589 active duty personnel, 1,253 reservists, and 39,422 family members.[5] The fort covers 1.12 million acres in both Texas and New Mexico. El Paso is so

Mountains loom near downtown El Paso. Shutterstock / Jose Sohm.

far west and so distant from the other major cities of Texas that it is in a different time zone, Mountain Time, while the rest of Texas uses Central Time. Both Fort Bliss and the US Customs and Border Patrol are large employers along with the City of El Paso and El Paso County. Along with government, El Paso's largest employment sectors are retail, health care, and food service, which are fueled by cross-border shopping and traffic. El Paso is also highly reliant on the wide-scale manufacturing activities in Ciudad Juárez conducted by maquiladoras, or twin plants. Maquiladoras assemble products and components under dual ownership with foreign companies, many of them US firms. About half of Ciudad Juárez' maquiladoras operate in the automotive industry, helping make El Paso a key gateway city in North America. More than half a million freight trucks crossed El Paso bridges in 2017. But the predominance of automotive factories producing components and parts makes Ciudad Juárez and El Paso vulnerable to the up-and-down automotive sales cycle and the resulting effects on production and employment.

Like other border cities with large immigrant populations, El Paso's wage and cost-of-living levels are below US and Texas averages, reflecting the area's relatively lower-skilled employment base. Education levels and skills are on the rise, however. The University of Texas at El Paso enrollment is about 23,600.[6] Lubbock-based Texas Tech University operates a health science center in El Paso, too, with about 660 students.[7] El Paso Community College enrolls more than 28,000 students.[8]

Midland-Odessa

Six hundred long miles separate Dallas–Fort Worth and El Paso. At the midpoint of that distance are the cities of Midland and Odessa, about twenty miles apart. Their West Texas location contributed to the fact that Odessa and Midland were established as transportation centers in a vast expanse of windswept land used mainly for cattle grazing. Indeed, that is how Midland received its name, being midway on Interstate 20 between two larger metros.

But Midland and Odessa have become the most affluent urban areas in Texas outside of the Texas Triangle. The reason is clear: Midland and Odessa sit astride a huge geological formation known as the Permian Basin. This is oil and gas country.

Midland and Odessa are separated into two metropolitan areas. The Midland metro has a population of 181,505 and occupies Midland County. The Odessa metro, in Ector County, has 165,230 residents. The two metros combined total 346,735 people. The city of Midland has a population of 144,600, while Odessa accounts for 125,720. Of the two, Midland has the most wealth with an economy of $32.82 billion. Odessa's GDP is $12.57 billion. But it is the land surrounding the cities that contributes the most to the region's economy. The Permian Basin energy fields cover twenty Texas counties and two counties in New Mexico.

Grasslands of value to farmers and ranchers were the initial attraction to the area in the 1800s, but as water wells were dug, oil and natural gas were detected. Commercial oil drilling commenced in 1921.[9] Deposits near the surface were drilled first, with production reaching a peak in 1973 under the drilling techniques at the time. In recent years, the advent of horizontal drilling and hydraulic fracturing technologies revived the Permian Basin. Independent drillers were the first to demonstrate the success of the new technologies in the Permian Basin before the "Big Oil" companies began arriving with their supporting casts of service companies and refineries. By 2018, Chevron Corp., Irving-based ExxonMobil, Royal Dutch Shell, and ConocoPhillips were highly active in the Permian Basin, some reporting record annual productions in the history of the companies.[10] Some of the companies upgraded their Gulf Coast refineries to process the light, sweet crude coming from the Permian Basin along with heavier-grade crude oils coming from Mexico and Canada.

The largest employer in Midland is Irving-based Pioneer Natural Resources, with about 3,600 employees, creating a direct tie to the Texas Triangle.[11] Other large employers are Halliburton and Keane Group, both energy service companies based in Houston. Industrial and pipeline construction companies also employ thousands of workers. Poverty is low in the area, 10.4 percent, but so is the

Oil and gas drilling is widespread in the Permian Basin, near Midland and Odessa. Shutterstock / G B Hart.

education attainment level. The percentages of the population with high school diplomas and college degrees are lower than the state average, but average incomes are higher than average at $75,646 in Midland and $61,541 in Odessa.[12] Average wages are volatile, fluctuating with the price of oil on the world markets. Energy companies pay high wages for field workers, occupations that do not require college degrees, although with new, more sophisticated technologies, higher skill levels are required.

The Midland-Odessa area is recognizable for other reasons. George H. W. Bush and his family, including son George W. Bush, lived in Midland. High school football is the most popular entertainment there, as it is across West Texas. Odessa Permian High School, known widely because of the book, movie, and television series *Friday Night Lights*, has been a schoolboy football powerhouse over the decades.

The economic outlook for Midland and Odessa is strong. The Permian Basin's many layers of shale formation—with some places containing a dozen layers—will continue to draw energy investments and employment. The US Geological Survey in 2018 estimated that the Wolfcamp Basin, only one part of the Permian Basin, has recoverable reserves of 46.3 billion barrels of crude oil and 281 trillion cubic feet of natural gas.[13] That alone makes the basin the largest single oil and gas reservoir in the United States and one of the largest in the world. In November 2018, about 3.6 million barrels per day of oil were produced across the Permian Basin. The Permian is regarded as a resource that will continue to boost the fortunes of Midland and Odessa as well as fuel the petroleum companies in the Texas Triangle.

Beaumont–Port Arthur

Like Midland and Odessa, the rise of Beaumont and Port Arthur is linked to oil and natural gas. The fabled Spindletop oil discovery in 1901 occurred near Beaumont. The four-county Beaumont–Port Arthur metro area adjoins the Houston metro to the east, an urbanized area called the Golden Triangle, referring to the rise of Beaumont, Port Arthur, and Orange. In the early 1900s, the area rose with oil drilling at first, accounting for the birth of oil giants Texaco (originally the Texas Co.), Gulf Oil Corp., and ExxonMobil (originally Humble). Now its main industries are downstream in the oil and gas process with refining and petrochemical plants, plus distribution through the Port of Port Arthur. As in Houston, the petrochemical industry in the Beaumont–Port Arthur area has expanded thanks to the shale-drilling revolution elsewhere in Texas.

The counties of Hardin, Jefferson, Newton, and Orange comprise the Beaumont–Port Arthur metropolitan area. The combined metro area population is 396,282. Beaumont is the largest city, with a population of 119,780. Port Arthur is second, with 54,440, and Orange has 18,847. The metro area's economic size was $30.68 billion. Interstate 10 runs through Beaumont between Houston and New Orleans, Louisiana.

Large employers in Beaumont and Port Arthur are directly tied to the Texas Triangle cities. Irving-based ExxonMobil, Houston-based Motiva Enterprises, and San Antonio–based Valero Energy

Oil refining is a large activity in Beaumont and Port Arthur. Shutterstock/ ZHMURCHAK.

employ more than four thousand workers combined. Motive Enterprises, whose parent company is Saudi Refining Inc., based in Saudi Arabia, operates the Port Arthur Refinery. It processes about six hundred thousand barrels of oil per day into various fuels. The refinery is the largest in North America and the fifth largest in the world. Activity in the ports of Port Arthur and Beaumont rose with the increase of Texas oil production. Both ports rank among the top twenty-five in the United States in annual tonnage. The giant German chemical company BASF, whose US headquarters is in New Jersey, runs an herbicide production facility that underwent a $270 million expansion. Houston-based Total Petrochemicals and Refining USA and BASF operate the world's largest steam cracker, which makes ethylene, in Port Arthur. Total Petrochemicals also planned a $1.7 billion ethane cracker in Port Arthur, which also would make ethylene. ExxonMobil operates chemical and polyethylene plants in the area. Manufacturing of electrical equipment and machinery in the area happens in above-average concentrations.

Wage levels in Beaumont and Port Arthur are below the state average. The energy and construction jobs in Beaumont and Port Arthur mostly do not require college degrees, but new investments in industrial expansions with newer technologies will require higher skills that will compensate better. Rising activity in the area stemming from Texas' shale drilling already drove wages higher in Beaumont and Port Arthur, up 13 percent in median household income between 2014 and 2017.

Panhandle

Lubbock and Amarillo are the two metro areas, 124 miles apart on Interstate Highway 27, on the windswept plains of the Texas Panhandle. Lubbock has 256,600 city residents. The Lubbock metropolitan area has a population of 329,581, who live in Lubbock, Crosby, and Lynn counties. The Lubbock area's economy is measured at $14.55 billion.

Lubbock in the late 1800s was a market center for farming, especially cotton and sorghum. Lubbock's growth jumped in 1923, when the Texas Legislature decided to establish Texas Technology College there. It now is called Texas Tech University and is one of the largest state-supported four-year universities in the state with an enrollment of about thirty-seven thousand students. Its athletic teams, the Red Raiders, play in the Big 12 Conference, giving Lubbock visibility through sports broadcasting. The university helped develop health care as Lubbock's top industry. Because of Texas Tech, education is Lubbock's second-largest industry. Agriculture still has a presence with crop production—mainly cotton and food manufacturing. In 2016, Monsanto, later acquired by the German firm Bayer, located a $140 million national-scale cottonseed processing center in Lubbock. Because of Texas Tech, Lubbock has higher education attainment than the Texas average, but large clusters of retail services and food processing push wages below the state average.

The five-county Amarillo metro has 269,397 residents. The counties are Armstrong, Carson, Oldham, Potter, and Randall. The

Amarillo-area economy is $13.76 billion. Amarillo evolved from the cattle market into energy with the discovery of oil and natural gas in its area early in the 1900s. Along with natural gas, helium deposits were discovered, leading to the creation of a US Bureau of Mines helium plant. During World War II, Amarillo became a weapons and ammunition center with the start of the Pantex Ordnance Plant, later expanding to become the top US nuclear weapons campus with 650 buildings. Bell Helicopter employs about one thousand people at a production factory. Service industries—retail, health, education, and food—undergird the Amarillo economy. The Panhandle's near-perpetual wind has blown in a new industry, electricity-generating wind farms that have sprouted up in the Panhandle. Electricity production from wind increased almost 500 percent between 2010 and 2016, boosting the area's share of statewide electricity production to 10 percent from 3 percent over that period. Amarillo's median household income level, $51,198 on average between 2013 and 2017, is higher than in Lubbock, $47,326, with the large presence of college students in Lubbock likely accounting for the difference. The best-known university in the Amarillo metro, a Texas A&M University branch campus, is in nearby Canyon, Texas.

Amarillo is the northernmost metropolitan area in Texas, receiving wintry weather that most of Texas rarely experiences. In Amarillo, there is a saying that there are only barbed-wire fences between the Panhandle and the Arctic wind. Amarillo sits closer to the state capital cities of three other states than to the Texas capital of Austin. Amarillo is 416 miles from Austin, while Santa Fe, New Mexico, is 233 miles away. Oklahoma City is 243 miles to the east from Amarillo, while Denver, Colorado, is 356 miles to the northwest. Topeka, the capital city of Kansas, is just 13 miles farther than Austin at 429 miles. Amarillo proves the point that Texas is a big state with far-flung urban centers.

Other Metros

The remaining ten Texas metro areas are market centers for regions of Texas and are home to specialized industries and services that serve the diverse economic sectors of Texas. These cities expanded from agricultural roots and became significant urban centers as they acquired railroad services, developed water for drinking and recreation, and, in many cases, became the site of a military installation. In recent decades, health-care companies gravitated to many of these cities to serve regional populations.

Corpus Christi is a South Texas coastal urban area with a population of 427,347 and an economy measured at $23.17 billion. The city of Corpus Christi has a population of 326,162. The metro area covers Nueces, Aransas, and San Patricio counties.

The Corpus Christi–area economy is served by Port Corpus Christi, opened in 1926. The port is the state's third largest in cargo tonnage, after Houston and Beaumont, and sixth in the nation, ahead even of the number-seven port at Long Beach, California. Tonnage in 2017 was 81.98 million.[14] Port Corpus Christi specializes in bulk cargo, like petroleum products and grain. It is now working to add roll-on and roll-off capabilities utilizing container vehicles and trucks. Port Corpus Christi employs 13,770 people directly and supports 16,212 jobs indirectly.[15] Related users, such as shippers taking freight to and from the port, employ 31,939 locals. Numerous towering refineries line the port's industrial canal that juts inland from Corpus Christi Bay, their lights illuminating the night like a fantasy downtown. Corpus Christi is connected to San Antonio 143 miles away by Interstate 37. Port Corpus Christi has significant relationships with San Antonio industries. The Corpus Christi area also serves as the favorite destination of San Antonians for beach and fishing excursions. Nearby towns and sites, including Aransas Pass, Port Aransas, Rockport, Fulton, Mustang Island, and North Padre Island, are popular weekend visits for San Antonians and South Texans. Tourism thus is another large industry for the Corpus Christi area. Another big employer since 1940 is the Naval Air Station at Corpus Christi, which now has direct employment of about 9,700 people.[16] The installation specializes in naval flight training.

Laredo is a critical inland port city on the Rio Grande. Because Laredo is the southern terminal point of Interstate 35, the city handles a vast amount of US-Mexico freight trade southbound and northbound along Interstate 35 to San Antonio, Dallas, Oklahoma City, and even to Minneapolis. The Laredo metropolitan area has a population of 281,964 and an economy valued at $11.71 billion. The city of Laredo population is 268,057. The Laredo metro covers only one county, Webb. Like other Texas border cities, a larger Mexico metro exists on the other side of the river. Nuevo Laredo, in the Mexican state of Tamaulipas, has an estimated population of 399,431. Combined, the Laredo–Nuevo Laredo area has a population of 681,395. The two cities are known as "Los Dos Laredos." The community began on both sides of the river in the 1700s as one city, but when the international border was fixed in 1848 along the Rio Grande, residents had to decide which country to live in. Most chose Mexico. Laredo, Texas, incorporated in 1852.

Daily life in Los Dos Laredos is characterized by long lines of trucks, passenger buses, and personal autos waiting to cross the border each way. Warehouses, rail yards, industrial parks, and *casas de cambio* (currency exchange offices) abound. About 4.04 million freight trucks cross the border in the Laredo area in 2019.[17] The cross-border traffic is driven by 220 freight forwarders, 274 trucking companies, and 120 US customs brokers. As the number-one inland port along the US-Mexico border, the Port of Laredo crosses more than $234 billion in imports and exports yearly.[18] The goods travel over two commercial bridges and a rail bridge. Of those, the most important is the World Trade Bridge in Laredo, crossing the largest number of freight trucks. A bridge about twenty-five miles upriver from Laredo called the Colombia Solidarity Bridge joins a narrow stretch of land along the Mexican state of Nuevo León, whose capital is Mexico's largest industrial city, Monterrey. About twelve thousand trucks a day cross the two commercial bridges. The Colombia Solidarity Bridge handles both truck freight and auto passenger traffic. Two other Laredo bridges are the Lincoln-Juarez International Bridge, which processes auto passengers, and the

Gateway to the Americas Bridge, which crosses auto passengers and pedestrian traffic.

*   *   *

Forty miles separate the two metro areas of Tyler and Longview, which are located in the scenic East Texas forests. Both cities initially grew from cotton and timber agricultural bases, were boosted by oil discoveries, and then evolved into new commercial sectors, especially health care. Tyler's metro area population is 230,086, and the Tyler city population is 107,549. The Tyler metro's economic size is $11.04 billion. Longview's metro area population is 289,854, and the Longview city population is 82,894. Longview's metropolitan GDP is $16.64 billion. The Tyler metro covers only Smith County, while the Longview metro encompasses the adjoining Gregg, Rusk, and Upshur counties. The two metro areas are highly interconnected economically and have a joint population of 519,940 and a combined economic size of $27.68 billion.

The health-care sector employs more than thirty-four thousand people in the area, underpinned by the UT Health Tyler medical school. Tyler is the headquarters for a grocery chain, Brookshire Grocery Co. Target and Dollar General operate distribution centers in the Tyler-Longview area. A machinery manufacturing cluster, which includes Trane Co. and Komatsu Ltd. Energy, made a comeback with the expansion of natural-gas drilling in the Haynesville shale formation in East Texas and Louisiana. The area is best known for its annual Texas Rose Festival in Tyler, showcasing the area's many rose growers.

Abilene may look on a map like it belongs to North Central Texas, but in its DNA, Abilene is all West Texas, sitting 141 miles west of Fort Worth on Interstate 20. It's in a region called "The Big Country." Abilene started as a cattle-grazing and railroad town in 1881 before expanding into oil services and military activities. The Abilene metro area has a population of 172,655. Abilene city's population is 123,403. The Abilene economy is measured at $7.57 billion. The metro area covers Taylor, Jones, and Callahan counties. Interstate Highway 20 runs through Abilene between Fort Worth and the Midland-Odessa area.

Abilene was founded at the crossing of two railroad lines and was named after a similar cattle town in Kansas. For decades, the area survived droughts and periods of poor agriculture prices. Its future was assured with the founding in the 1950s of Dyess Air Force Base, whose mission became bombers, missiles, and aircraft refueling tankers. Abilene continues to rely largely on the military operations at Dyess, about seven miles from the city. Direct employment at the base is more than six thousand. Dyess is home to one of two B-1 bomber aircraft wings. During the Gulf War, the B-1 bomber flew missions directly to the Middle East from Dyess.

Wichita Falls is the largest metro area in an area that calls itself Texoma, being the seat of Wichita County along the Red River dividing Texas and Oklahoma. Again, the arrival of railroad services in 1882 sparked the sale of land, and Wichita Falls incorporated in 1889. The city had its heyday in the 1920s and 1930s after the start in 1918 of numerous oil gushers in Burkburnett, just north of Wichita Falls. This episode was depicted in part of the plot of the 1940 hit movie *Boom Town*, starring Clark Gable and Spencer Tracy. The oil-drilling success led to nine refineries and forty-seven factories. Sheppard Air Force Base opened between Wichita Falls and Burkburnett in 1948, replacing a decommissioned army air force field at the site. Sheppard became a center for aircraft technician and flight training.

Wichita Falls' population peaked around 1955 at 110,000 and stabilized at about 100,000 in the decades that followed. The city now has a population of 106,362. The three-county Wichita Falls metro area has a population of 153,867. The area's economy is valued at $6.56 billion. The counties in the metro area are Wichita,

Clay, and Archer. Wichita Falls is the southern terminal for Interstate 44, which runs north and east to St. Louis, Missouri.

On April 10, 1979, a tornado ripped through the southern half of Wichita Falls. It killed forty-two people and destroyed about 20 percent of the city's residences, leaving about twenty thousand people homeless.

The tornado notwithstanding, health care emerged as a leading economic sector for Wichita Falls, anchored by United Regional Health Care System. The area also continues to rely heavily on the activities of Sheppard Air Force Base and its missions, which employ more than seven thousand people. A bicycle race called "Hotter'N Hell Hundred" is the city's largest annual event. Held in late August, the race is one of the largest bicycle events in the world, usually drawing between ten thousand and fourteen thousand cyclists.

One hundred and nine miles to the east of Wichita Falls is another Texoma metropolitan area, consisting of the two adjoining cities of Sherman and Denison. Sherman is the county seat of Grayson County, the only county in the metro area. Like Wichita County, Grayson County is bounded by the Red River. Both Sherman and Denison are well within the Dallas–Fort Worth orbit. Sherman and Denison are seventy-five miles north of Dallas. Dallas suburban growth in the neighboring Collin and Denton counties is rapidly spreading into Grayson County, with home builders platting new lots in Grayson. It is a sign that the Dallas–Fort Worth metro area will soon reach the Oklahoma border. Increasingly, Sherman and Denison leaders are marketing their cities as part of the Dallas–Fort Worth area for business investments.

The Sherman-Denison metro area has a population of 137,479. Sherman city's population is 44,192, and Denison's is 25,631. The metro area's economy totals $5.08 billion, the smallest of the state's twenty-five metropolitan areas. Like other Texas metros, the urban area grew after railroad services arrived in the 1870s. Sherman was the site of one of the nation's worst race riots in US history. In May

1930, white residents set the county courthouse on fire and dynamited a vault inside it to obtain the body of a Black farm worker who had been standing trial for rape. The body was then burned in the Black section of the city as the white mob continued a violent riot. Martial law lasted for two weeks after the riot. Two men were eventually convicted and sentenced to prison for rioting and arson.

Today, Sherman is best known as the site of 1,300-student Austin College, a private, liberal arts university affiliated with the Presbyterian Church. Denison is known as the 1890 birthplace of US President Dwight David Eisenhower, although he did not live there long. Eisenhower's father, a railroad employee, moved the family soon after Dwight's birth to Abilene, Kansas. The home where Eisenhower was born is now a museum. The Sherman-Denison economy is enhanced by Lake Texoma, formed by a Red River dam. The lake became a popular recreational area, attracting six million visitors yearly. The earthen dam was built during World War II, largely by the labor of German prisoners of war.

Almost exactly in the geographic center of Texas sits San Angelo, another city that won a race with surrounding towns to become the regional hub. San Angelo is 180 miles northwest of Austin. San Angelo, originally cattle and sheep country, was along the route of the 1870s cattle drives and the site of the US Army's Fort Concho starting in 1867. The first railroad arrived in 1888, and a second rail line came in 1909. Oil and gas drilling in the Permian Basin in the 1920s and 1930s became a positive economic factor. San Angelo was selected in 1940 for a second military installation, Goodfellow Air Field, later becoming Goodfellow Air Force Base. The base became the site of a $100 million Strategic Air Command long-range radar operation. The base employs more than seven thousand people directly.

The San Angelo metro area population is 120,224. San Angelo's city population is 99,794. The San Angelo metro-area economy is measured at $7.1 billion. San Angelo is the county seat of Tom Green County, and adjacent Irion County is also counted in the metro area. By the late 1980s, San Angelo had transformed into a regional health-care center. St. John's Sanitarium started in 1910, became a hospital, and later was absorbed into the Shannon Medical Center. Also in San Angelo are the Angelo Community Hospital, River Crest Hospital, Baptist Memorial Geriatric Hospital, and the West Texas Rehabilitation Center. San Angelo has also become known as a retirement area.

Victoria in Southeast Texas, situated between Corpus Christi and Houston, is one of the oldest cities in Texas. Victoria was founded along the Guadalupe River as a Mexican city in 1824 and was named for the first president of Mexico, Guadalupe Victoria, well before Texas became a nation in 1836. Victoria is about twenty miles inland from the Gulf of Mexico coast. Historic Victoria is characterized by majestic mansions from the 1800s with wraparound porches and balconies. Many of the mansions have Texas historic markers on them. Downtown Victoria is centered by a Spanish-style plaza.

The Victoria metro area population is 99,928, and the city itself has 67,326 residents. The metro-area economy is $5.57 billion. The Victoria metro comprises Victoria, Goliad, and Calhoun counties. The US military had a temporary role in supporting Victoria's growth, establishing Foster Army Air Field in 1941, which was decommissioned in 1957. The site of the base is now Victoria Regional Airport. Victoria is known for its 344-acre Riverside Park, where people paddle kayaks and canoes along the Guadalupe River. The park also features the expansive Texas Zoo. The best-known annual event is the Victoria Bach Festival held each June.

The city name of Texarkana describes itself, tucked into the northeast corner of Texas that borders on Arkansas and is a short distance from Louisiana. "Tex" stands for Texas, "ark" for Arkansas, and "ana" for Louisiana. The metro area itself spills into both Texas and Arkansas. The city arose naturally from a Red River location that also positioned it as a gateway to the Southwest as settlers moved westward. From the 1800s into the 1900s, the city was eventually served by four railroad systems. Texarkana's main industries flowed naturally from its surrounding forests, fertile soil, and abundant mineral resources. The military arrived during World War II and built the Red River Army Depot, which stored and issued ammunition, explosives, and US Army Corps of Engineer supplies. The Lone Star Army Ammunition Plant, a subsidiary of the B. F. Goodrich Rubber Corp., was an ammunition plant making bombs and fuses until 2009. The Red River Army Depot continues, directly employing more than 4,800 people. Onsite contractors at the depot employ thousands more workers.

The Texas population of Texarkana is 97,488, while the two-state metropolitan area population totals more than 150,000. The city of Texarkana, Texas, has a population of 38,816. The metro area comprises Bowie County in Texas and Miller County in Arkansas. The metro's overall economy in both states is valued at $5.84 billion. Many Texarkana residents live in one state and work in the other. The Federal Bureau of Prisons operates a low-security prison, with more than 1,200 male inmates, inside the Texas border at Texarkana.

Triangle Connections

The smaller metropolitan areas anchor population centers, educational facilities, and businesses that serve Texas. Although they are spread across the vast distances of Texas, they all have ties to the Texas Triangle. Jim Gaines states, "How well they [Dallas–Fort Worth, Houston, San Antonio, and Austin] do affects the overall state economy."

The smaller metros have specialized economic bases based upon their region's natural products and independent histories. Victoria and Corpus Christi, for example, thrive because of the Eagle Ford Shale energy fields. Laredo grows from the Interstate 35 corridor truck and rail trade that stretches to Chicago. The economies of Lubbock and Amarillo are Panhandle centers of regional banking.

Midland and Odessa have unique challenges caused by the energy boom in the Permian Basin. Gaines describes how a teacher shortage in Midland and Odessa resulted in the importation of three hundred teachers from the Philippines: "The teachers were living in their cars. They literally had no place to put them," Gaines says of the subsequent housing shortage. "The boom was so fast-hitting. But Midland and Odessa know that the boom is not going to last, so there are no long-lasting public commitments" of infrastructure.

Texas is the second-largest state in land after Alaska. Texas also is the second largest in population, after California, and, as noted earlier, is second in the number of metropolitan areas, with twenty-five, after California's twenty-six. It is logical that Texas' metropolitan areas would cover every corner of the state and anchor their respective regions.

The smaller twenty-one metropolitan areas described in this chapter and the previous chapter interact with the Texas Triangle through commercial ties and in the development of the state's workforce. And common threads tie all twenty-five Texas metros in history and in prospects. Urban Texas was shaped by the availability of water, the routes and crossroads of the railroads in the 1800s, the discoveries of oil and gas, and the decisions by the US military to locate numerous bases and forts across Texas. The building of the US interstate highway system starting in the 1950s linked Texas' metro areas, helping them grow as manufacturing and distribution centers. The development of health-care facilities, colleges and universities, airports, seaports, and border ports of entry further creates networks of interconnected interests. The bonds connecting Texas communities of all sizes and locations can work to the mutual benefit of the Triangle metros, the smaller metropolitan cities, and the rural counties of Texas.

Rural Texas

Perhaps the contrast between urban and rural Texas can be illustrated best by two parallel, north-south highways not far from each other. Interstate 35 and US Highway 281 converge in San Antonio. North of San Antonio, I-35 angles on a northeasterly track through the state, while Highway 281 heads directly north to Oklahoma.

I-35 is the backbone of Texas, forming the western boundary of the Texas Triangle. Eighty-seven percent of the Texas population lives east of I-35, including urban and rural counties. But driving from San Antonio to the Oklahoma border on I-35 is to experience urban Texas. Almost no undeveloped land exists between San Antonio and Austin as drivers pass through New Braunfels and San Marcos on a divided highway with six to eight lanes. Fast-food restaurants line the route, as do shopping centers, some of the largest in the state. A gigantic convenience store named Buc-ee's in San Marcos, with dozens of gasoline pumps, a grocery store, a food court, and clothing, is bigger and busier than many department stores. Buc-ee's is known for its dependably clean and ample restrooms for travelers. More shopping centers buffer the highway from the residential areas of Buda and Kyle between San Marcos and Austin. Interstate exit and entry ramps are spaced at almost every mile, sometimes closer. I-35 traffic is severely congested nearly around the clock in Austin as drivers creep slowly past the layered cloverleaf highway intersections, the ever-growing higher downtown district, the state government office building cluster, and UT Austin with its massive, one-hundred-thousand-plus-seat, upper-decked football stadium. Traffic doesn't lessen until drivers pass through Georgetown, but soon after is the Temple-Belton area and then Waco, with Baylor's huge football stadium at I-35 and the Brazos River. To accommodate the duality of the Dallas–Fort Worth area, I-35 splits south of the metro into two parallel interstate highways, rejoining into one I-35 north of the sprawling urban area. On either route, there is a large core city for drivers to navigate—Dallas or Fort Worth—along with numerous suburban cities. All along I-35, freight trucks are constantly in view as they head to and from

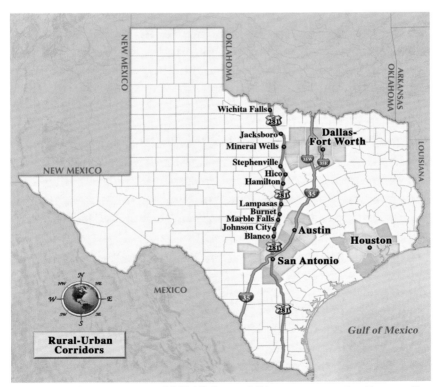

Interstate Highway 35 and US Highway 281 are near each other on the Texas map, but the highways could not be more different. One connects three of the nation's largest urban areas, while the other is a rural, small-town connector.

Laredo, conveying US-Mexico trade into the US heartland as well as intercity trade circulating within the Texas Triangle.

Running parallel to the west, Highway 281 is never far away from I-35, but it seems to traverse another time. Highway 281 divides the entire state but is congested only at San Antonio. Between San Antonio and Oklahoma, the lone metropolitan area is Wichita Falls, barely more than a dozen miles south of the Oklahoma border. Between San Antonio and Wichita Falls are 336 miles of pure rural Texas. After clearing San Antonio's dense North Side traffic, northbound drivers immediately encounter a two-lane highway, one lane in each direction, through the open, rolling landscape of the Texas Hill Country. Blanco is a one-stoplight town. A 1960s-era sign proclaims Johnson City as the home of previous US president Lyndon B. Johnson, although the town bore the name before Lyndon was born. This part of Texas is known for broad fields of bluebonnets and Indian paintbrush each spring. The towns of Marble Falls, Burnet, Lampasas, Hamilton, and Hico break the pattern of Central Texas' pastures. Pickup trucks vastly outnumber the relatively few freight trucks that use Highway 281. North of Stephenville, Highway 281 is elevated enough to offer long vistas of natural, virtually pristine land leading into the photogenic Dobbs Valley in Palo Pinto County, where the Brazos River meanders. Cell service strengthens dramatically where Highway 281 intersects with Interstate 20 between Fort Worth and Abilene, the only hint that urban areas are nearby. The abandoned Baker Hotel looms above the horizon on the approach to Mineral Wells. Built in the 1920s, the fourteen-floor, 450-room hotel once drew Hollywood stars, including Clark Gable and Judy Garland, wishing to enjoy the health spa's mineral waters. Now the sand-colored brick hotel sits silent and empty with broken windows, a ghost of past opulence. Several renovations have been announced since its 1972 closing. The latest $65 million plan is scheduled for a 2022 reopening. A little further north, the town of Jacksboro seems to preside over a vast wind-energy farm spreading in every direction, even north into Archer County just south of Wichita Falls. The wind-energy leases provide a new avenue of income for landowners in the area. All up and down Highway 281 are picturesque farms and ranch houses surrounded by cattle, goats, and horses. The dirt-road entries to the farms sometimes carry names like "The Back Forty," often displayed in fancy wrought-iron archways. Hay bales sit in rows on the agricultural properties, either for consumption by on-site livestock or for distribution elsewhere. A common sight along Highway 281 is the old-fashioned, rusting farm windmills with sucker rods that once brought up precious groundwater to nourish the windswept fields.

Rural Dimensions

As we've noted earlier, Texas has the nation's largest rural population even though only about 15 percent of its residents live in rural areas. According to the 2010 national census, the Texas rural population totaled 3,847,522, comprising 15.3 percent of the state population.[1] North Carolina has the second-largest rural population, numbering 3.23 million, or 34 percent of the state. Pennsylvania, Ohio, Michigan, Georgia, New York, and Tennessee are the other states with rural populations of more than two million each. The most rural states as percentages of total population are Maine (61.34 percent), West Virginia (51.28 percent), and Mississippi (50.65 percent). At 15.3 percent, the rural population share in Texas is below the rural population share of the nation as a whole, 19.3 percent. Texas' rural population constitutes just over 5 percent of the total US rural population of sixty million.[2]

If the Texas rural population was a state unto itself, it would rank twenty-seventh in population, ahead of Oregon and neighboring Oklahoma in the 2010 census.[3]

Even though the Texas rural population is growing in absolute numbers, from 2.46 million in 1980 to 3.84 million in 2010, the state's rural population share is shrinking. As recently as 1980, 20.4 percent of Texas was rural; in 2010, the rural percentage had declined to 15.3 percent.[4] The most obvious reason for this is the fact that urban Texas is growing so much faster. But in addition, ninety-two Texas counties lost population between 2010 and 2017, according to the Texas Demographic Center. Almost all of them are counties outside of the twenty-five MSAs. The counties losing people are mostly concentrated in the Panhandle and West Texas, but some counties in East and South Texas have lost population as well.

Statistics from the US Department of Agriculture Economic Research Service help explain the trend. Rural populations are growing slowly. On the whole, they are characterized by lower income levels, less education attainment, less access to health care, and slower job growth.

In 2016, rural Texans' per-capita income was $37,629 compared to $47,339 in urban Texas. The poverty rate in 2017 was 17.6 percent in rural areas and 14.4 percent for urban Texans. While rural and urban Texans both attended college beyond high school at a 29.2 percentage between 2012 and 2016, only 16.1 percent of rural residents received degrees versus 29.7 percent of urbanites. The unemployment rate among rural Texans in 2017 was 4.8 percent compared to 4.2 percent in urban Texas.

Rural Texas is generally underserved in terms of health-care facilities. Of 177 rural counties in Texas as measured by the UNT, 50 counties have no hospital.[5] Ninety-nine counties have one hospital, and 28 counties have two or more. Fifteen counties have never had a primary care physician at any time. Rural Texas is critically short in mental health, dental, and pharmacy services, according to the UNT study.

Agriculture

Thanks to the productivity of Texas agriculture, rural Texas is economically stable. The number of Texas farms grew to 248,809 in 2012 from 228,926 in 2002. Total farmland remained constant over the same period at 167 million acres. Farm income rose to $4.44 billion in 2017 from $2.96 billion in 2016. Cattle and calves accounted for the highest farm revenues, followed by cotton, chicken broilers, dairy products, and miscellaneous crops. Texas agriculture reaches far beyond the state. Exports totaled $7.19 billion in 2017, led by cotton. Other agricultural exports included plant products, beef and veal, dairy products, and feed grains.

Much of rural Texas is wide-open farmland, such as this location in Justin, near Fort Worth. Shutterstock/Jiujiuer.

The challenge for rural Texas will be stemming population losses. Outside companies tend not to invest in small, rural Texas towns because the areas typically do not have the labor force they need.

Jim Gaines says rural job creation will predominantly take place in occupations that are not tied to fixed industries, such as home-based businesses that need only an internet connection. Providing better internet and Wi-Fi connections will help small towns retain their populations. According to Gaines, "If you are twenty-seven, and you are not the head of the family business, like a farm, in small-town Texas, there is nothing for you to do. You are going to leave unless you stay and start a business. Agriculture is limited and is not going to be the answer." One answer found by some small towns has been to create tourism centered on a distinctive culture or arts scene, as Marfa in remote West Texas has achieved. Another possibility is becoming a destination for second homes away from urban density, Gaines points out.

Rural Texas has one other competitive advantage, says San Antonio consultant Trey Jacobson: "They are without regulations."

Jacobson says that industries that are not compatible with dense populations, such as food production plants dependent on nearby agriculture, are a good fit for rural sites. But rural Texas will not offer enough for many people, Jacobson says. However, some rural Texans will find ways to connect to the more prosperous Texas Triangle. Jacobson explains that "with today's technologies, people have the opportunity to do a lot of work anywhere. There can be small concentrations for distribution of goods and services, such as groceries, insurance. Towns sixty miles outside of Dallas can find ways to inject incomes into their communities by finding ways for residents to work, to connect the workforce to the big cities through passenger rail options. Or there can be tourism from the large cities." Jacobson cites Fredericksburg for its shopping and bed-and-breakfast rooms popular for residents of San Antonio and Austin: "You can bring in money from the big cities or you can get the people in the big cities to come to them to spend."

"Man, that's a tough one," says Bernard Weinstein on how urban prosperity can expand to rural regions:

> This has been a challenge to folks doing economic development at a macro level. How do you spread the benefits of growth? Can you encourage businesses in Austin or Dallas to put a plant in Abilene, or in a rural county? Probably not. To some degree, we have to accept the fact that rural depopulation is going to continue. It's not just here. It's the whole country, and it's been happening for a hundred years. It's happened in large part because you don't need as many people on the land to grow food or to herd animals because we've gotten so productive. If you are fortunate enough to be in the Permian Basin of course, and you have mineral rights, you don't have much to worry about. In the Permian Basin you now have a 2 percent unemployment rate. That goes up and down, depending on what is happening in oil and gas. If the core regions of urban Texas are doing well economically, that does generate revenue that the state can use to help sustain communities that are losing population, but at some point, what does that mean? You can

keep the roads up. We're paying the road taxes. They are all over the place. The future of rural Texas is to be determined. You have to make sure everyone in Texas and everyone in the country has access to high-speed internet. That can help. If it's not on the grid, you can't participate in the market. There are places in Texas where you can't get a cell phone signal. If every county in Texas is 5G, does that stop the population decline in those ninety counties? Some counties are driven by opportunities in urban areas but are still nonmetropolitan.

Although economic activity and population in Texas are concentrated in the Texas Triangle urban areas, many rural areas are self-sustaining as well as performing supportive roles that fuel the Texas Triangle's growth. Petroleum-producing counties extract oil and gas feed stocks that are processed and distributed by petrochemical plants and refineries in the Houston area. Higher education institutions in rural areas educate young Texans from across the state, building skills and knowledge that often become assets for Texas Triangle businesses. Rural areas produce raw materials and foods that are processed, consumed, and exported by companies mainly in the state's large metropolitan areas.

Critical Roles

At key periods in US history, national leaders have understood the importance of healthy rural areas to the nation's well-being. That concern, for example, led to a decades-long effort beginning in the early 1900s to extend electrical power to rural communities and farms, which resulted in the creation of the Rural Electrification Administration during the Great Depression. In the lead-up to the effort, numerous national studies proposed ideas to make rural life as convenient and productive as life in the nation's cities. President Theodore Roosevelt wrote in his introduction to a 1908 report by the Commission on Country Life that "the great recent progress made in city life is not a full measure of our civilization;

for our civilization rests at bottom on the wholesomeness, the attractiveness and the completeness, as well as the prosperity of life in the country."[6]

Although much progress has been made to extend the comforts of modern life to rural areas in Texas, there are still vast disparities in economic opportunities and access to essential human services. Modern disparities require modern solutions. In an era when so much of the prosperity of Texas is generated in the Texas Triangle metros, better solutions, better policies, networks, and links must be created to extend that prosperity to the rural areas of Texas.

The Texas Triangle's Economic Reach outside of Texas

A good example of the extraordinary reach of the Texas Triangle is the deep business ties between Houston and New Orleans, Louisiana. Some studies of US regional urban clusters link Houston to the Texas Triangle and also separately to a string of Gulf Coast urban centers that include Beaumont–Port Arthur, Lake Charles and New Orleans in Louisiana, Gulfport and Biloxi in Mississippi, and Mobile in Alabama, all seaport cities involved in the transport of oil and petrochemicals.

In that region, the volume of commercial and cultural interactions between Houston and New Orleans exceeds all others. The two cities were the twin kings of the oil industry in the 1980s, each with large ports and refinery complexes. But drastic drops in oil prices that decade and the next, falling at one point to $10 a barrel from a normal range of $40 to $60, caused a wave of consolidation of energy industry operations. Companies with offices in both New Orleans and Houston shrank in employment, almost always in favor of Houston, which they saw as a strong headquarters city, with stronger infrastructure and public institutions.[1] If New Orleans–based energy companies did not move to Houston, they at least opened satellite offices in Houston. In 2003, Irving-based

ExxonMobil decided to move its offshore production operations to Houston from New Orleans, a large setback for New Orleans and Louisiana.

But nature soon delivered an even bigger blow. The eye of Hurricane Katrina struck near New Orleans on August 29, 2005. The storm flooded the Crescent City, killing almost 1,500 people, forcing the evacuation of most of its residents, and causing damages in the tens of billions of dollars.[2]

Katrina had multiple effects on Texas. Up to 250,000 New Orleans evacuees were transported west on Interstate 10 and ended up in Houston shelters. The Houston mayor's office several years later estimated that 90,000 of them remain in Houston today.[3] They found jobs and started businesses, adding a large dose of New Orleans culture as they settled into apartments, homes, and retirement communities. They mixed into a city already known for its diverse, global cultural base. Tens of thousands of other New Orleans evacuees went elsewhere, to San Antonio, Dallas, and as far as Phoenix, Arizona. San Antonio, also along I-10, received 25,000 to 35,000 evacuees in four shelters.[4] But Houston was the main recipient of hurricane victims who had nothing to return to in New Orleans.

Katrina did something else for Houston. The New Orleans–based energy companies sent their executives to Houston temporarily until their New Orleans offices could resume operations. Once in Houston, many executives did not want to leave. Texas, unlike Louisiana, has no state income tax. Energy industry deals between companies were easier to transact in Houston. Houston increasingly became recognized as the world's energy capital. Some New Orleans companies relocated their headquarters to Houston, partly to keep a better eye on competitors. Others allowed many of their executives and other employees to stay in Houston. Before Katrina, Chevron had more than one thousand employees in New Orleans; afterward, it had fewer than six hundred. One thousand Shell employees returned to New Orleans, but four hundred remained in Houston. Smaller energy companies made similar decisions. W&T Offshore had one hundred employees in Metairie, a New

Orleans suburb, before the storm and twenty-five in Houston. Those numbers reversed after Katrina. Houston had become a magnet, pulling in New Orleans' energy companies and operations. According to the US Census Bureau, the job losses contributed to a population decrease in the New Orleans MSA, from 1.34 million in 2000 to 1.19 million in 2010.

Particularly painful for New Orleans was the gradual move of Tidewater to Houston. The global offshore services company, perhaps the largest of its kind anywhere, had been based in New Orleans for more than sixty years. In the aftermath of Katrina, Tidewater seriously considered moving its headquarters to Houston in 2007. At the time, it decided to keep 85 employees and the headquarters in New Orleans. That number dwindled, however, and when the company decided in 2018 to shift the headquarters to Houston, only 30 employees were left in New Orleans out of 4,600 worldwide.[5] By 2018, however, the main reason for the headquarters move had changed somewhat. Offshore activities in the Gulf of Mexico had declined in recent years, while ocean drilling was on the upswing elsewhere, such as the North Sea and off the South American and West African coasts. Houston's airports offered better global access to those and other locales than did the New Orleans airport.

Dallas–Fort Worth–Austin–San Antonio

The business activities based in the Dallas–Fort Worth metro also radiate regionally across state lines. The Federal Reserve Bank of Dallas's district extends into New Mexico and Louisiana. An example is Dallas-based AT&T, which has more than 15,800 employees in the Dallas area,[6] 5,800[7] of them at the four-acre headquarters complex in downtown Dallas. AT&T, however, is one of Oklahoma City's largest employers, too, with 2,700 workers.[8] Round Rock–based Dell, the Austin-area computer company, is another direct tie between the Texas Triangle and Oklahoma City. Dell employs a sales and business services force of 1,800 people in the Oklahoma capital. Jim Gaines notes that Oklahoma's oil industry is another link to the Texas Triangle, mainly through refineries and petrochemical plants in the Houston area.

San Antonio has an economic influence in North Mexico. The family-owned H-E-B grocery chain based in San Antonio operates more than three hundred stores in Texas and more than fifty in North Mexico. As a manufacturer of many of its products, H-E-B works with suppliers in both countries and beyond.

A few years after Toyota opened a San Antonio–area assembly plant in 2006, Bexar County established the Texas-Mexico Automotive SuperCluster, a consortium of automakers and suppliers in Texas and Mexico. The consortium markets Texas and Mexico globally for additional automotive industry investments, promoting its middle position in an automaking corridor stretching from Detroit to the US Southeast and further south all the way to the Mexico City area.

Texas Triangle–based companies like AT&T and Dell operate nationally and beyond, and many other Texas Triangle companies do business worldwide, such as ExxonMobil and American Airlines.

"Texas also is the largest export state, period," Gaines says. "With Houston as a port city, and Dallas considered a port city, too, even though it is inland, the commerce in and out and through them is phenomenal."

Texas Triangle Challenges

No cluster of urban areas can sustain rapid growth rates indefinitely. Local economies can certainly keep growing, but a city's growth rate in percentage terms is likely to slow down as the sheer size of an urban area increases. The Texas Triangle is better positioned than most other megaregions to grow in land-area terms, as it faces no significant constraints from coastlines, state borders, or topography. While the Triangle metros all have work to do in preparing their physical infrastructure to accommodate continued growth, they're all focused on developing sound technical plans for building their water, energy, and transportation capacity. In many ways, the Triangle is well positioned for its projected growth.

However, potential obstacles to the Texas Triangle's ability to sustain rapid economic growth loom on the horizon. Major challenges include housing adequacy, education quality, and transportation accessibility. For the short term, Texas must recover from the economic slump caused by the COVID-19 pandemic. Climate change poses additional challenges in the forms of reduced rainfall, extreme heat, and rising sea levels.

Housing

Each of the Texas Triangle urban areas has gone through the familiar stages of housing expansion from inner neighborhoods to suburban rings and a revival of the urban core. Each of the Triangle cities faces challenges from rapidly rising property values and property tax rates that render housing increasingly unaffordable for moderate- and low-income residents.

These patterns closely resemble what's happening elsewhere in the United States' thriving metros, particularly in the large cities of the West Coast and the Northeast, where residential property values have rocketed to sky-high levels. These housing pressures have unfolded more slowly in the Texas Triangle cities than in the most expensive metros, both because the natural geography of Texas has better permitted physical expansion and because each of the Triangle metros has generally pursued more permissive land-use policies than most peer metros on the coasts. Consequently, housing supply has kept up with rising demand to a greater degree in the Triangle metros. Better matching of supply and demand in turn means housing remains relatively affordable in the Triangle compared to the urban giants on the coasts.

But the Triangle metros are facing worrisome trends. Increasingly high labor and materials costs, complex permitting processes, and other cost pressures have made new construction more expensive than ever in the Texas Triangle. Some cities in the Triangle—above all, Austin and Dallas—have implemented policies that in practice raise obstacles to new housing supply, particularly in the lower-priced segment of the market. Each of the core cities in the Triangle have neighborhoods that have recently experienced high-displacement forms of "gentrification," where rapid influx of new development and higher-income families have driven up rents and property tax obligations for longtime residents. These housing-market dynamics have given rise to urgent community-wide discussions about how the Triangle's cities need to shift policies to prepare for ongoing population growth.

Austin stands out among the Texas Triangle cities for the severity of its affordability challenges. Even more than in the other

Triangle cities, a median-income person in Austin cannot afford the rent for a one-bedroom apartment without being "stressed," defined as having to spend more than 30 percent of income on housing. The average one-bedroom apartment rent in Austin of $1,353 per month is more than 40 percent of the city's median household income.

"Austin is different from the other three markets," says Noel Poyo, executive director of the National Association for Latino Community Asset Builders, with offices in San Antonio and Washington, DC:

> Part of that is that Austin is smaller geographically. It is a more concentrated city. The speed of change is further along. The technology money that came in played a big role in that. The extent to where the University of Texas owns so much of the downtown, and so much of the state functions own so much of the downtown takes stuff off the table in some ways. Austin has just been on this trajectory longer than San Antonio, Houston, and Dallas. The [housing policy] advocacy in Austin has been more conventional, in line with the traditional views that those are the good guys and those are the bad guys. But Austin also is ahead in thinking about displacement policy and thinking about mobilizing private capital for the public good. I just think the dynamics are further along in Austin, which means the challenge is harder to solve.

Moderate- to lower-income people in Austin who have difficulty affording a one-bedroom apartment typically either settle for an older, less attractive apartment or move to the suburban edge of the city, sometimes far from job centers. "People are doing whatever they can, but that population move is happening. You get all the things that come with that, overcrowding, substandard housing, insane traffic conditions," Poyo says. "The transportation planning in Austin—people point to Austin and say that is a place that is really thinking ahead—is so far off where the market is. It is so dramatically bad. People are moving out of the city and commuting, particularly families with children."

Affordability challenges are much less severe in San Antonio, but San Antonio's city government has nonetheless acknowledged that it needs to focus on housing policy. The homeownership rate in San Antonio fell from 61 percent in 2005 to 54 percent in 2016.[1] About 165,000 San Antonio residents were "housing stressed" as of 2016, based on the standard of paying more 30 percent of income on housing.

San Antonio appointed a Housing Policy Task Force in 2017, and the City Council approved the task force's recommendations in 2018. The plan calls for incentives for developers to build afford-able housing, requires the city to organize more housing counseling programs, and mandates changes in regulations that have made housing more expensive.

Poyo says, "The fact is San Antonio is still a city that is reason-ably affordable, for people living here and people moving here. I think there is a long way for the city to go in terms of policy and investments and things they can do. But the fact that the conversation is where it is, in comparison to where the market is, is great. One reason San Antonio can have these conversa-tions is that San Antonio is in a very good financial position." Poyo cites almost a decade of triple-A bond ratings for the city, allowing City Hall to spend less on bond debt service: "Having a good bond rating is important to low-income people. It puts the city in a position to be able to use resources to [fund housing programs], to make dollars go further for the kinds of invest-ments the city needs to make."

Houston's position is different from San Antonio's. According to Poyo,

Financially, Houston is a disaster. There is no money in Hous-ton to fill a pothole, much less think about affordable, innova-tive housing. [Hurricane] Harvey made the market conditions worse, but Harvey also put $1.2 billion in the hands of the city. The mayor [Sylvester Turner] did something incredibly important. All that disaster recovery money went to the state. Before the governor [Greg Abbott] closed the deal with the [federal government], the mayor stepped in, in a savvy way, and negotiated a pass-through amount directly to the city, $1.2 billion to the state, $1.2 billion to the city, and $1.2 billion to Harris County. If he had not done that, if the mayor had wanted to do anything in Houston, he would have had to ask the governor for permission. Now the natural disaster recovery money is in the mayor's hands. Houston now is in a position to think about these issues and has money for these issues in a way that was not the case before. Houston's housing department is making up for the lost time. There is some interesting policy thinking that is driving immediate investment. Dallas is a little different because there is this acknowledgement of this stark divide between Black South Dallas and white Dallas. No one has known what to do about it. There are these housing plans that have been passed. They sort of start and stop. They are still trying to figure their way through this.

Poyo argues that the business community should take the lead in addressing affordability challenges in Dallas:

The private-market forces in Dallas are outsized. The business community really drives this, and in powerful ways. The public sector has to look for permission. We'll see how it develops. They [the business community] worry about the workforce. That's the issue that motivates the business community and appropriately so. If half of your workforce is driving an hour to go to work in the Dallas–Fort Worth area, then as a company, you are at the mercy of employee's mufflers and brakes and taillights. You track that inefficiency back, and it scares CEOs. Dallas is going to bust a lot of the orthodox views about the roles of the public and private sectors, that all the private-sector folks are just corporate bastards who want to make money, and all the public-sector folks are fighting for the people. That's not true in Texas. I think it is going to be really interesting in the next few years to see how it confounds all those traditional political ways of looking at this that unfortunately all of our political parties and lots of the media try to reinforce.

Home prices and rents in Dallas have grown even faster in the lower-priced segment of the market than in the luxury segment, reflecting an extreme shortfall in new development in the lower-priced part of the market. In 2009, a quarter of the homes in the Dallas-Plano-Irving area were priced below $95,000. By 2018, only one quarter of the market was priced below $221,000.[2]

This pattern has played out in all the large cities of the Texas Triangle. In each city, the private sector has struggled to address the need for new housing in the lower-priced segment of the market. Poyo states,

> The private-sector response in the past decade has been to over-supply the luxury market and undersupply the 50 to 60 percent of the market that serves most people. What we are seeing, depending on the business cycle, is a glut in the luxury market and a very consistent increase in prices in portions of the rest of the market. In a scary way, there are disconnected market valuations. Bridging those market dynamics has to be a public-sector endeavor. . . . You end up with all the problems that ultimately all of the public ends up paying for in different ways.

Poyo stresses, "Let's take the bottom third of the income earners in the state. Those people are living on the edge with regard to their household expenses. Very small movements in the market have dramatic impacts on their households because they can barely afford what they are in, and then appreciation from year to the next is 10 percent or more, then very quickly rents go up, and taxes go up. They become stressed. They have to move."

Weak levels of new development in the lower-priced segment of the housing market reflect basic economic forces. In any place and time there is some price point below which it isn't economically feasible to build new housing units, and the threshold price point has been rising faster than most people's incomes in the major cities of the Texas Triangle.

*   *   *

Most local governments in major US cities play a role in subsidizing the "affordable housing" for lower-income residents and families. These subsidies typically take one of two forms: subsidies to demand, such as "Section 8" rental housing vouchers, which come from the federal Department of Housing and Urban Development but are administered at the local level, and subsidies to new supply, coming either from state and local budgetary resources or from federal sources like the Low-Income Housing Tax Credit program. Like large cities throughout the United States, the major Triangle cities have to make choices every year about how to deploy these scarce resources, where to locate affordable housing, and whom to help.

Research by Raj Chetty validates the social significance of getting these decisions right. Chetty's work, for instance, shows that the neighborhood in which a child grows up has powerful, lasting effects on how they fare as adults more than two decades later. It also offers evidence that the children of lower-income families who move to a "high-opportunity" neighborhood when the children are young experience remarkable benefits in education attainment and other measures of upward mobility.

As Chetty wrote in a 2020 US Census Bureau report,

> The lesson from these findings is not necessarily that moving is the best solution to increasing upward mobility, but rather that the low rates of upward mobility observed in some areas can be changed. By studying the places that produce the best outcomes for low-income children, one may be able to replicate those successes in other areas through place-focused investments. . . . What matters for upward mobility is not proximity to jobs, but growing up around people who have jobs. . . . The availability of low-rent, high opportunity neighborhoods suggests that affordable housing policies could be redesigned to produce larger gains for children without increasing government expenditure.[3]

This can only happen in the Texas Triangle if advocates for more expansive affordable housing policies can incorporate sophisticated policy expertise, Poyo says:

You are going to continue piling people into the cities. We are going to see higher growth in lower-income populations. All of those are going to continue for forty to sixty years. What I hope happens is that municipal governments in these Texas cities lead the nation in undertaking clear-eyed policies and take them seriously so that it engages the private sector in a way that allows us to leverage the kind of capital necessary to make a dent in it. There is a range of policy and programmatic solutions that can have an impact. There is this need for advocacy that can match the technical expertise about how to do some of these things. It is a political barrier to getting something done if politicians don't have the confidence that anyone knows how to do it. We have the benefit of forty years of trying to figure out some of these challenges but also a much bigger base of technical experts out there who are working on these issues. That is different than decades ago. That and the electorate are more reflective of the people who want change. It matters the percentage of people who are Latinos and blacks and of moderate income. Those electoral movements eventually will drive this. And it matters whether it is tomorrow or ten years from now.

Some experts believe the core cities of the Texas Triangle need to rethink architectural forms to address their housing supply challenges—and particularly to address the problem of the "missing middle" in the housing market. James Michael Tate, an assistant professor of architecture at Texas A&M University, argues for policies to promote the development of more townhomes in Texas cities: "The Texas Triangle only has two scales of housing: Detached houses and apartments grouped in private subdivisions and apartment complexes. Within each development, limited housing options exist in costs and unit groupings. But what about the middle? Townhomes—two to six family unit buildings—make up less than 10 percent of the available housing. Outside of downtown areas, there are very few options to get a shared house or live in a neighborhood with shared yards and parks." Tate and his team are working to design what he calls "alternatives to the single-family homeownership model that are just as appealing as the classic post-war American dream of owning your own land with a detached house." His designs call for structures with two to four units in new arrangements that create "more diverse cultural and physical communities in the Texas Triangle."

Tate goes on:

> At the scale of a room, we'll explore how lifestyle and functional requirements of houses are changing over time. Studying rooms lets us consider the intimacy of spaces in residential architecture, where people interact and where they retreat. At the scale of the building, we will consider households of different sizes and social dynamics. We will develop new ways in which multiple families can live together in a building with separate and shared spaces. We will explore how a residential building creates meaningful connections with its surroundings—even beyond the property line. Finally, at the neighborhood scale, our research will focus on connections between groups of buildings. We'll create new models of space between buildings, the block and the full neighborhood.

While the Texas Triangle metros are right to focus on how to accommodate increasing populations within their large core cities, they must also not forget that they are continuing to benefit enormously from another model that has played a tremendous role in maintaining relatively good affordability compared to the large metros of the coasts. This second model for preserving affordability is embodied by the high-growth suburban cities and towns within each of the large Triangle metros—in places like Collin, Denton, Williamson, Hays, and Fort Bend counties. These booming communities are generally very affordable, relative to nearby core cities, with good schools, excellent public safety, and ample open space. A number of them represent "urbanizing suburbs," with growing diversity of housing types, abundant job opportunities, and increasingly diverse populations. For the most part, they maintain business-friendly, growth-oriented policies. The extraordinary growth of these cities and towns has acted as a pressure valve in the

Triangle metros as a whole, offering affordable housing options on the edges of each metro area and thereby helping maintain some degree of affordability in the core cities as well.

The policy challenge posed by the growth of cities like Frisco, Round Rock, and Katy is that as they grow, each of the Texas metros becomes ever more enormous in geographic extent, even as the economics of each metro require that it function as an integrated labor market. To put it simply, people increasingly need to travel a very long way to get to work, and that's going to require a lot more infrastructure.

Addressing these housing challenges is essential to the future prosperity of the Texas Triangle. The Triangle's edge in afford-ability has been a key driver of the megaregion's success. Young professionals have been coming to the Triangle because urban Texas offered them an unparalleled combination of economic opportu-nity, quality of life, and affordability. In short, the Triangle has been a great place to achieve the middle-class American Dream. But the Triangle's affordability edge relative to large coastal metros has been narrowing since early in the last decade as home prices and rent levels rise. The future of the Triangle depends on maintaining a strong edge, which in turn will require fresh thinking on housing and land-use policies.

Education

Education in the Texas Triangle and the rest of the state is a continuing challenge. The main issue is preparing all students equally for careers in a state where ethnic minority populations, especially the Hispanic community, are increasing as a share of the population but mostly live in low-income school districts dependent on inadequate funding mechanisms. Higher-income households generally want to live in the best-funded, best-performing school districts. That raises the demand for housing in those districts, increasing property values and property-tax revenues in high-performing districts. In turn, housing in those districts becomes affordable only for higher-income families. This has caused the quality of public education within the Texas Triangle metros to vary dramatically across school districts, even within the core cities. The state of Texas has enacted funding formulas to address these inequities, including the mechanisms known as "Robin Hood" and "recapture," in which the state redistributes some of the property tax revenues generated in wealthy school districts to lower-income school districts. These funding mechanisms have come under repeated challenge in the courts. Meanwhile, the state of Texas, which partially funds public education, has over time reduced the share of statewide educational expenses it pays for out of general funds. From 2008 to 2017, the state legislature cut its direct spending on K–12 education by 12.6 percent per student, adjusting for inflation, increasing the reliance of school districts on property tax revenues.[4] Texas Triangle residents paying property taxes are well aware that school district taxes account for the largest chunk of their annual property-tax bill, far more than they pay in property taxes to their city government.

Other points of contention exist within the school systems, including the system for holding teachers accountable through statewide standardized testing at various grade levels. Some critics argue that standardized testing has forced teachers to "teach to the test" instead of having the flexibility to meet the needs of each student. In addition, dropout rates are consistently high in each of the Triangle's core urban school districts.

Texas has a growing K–12 student population of 5.4 million students, about 10 percent of the national student population of 50.8 million in public schools and 5.8 million in private schools.[5] About two-thirds of Texas students are school-lunch eligible under federal standards, a proxy for coming from low-income homes. This number is more than the entire population of twenty-one states, according to the Intercultural Development Research Association (IDRA) in San Antonio.[6] Although three hundred thousand students graduate from Texas high schools each year, most troubling is the dropout rate. IDRA found that in the mid-1990s, the Texas dropout rate was one in three students. By 2019, the rate had fallen to one in five students, still unacceptably high in a state that needs to make special efforts to educate lower-income students to raise incomes and reduce poverty rates. The dropout rate for Hispanics and Blacks is twice that of Anglo students.

Says Lloyd Potter, "One of our big challenges is that we have to continue pressing to educate young Latinos if we want our labor force to be filling the jobs we are creating here. If we don't do that, we're looking at having an increasing percentage of our population with low levels of education attainment and low levels of income. That generally is not a good thing for any population if you have that sort of process happening."

Celina Moreno, IDRA CEO and president, says there is no lack of capability among the students:

> It is the public institutions that are not set up to adequately serve them. Going back to after World War II and the baby boomers, we saw this huge investment in public education dollars in K–12 and also higher education, throughout the state and the country, in response to that demographic shift. Now unfortunately, we are seeing a huge divestment in public funding both in higher education and K–12 levels. Over the last ten years alone, the state share in public education funds has significantly decreased. It used to be that the state and local share was about the same, at about 50 percent, and now the state only provides about a third of the funding for public schools. It tells us about what priorities are, not just how we fund them but how equitably we fund them. There are districts in the state with a $1,000 difference (in spending) per student from the lowest 10 percent in property wealth compared to the wealthy districts. Think about what that means for each classroom. If there is a class of thirty, you can do a lot with $30,000.

In 2019, the Texas Legislature approved significant modifications to its K–12 school funding formulas, based loosely on recommendations from a blue-ribbon commission. While the commission argued for increasing the state government's share of total school funding to give property owners a break, finding money to boost the state's share proved difficult for state lawmakers. In the end, the legislature settled on a bill that raised schoolteacher salaries, boosted per-student funding, reduced property taxes, and decreased transfers under the "Robin Hood" program.[7]

In addition to addressing the puzzle of school finance, Texas needs a fresh approach to educating students from low-income neighborhoods, many of them learning English as a second language. IDRA Operations Director Hector Bojorquez recalled when he taught at a school in a largely Hispanic low-income area in San Antonio. Some teachers, he says,

> didn't understand the gifts the children themselves bring to class. This student brought pieces of his culture to the classroom. I saw the brilliance in the way they play with words, the way they express themselves. That is a fund of knowledge that goes beyond. Those are different gifts. If, as an institution, I do not recognize that student and the gifts he is bringing, then I am going to lose out. I see that time and again. We have to take off our middle-class lenses to understand the kids. There's nothing good about poverty. It is not ennobling. It's also not a condemnation that should ruin the rest of your life.

Another issue that's becoming more prominent in education discussions in the Texas Triangle is how to provide widespread, quality prekindergarten education. In 2012, San Antonio voters approved setting aside a one-eighth-cent-per-dollar city sales tax for a citywide pre-K program aimed at four-year-old children. The third-grade reading scores on standardized tests of the first students who attended the Pre-K 4 SA program were higher than the third-grade scores of students who attended other pre-K programs and of students who had no prekindergarten education, according to a study funded by the Raise Your Hand Texas Foundation.[8]

But pre-K education is not a miracle solution for improving public education in Texas cities, Bojorquez says: "Pre-kindergarten should be seen as the absolute, most important, basic foundation on which all of the other things must be built, not as a silver bullet that allows you to walk away. There's first grade, second grade and third grade. Were those as excellent as they should have been?"

IDRA's Moreno says,

We have to change the unfair institutions, the funding system. We ought to shift the way we look at accountability and focus on teaching and learning and not scores on tests that narrow the curriculum and are not sure indicators of college preparedness. We have to focus on the changing demographics and providing more support for teachers who are teaching English learners. You are seeing a lot of disproportionality in who is disciplined, especially Black students and special education students are being suspended, expelled, and sent to alternative schools more than their peers. You have to stop watering down the curriculum and prepare students for college and keep those expectations high. More and more jobs require a college degree or some level of college.

Like the K–12 public education sector, the state's higher education community is striving to increase graduation rates. In 2013, 35 percent of Texans aged twenty-five to thirty-four held associate's degrees or higher. Adding certificates for certain technical skills that students typically earn at community colleges, this figure rises to 38 percent. In 2015, the Texas Higher Education Coordinating Board started an ambitious plan aimed at raising the proportion of Texans between twenty-five and thirty-four with an associate's degree or higher to 60 percent by 2030, calling the plan "60x30TX."[9] This objective translates into the specific goal that 550,000 Texas higher education students complete a certificate, associate's, bachelor's, or master's degree from a Texas institution of higher education in the year 2030. Another 60x30TX goal is that student loan debt should not exceed 60 percent of first-year wages for graduates of the state's public higher education institutions. The plan recognizes the need to concentrate on higher education attainment for Hispanics and African Americans. The Texas Higher Education Coordinating Board is asking colleges and universities to provide professional development in teaching methods for doctoral candidates so they will have a foundation in instruction within higher education.[10] The board is also encouraging more student-professor contact during faculty office hours, especially with at-risk students.

According to Bernard Weinstein,

> Educating everybody is a challenge because of where the population is growing the fastest. It is among the lower-income minorities, who are now a majority, and they have different education needs. We're going to have to spend more. It's not a popular thing to say. We're in the bottom quintile when it comes to education spending. But I know we're going to need an educated population. You need the basics. You need to be able to read and write and think and compute. If a kid gets a high school diploma but can't read, write, think, and compute, it won't do him or her any good in the job market. We are going to need people up and down the skill chain.

Transportation

Transportation is a pressing problem in the Texas Triangle. Congestion, a way of life throughout the urban United States, is increasing. Dallas in the 1970s. Houston in the 1980s. Austin in the 1990s. San Antonio since 2000. One Texas city after another has had to acknowledge they have a serious problem. The future growth of the Texas Triangle economy depends on successfully moving people to their jobs and goods from one corner of the megaregion to the other and beyond. And the economic cohesion of the Triangle depends on the physical connections among the Triangle's three corners.

Traffic congestion is costly. Ninety-two of the one hundred top congestion chokepoints in the state are in the Texas Triangle, according to the Texas A&M Transportation Institute. Houston has the most chokepoints, thirty-eight, followed by Dallas (twenty-four), Austin (thirteen), San Antonio (ten), and Fort Worth (seven). Fully 93 percent of Texans use personal vehicles as their primary means of transportation.

Texas drivers in Triangle cities are often delayed by traffic congestion, such as in this scene in Houston. Shutterstock / Trong Nguyen.

The Texas A&M Transportation Institute estimated in 2018 that the state's top twenty high-congestion corridors cause 83.6 million hours of delay a year for passenger cars at a $1.67 billion cost.[11] Congestion slows freight trucks, too, with 4.5 million hours lost at a cost of $225 million per year. The estimates for the state's one hundred most-congested corridors were just as staggering. For passenger vehicles, the costs amount to 201 million delay-hours and $3.97 billion a year. For freight trucks, delays amount to 9.7 million hours at a cost of $489 million per year. No one has estimated how much air pollution Texas congestion has caused, although these delays result in billions of gallons of fuel waste each year. Measured another way, congestion costs more than $1,000 a year per commuter in the Texas Triangle (see table 16.1).[12]

For drivers, Houston has the most congestion delay, sixty-six hours per year per commuter. Dallas–Fort Worth is second with fifty-five hours yearly, followed by Austin, fifty-three hours, and San Antonio, forty-six hours. As trucking freight volumes increase in coming decades, these problems are likely to grow considerably worse.

Table 16.1

Annual costs of congestion per auto commuter

Houston	$ 1,490
Dallas–Fort Worth	$ 1,185
Austin	$ 1,159
San Antonio	$ 1,002
US average	$ 960

Source: 2017 Texas Infrastructure Report Card, American Society of Civil Engineers.

One of the most congested highway stretches in Texas is Interstate 35 between the fast-growing Austin and San Antonio metros. The highway already has three to four lanes in each direction. One possibility, under discussion by transportation experts for decades, is to create a passenger railway connection between the two city centers. But an effort to make this happen fell apart in 2016, due both to funding challenges and to disagreements over how freight and passenger services would share the same tracks. With passenger rail service off the table, the Austin and San Antonio metropolitan planning organizations began work on a joint plan in 2018, expected to last several years, on a project to add two lanes to I-35 in each direction, with the further idea of setting the new lanes partially or fully aside for self-driving vehicles. As there is insufficient right-of-way space to execute this plan at grade, it would require construction of elevated lanes for much of the route, costing some $8 billion to $9 billion. It's also unclear whether the addition of more lanes would lead to what economists call the "law of induced demand": with more lanes, drivers might take more trips on the highway until it's just as congested as before.

Better transportation between the two largest Texas Triangle metros—Dallas–Fort Worth and Houston—is another matter. Interstate 45 is not as busy or congested as I-35, but cutting down the 3.5 hours of driving time with a high-speed passenger train service would yield enormous economic rewards, benefiting the transportation of both goods and people. Texas Central Partners, with offices in both Dallas and Houston, is planning a project to build a "bullet train" that would travel at speeds up to two hundred miles per hour along the 240-mile route, offer just one stop at College Station Texas A&M University, and shorten Dallas-Houston travel times to ninety minutes.[13] Texas Central aims to build the system by 2026 at a cost of $12 billion to $15 billion and suggests it would provide ten million trips a year by 2050, or almost one-third of all trips between the two metros.[14] The plan faces resistance, since the train's route would run mostly on berms, possibly causing erosion and water-supply problems for cattle ranchers. The outcome of the debate will signal whether the time for intercity passenger rail in Texas has arrived.

Each of the Triangle's core cities is actively studying how to reduce congestion on its city streets as well. San Antonio has bypassed consideration of local light rail to move on to an urban transportation strategy using newer ideas and technologies. One possibility is a combination of bus rapid transit and trackless, self-driving trains. Bicycles and ridesharing enabled by Uber, Lyft, and other companies are also likely to be a growing part of the city's urban mobility system.[15]

Like large cities throughout the world, the Texas Triangle metros will need to rely on a combination of entrepreneurship and invention to produce transportation solutions as the population grows in the coming decades. One advantage: the flat geographic layout of the Texas Triangle might make new systems possible that other megaregions around the world could adapt.

COVID-19

The COVID-19 pandemic hit Texas and the Triangle cities hard, in terms of both illness and death in the population and the blow to the state's economy.

Although a San Antonio military installation early on helped isolate people who had been infected on Pacific cruise ships, the first community spread of the illness in the Texas Triangle happened in Houston in late February 2020.

Gov. Greg Abbott declared a state of emergency on March 13, 2020, leading mayors and county officials to announce stay-at-home rules in cities across the state. Schools switched to online class regimens. Tourism came to a halt, devastating companies in the hotel, airline, and other hard-hit industries. Restaurants had to shift to drive-through, curbside, and home delivery only. Soon, staggeringly long lines of autos formed so that unemployed, low-income residents could collect food from their local food banks. In San Antonio, the convention center lost almost all of its bookings, and leisure tourism evaporated. Austin's reputation as a live-music capital became endangered as concert venues closed permanently and performance groups disbanded. Performing arts organizations across the Texas Triangle, including symphonies, theater groups, and ballet and opera companies, went dormant. The ripple effects extended outward to suppliers and service companies.

On May 1, 2020, Abbott announced the first phase of a gradual reopening of activities, allowing partial patronage of stores and restaurants. Later, he allowed gyms and salons to reopen on a limited basis, but rising infection numbers led him to roll back the reopenings in late June, closing bars and tightening capacities at restaurants. New cases, hospitalizations, and deaths peaked in July. By early October, however, as Abbott issued executive orders allowing more activities and schools to open for limited in-person classes, COVID cases began to trend back up, as in much of the rest of the United States.

By the first week of October, cumulative cases in Texas had reached 805,560, while the state's death count attributed to the pandemic stood at 16,573. As of October 7, 2020, deaths in Harris, Dallas, Tarrant, Bexar, and Travis counties totaled 6,328. This amounts to 38.2 percent of the deaths statewide, while these counties account for 43.9 percent of the Texas population. One possible reason for the difference was the high rate of deaths in the Rio Grande Valley, outside the Texas Triangle.

Texas statewide had a higher percentage of COVID cases than the national average but a slightly lower percentage of COVID deaths. As of October, 2.99 percent of the Texas population had been infected in Texas—higher than the 2.47 percent nationally. In deaths, 0.060 percent of Texans, more than 17,000, had succumbed to the virus. Nationally, 0.067 percent of the population, or more than 220,000 people, had died.

Although Texas counties kept data on cases, hospitalizations, and deaths differently, it became apparent that the state's Hispanic, Black, and low-income populations were suffering disproportionately in the pandemic, both in infection numbers and in economic effects. Based on a study released by the Texas Health and Human Services Commission in October 2020, Blacks accounted for 16.6 percent of cumulative statewide COVID cases but just 11.8 percent of the population as of the time of the study. Whites accounted for 30.1 percent of total cases compared with their 41.8 percent population share. Hispanics, meanwhile, accounted for 39.5 percent of cases and 39.3 percent of the state's population. Twelve percent of cases statewide were deemed as unknown in ethnic origin.[16]

In the Texas Triangle's core counties, the disparities were especially stark. According to data published by the TMC in Houston in September 2020, Hispanics accounted for 54 percent of the 823 Houstonians who had died as of September 1 but were 45 percent of the city's population. Blacks accounted for 23 percent of Houston deaths and the same share of the population. Whites and Asians experienced a death toll below their population shares. In Bexar County, Hispanics accounted for 76.1 percent of cases as of September 14, 2020, far ahead of their 60.3 percent population share. Whites, amounting to 27.3 percent of the county's population, accounted for just 17.2 percent of cases.

According to a September 2020 report by the Texas Demographic Center, the state also saw significant racial disparities in the economic consequences of the COVID-19 crisis. The state's Black and Hispanic households experienced greater job losses, food insecurity, evictions, and uninsured medical expenses than white households in the early months of the recession.[17]

Overall, total employment in the state stood almost nine hundred thousand below its prepandemic peak level as of July 2020, according to data from the Real Estate Center at Texas A&M University. The Federal Reserve Bank of Dallas estimated in July that total employment in Texas would remain 5.2 percent below the pre-COVID peak level at the end of 2020. As the state headed toward seasonally colder weather in October 2020, it was clear that the COVID-19 recession was the most severe blow to economic output since the Great Depression of the 1930s in Texas and throughout the United States.

Unemployment was particularly acute in Houston, where the jobless rate stood at 9.3 percent as of July, the highest among the Triangle cities. The city's energy sector laid off workers in large numbers as oil production collapsed in the spring of 2020 in response to the sudden falloff in oil demand around the world. At one point in the spring of 2020, oil prices in the futures market entered negative territory because of the sudden glut in supply. The Texas rig count fell to an all-time low of 107 as producers slashed drilling activity.

In San Antonio, the tourism sector suffered from closed theme parks, canceled conventions, and idle hotels. In Austin and other Triangle cities, higher education institutions reeled from the consequences of closing campuses and moving to online learning. In Dallas–Fort Worth, furloughs and layoffs by American Airlines and Southwest Airlines sent unemployment rates skyrocketing.

By late 2020, some cities started to set out long-term plans for economic recovery. On November 3, 2020, San Antonio voters approved a $154 million job-training program to help ten thousand residents obtain employment in the construction, health-care, and manufacturing sectors, with a focus on the thousands of people whose jobs in the tourism sector were not likely to return before 2023 or later.

At the same time, the Texas Triangle metros had all outperformed the US economy as a whole by some measures half a year into the COVID-19 crisis. As of August 2020, the unemployment rate stood at 5.5 percent in the Austin metro area, 6.3 percent in the Dallas–Fort Worth metro, 6.6 percent in the San Antonio metro, and 8.1 percent in the Houston metro compared with 8.4 percent for the nation in aggregate.[18] All four Texas Triangle metro areas were ahead of the average for the United States' top forty metros on their recovery in foot traffic in commercial locations relative to prepandemic levels as of October 2020, based on Google data tracked by the American Enterprise Institute.[19] There were also signs of an accelerating movement of families from the dense cities of the Northeast and California to the Triangle metro areas.

The COVID-19 crisis raised profound questions for metropolitan areas throughout the world, including in the Texas Triangle. How many of the millions of professionals who worked from home during the crisis will return to office-based work? What will these changing work patterns mean for the Triangle's housing and infrastructure priorities? How will they affect oil and gas demand and prices in the long term? What are the implications for office and retail real estate?

Climate Change

Texas is also likely to face growing challenges in coming decades from climate change. Warmer global temperatures might cause a rise in sea levels, flooding parts of Southeast Texas, especially in the Galveston area, and making part of the current coastline uninhabitable. At the same time, parts of inland Texas, including a large section of the Texas Triangle may become more arid because of declining rainfall. This could deplete drinking-water supplies for the state's large metros even as population growth imposes new demands on the region's aquifers and reservoirs.

Historically, the north-south 100th meridian has generally served as the boundary between US land that requires irrigation for farming, to the west, and farmland that does not require irrigation because of sufficient rainfall. The 100th meridian, one hundred degrees longitude from the prime meridian in Greenwich, England, stretches from the North Pole to the South Pole and crosses the United States across the Midwest great plains. It divides Texas nearly in half. Indeed, the 100th meridian defines the north-south border between the Texas Panhandle and Oklahoma. West of the 100th meridian, rainfall generally is less than twenty inches a year. To the east, rainfall is considerably higher, more than forty inches per year in some parts of the state.

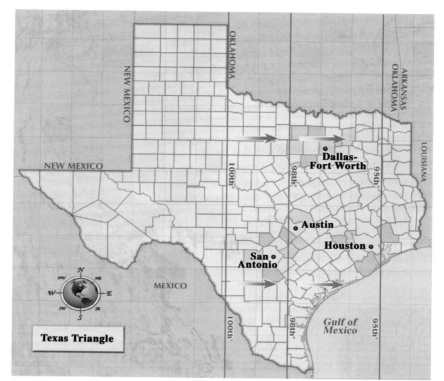

A long-projected shift in the Texas rainfall line is underway, moving from the one hundredth parallel to the ninety-eighth parallel, which covers the west end of the Texas Triangle. In the coming decades, the rainfall line could continue shifting eastward to cover the entire Texas Triangle, expanding the amount of arid land. Rainfall generally is less than twenty inches per year west of the rainfall line.

Historians credit the idea of the 100th meridian as an important dividing line to John Wesley Powell, who was the first white explorer to see the Grand Canyon and who wrote an 1878 report on the United States' desert regions.[20] Powell's report observed that varying rainfall levels to the east and west of the line are associated with differences in naturally occurring vegetation and crop yields. His observations had long-lasting economic effects. Landowners west of the 100th meridian historically have had trouble obtaining farm loans and buying crop insurance.

New research shows that the "twenty inches of rain per year" dividing line is moving east. A team of scientists and researchers affiliated with Columbia University's Lamont-Doherty Earth Observatory ran calculations on the changes of aridity between 1979 and 2016. The team found that the dividing line had moved east to the 98th meridian. For the Texas Triangle, this could spell future trouble. The 100th meridian comes closest to the Texas Triangle when it passes just west of Uvalde, Texas, about ninety miles to the west of San Antonio. If the 98th meridian is now the new dividing line, it crosses through the Austin metropolitan area and to the east of almost all of the San Antonio metropolitan area, reducing the expected amount of annual rainfall in these metros. The scientists predicted the arid dividing line could continue to shift east another two to three degrees by 2100. If the rainfall dividing line reaches the 95th meridian, it would cross just east of the city of Houston, positioning nearly all of the Texas Triangle, including Dallas–Fort Worth, in an arid region. Lower annual rainfall would have a profound effect on the Texas Triangle's urban areas as river-fed reservoirs shrink and supplies for drinking and irrigation water are reduced. The likely result would be higher water-utility rates for residences and businesses to encourage conservation and assure availability. But the higher rates could also cause ripple effects in prices for food and other products. One hope is that emerging technologies might reduce the cost of desalinating seawater and brackish underground water.

Sea Rise

While the middle of the state might become more arid, rising sea levels might transform the Texas coastline. Areas likely to suffer grave effects include Galveston Island and the stretch of coast nearby.

Florida State University scientist Matthew Hauer has estimated the extent of possible population displacement in coastal areas by the year 2100. Starting from a hypothetical increase in sea levels of one to two meters by 2100, Hauer estimates that total displacement in the United States would amount to some 13.1 million people. About half of them would be Floridians. Texas, meanwhile, would see displacement of about five hundred thousand people, making it the sixth most affected state.

During a 2018 presentation at a Texas Demographic Center conference, Hauer said, "It will be a reordering of the US population similar to the Great Migration of southern Americans moving out of the US South to the north and California. This is going to be greater than the Great Migration. We know this migration is going to happen. If you don't have coastal defenses, your house is going underwater. That's motivation to move. That's pretty direct. Migration research and scholarship have come a long way. We are well equipped to know how this migration is likely to unfold."

Hauer predicts that Texas will see the largest population gain of all US states from this migration, with large numbers of migrants from Florida and Louisiana. Based on Hauer's projections, Texas could receive more than 1.5 million additional residents. He further projects that the 20 US counties receiving the most migration will include Travis, Harris, Fort Bend, Dallas, and Tarrant counties. So a more arid Texas and a flooding coastline will not necessarily scare away people from the Texas Triangle cities.

The Texas Triangle has overcome significant challenges in the past involving housing, education, and infrastructure. But the tremendous demographic and economic growth of recent decades has created new challenges that are different in character and intensity. Whether the Texas Triangle metros can keep pace with these challenges depends on how well they plan for continuing population growth and how creative they are in responding.

The Texas Triangle in the Coming Decades

Ready or not, the urbanization of Texas will intensify, with most of the growth in the urban counties of the Texas Triangle. Growth in the thirty-five counties of the Texas Triangle metros was exceptionally rapid between 2010 and 2020. The total population of the Triangle metros jumped from 14.2 million to 19.9 million. As a share of the state's population, the Triangle grew from 56.5 percent to 67.1 percent in just ten years.

Looking ahead, the Texas Demographic Center projects that the Triangle metros will grow to 35.3 million people by 2050, an increase of 148.5 percent. The state, meanwhile, will grow 88.3 percent, to 47.3 million. Based on these projections, the Triangle will account for three-quarters of the state's population. Table 17.1 presents the Texas Demographic Center's projections.

Table 17.1

Projected Texas Triangle share of the total Texas state population

Year	Texas population total	Proportion within the Texas Triangle (%)
2010	25,145,561	56.54
2015	27,326,252	65.78

Year	Texas population total	Proportion within the Texas Triangle (%)
2020	29,677,772	67.19
2025	32,204,904	68.57
2030	34,894,429	69.93
2035	37,716,507	71.26
2040	40,686,490	72.5
2045	43,867,040	73.61
2050	47,342,417	74.63

Source: Texas Demographic Center 2018 projections and author calculations.

Table 17.2 shows the Texas Demographic Center's projections for each of the four Texas Triangle metro areas, while table 17.3 shows the projected population totals for the Texas Triangle as a whole.

Table 17.2
Projected population growth of Texas Triangle metropolitan areas

Austin–Round Rock–Georgetown

2010	1,716,289
2015	1,970,861
2020	2,246,558
2025	2,541,538
2030	2,867,566
2035	3,228,364
2040	3,624,734
2045	4,059,824
2050	4,542,827

Dallas–Fort Worth–Arlington

2010	6,366,542
2015	7,007,291
2020	7,689,051

(*continued*)

Table 17.2 (*continued*)

Dallas–Fort Worth–Arlington

2025	8,438,307
2030	9,264,580
2035	10,152,883
2040	11,092,356
2045	12,088,874
2050	13,173,646

Houston–The Woodlands–Sugar Land

2010	5,920,416
2015	6,619,365
2020	7,372,325
2025	8,193,523
2030	9,074,797
2035	10,005,595
2040	10,986,620
2045	12,030,094
2050	13,155,993

San Antonio–New Braunfels

2010	2,142,508
2015	2,376,822
2020	2,633,014
2025	2,908,684
2030	3,196,106
2035	3,489,260
2040	3,792,616
2045	4,113,623
2050	4,459,030

Source: Texas Demographic Center.

Table 17.3

Total projected population growth for the Texas Triangle

2010	14,217,755
2015	17,974,339
2020	19,940,948
2025	22,082,052
2030	24,403,049
2035	26,876,102
2040	29,496,326
2045	32,292,415
2050	35,331,496

Source: Texas Demographic Center 2018 population projections and author calculations.

    The Dallas–Fort Worth and Houston metro area populations will be almost identical by 2050, based on the center's projections. The Austin metro-area population will surpass that of the next-door San Antonio metro by 2050. The combined populations of the Austin and San Antonio metros will be just more than nine million in 2050, still the smallest population among the three corners of the Texas Triangle, as the Dallas–Fort Worth and Houston metros will each have populations of more than thirteen million. Even then, the combined Austin and San Antonio metros will account for 19 percent of the entire Texas population. The Dallas–Fort Worth and Houston areas will each hold about 27.8 percent of the state's population, together accounting for more than half of the state's population in 2050.

    Most of the population growth will occur in the suburban counties surrounding the core urban counties of Dallas, Tarrant, Harris, Travis, and Bexar counties, according to the Texas Demographic Center.[1] Twenty-seven of the thirty-five Texas Triangle counties will more than double in population. Harris County (Houston), Bexar (San Antonio), and Dallas and Tarrant (Fort Worth) counties will each add more than one million residents between 2010 and 2050. But the suburban counties of Fort Bend and Montgomery (near Houston),

Collin and Denton (near Dallas), and Williamson (near Austin) together will add 15.5 million people from 2010 to 2050.

The Texas Demographic Center projects that nineteen of the smaller twenty-one metro areas of Texas will see an increase in population, the exceptions being Potter County (Amarillo) and Wichita County (Wichita Falls). The center projects that, in all, 99 of the state's 254 counties will lose population, almost all of them rural. The El Paso and Rio Grande Valley urban areas will grow at slower rates than the state as a whole.

Turning to the state's ethnic composition, the Texas Demographic Center projects that the state's Hispanic and African American populations will more than double in size between 2010 and 2050. The Hispanic population will grow from 9.5 million to 21.5 million by 2050. The state's Hispanic population will surpass its Anglo population in 2022 but won't quite have reached a majority of the state's population in 2050. Hispanics will be the largest ethnic group in each of the three corners of the Texas Triangle. The African American population statewide will grow from 2.9 million in 2010 to 4.1 million in 2050. Most of the growth of the Black population will occur in the suburban counties of Dallas and Houston. As a share of the population, the Asian American population will be the fastest-growing ethnicity in Texas, reaching almost six million people by 2050, about five times larger than its 2010 population. By 2050, Asian Americans will account for 12 percent of the state population.

The state's Anglo population will shrink over coming decades—rising from 11.4 million in 2010 to 11.8 million in 2028, then falling back to 11.3 million by 2050. The white population in rural Texas, in particular, will experience significant declines.

Table 17.4 shows the scale of projected ethnic changes in the Texas Triangle.

These population projections from the Texas Demographic Center are based on migration trends measured in the 2010–15 period and the assumption that those trends will hold steady.[2] Population estimates issued since 2015 tend to reinforce the assumptions used in the 2050 projections.

In April 2019, the US Census Bureau issued a special report reinforcing the population trends used by the Texas Demographic Center.

Table 17.4

Projected percentage changes in the Anglo, Hispanic, African American, and Asian American population shares in five core Texas Triangle counties

Bexar County	2010	2050
Anglo	30.27	19.59
Hispanic	58.72	61.25
African American	6.91	8.22
Asian American	2.31	7.34
Dallas County	2010	2050
Anglo	33.14	18.32
Hispanic	38.26	39.8
African American	21.9	21.81
Asian American	4.97	16.48
Harris County	2010	2050
Anglo	32.98	20.81
Hispanic	40.84	42.38
African American	18.43	17.64
Asian American	6.11	14.5
Tarrant County	2010	2050
Anglo	51.8	29.37
Hispanic	26.7	34.51
African American	14.51	20.41
Asian American	4.61	11.25
Travis County	2010	2050
Anglo	50.54	39.76
Hispanic	33.46	34.25
African American	8.08	8.03
Asian American	5.7	8.29

Source: Texas Demographic Center and author calculations.

The Dallas–Fort Worth metro area grew more in absolute terms than any other metro area in the nation between July 1, 2017, and July 1, 2018, with population growth of 131,767.[3] The Houston–The Woodlands–Sugar Land metro grew the third most over that period with a gain of 91,689. The Austin–Round Rock metro was seventh, with a gain of 53,086. The San Antonio MSA was not far behind, ranking fourteenth with a 43,762-person gain. Florida had two metros in the top ten in absolute growth over that year—Orlando and Tampa—but no other state had more than one metro in the top ten.

The Texas Triangle was easily the fastest-growing region nationally between 2010 and 2018. The Dallas–Fort Worth metro again saw the greatest absolute population gain in the nation, with a gain of 1.11 million. The Houston–The Woodlands–Sugar Land metro registered the second-highest absolute gain over that period with a rise of 1.08 million. In the third corner of the Texas Triangle, the Austin–Round Rock metro was the ninth-fastest-growing metro in the nation with an absolute gain of 451,995. The San Antonio metro came in at number fifteen nationally with a 375,515 gain. The Texas Triangle, then, had three metro areas in the top ten, while Florida was second with two metros areas in the top ten. Again, no other state had more than one.

The four core Texas Triangle counties were all in the top ten nationally for absolute population growth between 2010 and 2018. Harris County ranked first with an absolute gain of 605,431, Tarrant was sixth with 274,276, Bexar was seventh with 271,277, and Dallas was eighth with a gain of 271,089. California had two counties ranked in the top ten, while no other state had more than one county ranked.

The Future of the Texas Triangle

"I'm not a cheerleader, but I'm really bullish about Texas and particularly the Triangle. We have so much going for us," says Bernard Weinstein. "We used to say all booms turn to bust, but there's a lot going on here. It doesn't feel so much like a boom as it does just organic growth that is continuing, where growth begets growth and the economy fills in. I am not thinking just in geographic terms, but the economy filling in with more suppliers filling in with the basic industries. There's the growth of the health-care sector and a huge logistics industry, more oriented to domestic and global trade. Texas is now the number-one exporting state."

Weinstein expects that global oil demand will continue to grow through 2035 or 2040, providing an ongoing boost to the state's economy over the next two decades—though the sector will continue to see sharp cyclical swings.

According to Weinstein, globalization will continue to be a driver of the Texas Triangle's growth:

> Most of the growth in Texas is going to be in the Triangle. You have some pundits, even the *Economist* [magazine], writing about deglobalization. I hope not because most of the success of the US and Texas economies has been the result of globalization. With our more global orientation, I sure hope deglobalization is not happening. If there is a global recession, that will affect us here. It's great being part of the global economy, but that means as the economy goes, you go. We can't be booming in Texas if the rest of the country is in recession or a global recession.

The Texas Triangle's 2050 Destination

In the coming decades, Texas will solidify its role as one of the nation's leading urban states. Hispanics will constitute the largest ethnic group. The Texas Triangle economy will be larger, but how much larger will depend on how well the urban education system prepares students for industries in the Texas Triangle metros. Other factors will be how successful the Triangle turns out to be in housing its expanding urban population and ensuring geographic mobility for them as well. The Texas Triangle may not be fully prepared yet for the population and economic growth to come, but its large cities have track records of planning, investing, and executing solutions.

Technological changes, from autonomous vehicles to mass transit to new materials to ubiquitous communications, will play a role.

The certainties are these: The Texas Triangle will be an ever more powerful urban economic force nationally and globally in the coming decades. As an interconnected, three-cornered region, the Texas Triangle will take its place among the world's constellation of leading urban megaregions.

Old Texas versus New Texas

I f we look back to 1960, less than one lifetime ago, we get a glimpse of a very different Texas than the one we see today. The state's population was large—nine million people, sixth-largest in the nation—but 60 percent of those people lived *outside* the Texas Triangle, most of them in smaller cities, towns, and rural areas. Hispanics made up less than 15 percent of the population and an even smaller share of the urban populations of Houston, Dallas–Fort Worth, and Austin. The largest airport in the state was Love Field in Dallas. American Airlines was still headquartered in Manhattan, and Southwest Airlines did not exist.

Oil and ranches dominated not only the state's economy and politics but its very sense of itself. Though cities were starting to play a larger role in Austin, rural political leaders dominated the legislature. Democrats controlled the politics of Texas—they held all statewide offices and all but two state legislative seats—but most of them represented a conservative strain of Democratic politics decidedly different from the more progressive approach we see today.

The priorities of the oil and gas and agriculture sectors topped the agenda of the state government. The legislature grappled with things like maintaining farm-to-market roads, building a first-class highway system, converting the University of Houston from a semiprivate to public university, and passing the first-ever state sales tax in order to adequately fund schools. The Texas A&M System, as a land-grant institution, focused on supporting agricultural and engineering training and extension work. No one except a few visionaries could foresee Texas' future as a giant in technology, space, and medicine. Jim Crow racial segregation was still the law of the land.

Fast-forward sixty years, and we find a very different Texas. The state's population has tripled, and Texas is now one of the most urban states in the nation. In contrast to 1960, today two-thirds of the state's population lives in the Triangle. Indeed, over the last sixty years, fully 80 percent of the state's growth—fifteen million people—has occurred in the Triangle. Five of the thirteen largest cities in the United States are in Texas—all in the Triangle. The state's population is now almost 60 percent nonwhite, and Hispanics will soon become the predominant racial/ethnic group in the state.

Petroleum and agriculture continue to be important industries in Texas, but newer industries—technology, communications, biomedicine, transportation, hospitality, new media, and countless business services—are now also drivers of the economy. Texas is more closely linked to the world economy, and through a more complex web of connections, than ever before. Two of the four largest airlines in the nation are based in Texas—American and Southwest. All these new engines of Texas prosperity operate primarily in the vast metro areas of the Texas Triangle.

Texas politics have also changed dramatically over the last sixty years. While Democrats had held all the state government's constitutional offices as recently as 1995, Republicans hold all these offices today, including all statewide elected judgeships, and they've appointed every member of every statewide board and commission.[1] The rise of the Republican Party in Texas is primarily due to two factors: the in-migration of many Americans fleeing what they view as intrusive government and high taxes in other states and the success of key leaders—including Gov. Bill Clements, US Sens. John Tower and Phil Gramm, and the two presidents Bush—in persuading conservative Texans that they really are Republicans at heart. Over the past couple of elections, however, Texas has been gradually trending toward a middle ground between Republicans and Democrats.

Evolving Challenges

Even as Texas has built a modern urban economy and a conservative Republican political structure, it faces a very different set of public challenges than it did sixty years ago.

Ironically, many features of the "Old Texas" that have fueled the state's success have the potential to undermine the future success of the "New Texas." Recent economic success owes much to Texas' small-government tradition, including the absence of a state income tax, flexible labor markets, and a relatively light-touch approach to business regulation (though federal investment has been critical in several economic sectors).

At the same time, however, Texas underfunds its schools, and education attainment is low compared to other powerful states. Texas ranks last in the percentage of residents with health insurance. Housing affordability is a growing problem even in a state traditionally known for inexpensive housing, and traffic congestion is a major issue in all of the Triangle's cities. Texas also struggles to ensure that its water and energy infrastructures keep up with the demands of a rapidly growing population.

Now that Texas is an urban state, it must shed its own self-image as rural. Texas' enormous growth requires new thinking about policies and priorities—thinking that embraces Texas' urban growth, especially in the Triangle.

Investing in Education

Modern Texas recognizes the need to invest in human capital, but it faces major challenges regarding public schools and higher education.

As stated previously, education attainment is the one area in which the Triangle lags behind the United States' other megaregions. And that lack of education attainment is focused primarily on one group: Hispanics, who will soon be the largest racial/ethnic group in the state.

If public schools continue to serve populations of color poorly, Texas will undoubtedly pay a tremendous price in terms of future productivity and economic growth. The question is whether these populations of color will be undereducated, underperforming, underproductive, and alienated, leading to an impoverished and contentious future for all citizens. Or, alternatively, is it possible to enact policies enabling these large populations to be well educated, entrepreneurially successful, and highly productive, forming a growing magnet for economic activity from across the world?

Perhaps most important, Texas must address the question of adequate and equitable funding for K–12 schools. For decades, the state government has worked around court mandates requiring greater equity in school finance. In 2019, the Texas Legislature passed, and the governor signed, meaningful school reforms, but at the same time, Texas also passed limitations on local property taxes, which are the primary source of funding for schools. The state ranks thirty-ninth among the fifty states in the per-capita level of school funding.[2] Increased funding would enable smaller class sizes, modern lab and computer equipment, higher teacher pay and incentives, advanced training for principals and superintendents, and incentives for students to graduate high school and attend college. In particular, universal pre-K has proven to be a successful strategy—and must be fully implemented.

Postsecondary education is also vital to the Triangle's future, as a high school diploma is less likely to lead to upward mobility. The state has set an ambitious "60x30TX" goal—calling upon 60 percent of young Texans to complete some type of postsecondary program by 2030.

Texas has enormously powerful higher education assets—not just prestigious institutions such as the University of Texas, Rice University, and Southern Methodist University, but a powerful network of 114 community college systems. Yet even with all these assets, only 29 percent of young Texans currently complete a postsecondary program within a reasonable period of time—barely half the 60x30TX goal with less than a decade to go. Among other things, Texas must expand access to postsecondary counseling for students—and do so earlier in their high school careers. This proven technique will help the state and its students make huge leaps toward meeting 60x30TX's goals.

Housing

Especially compared to the expensive coastal metros, the metropolitan areas of the Texas Triangle have always had a big advantage in the cost of housing. Even in the biggest Triangle cities, housing has always been affordable, putting the traditional American dream within reach of most families. Abundant land, light land-use regulation, and a market-oriented approach have helped keep housing abundant for most Texans.

In the past few years, however, the Texas Triangle has gradually begun to lose its affordability advantage. Austin—under tremendous pressure due to in-migrants from California and other expensive housing markets—has seen average home prices double, to more than $400,000, just in the last decade. Though they are still more affordable, home prices in Dallas–Fort Worth and Houston have risen as well, and homeownership rates in the Triangle have dipped below the national average.

Meanwhile, half of all renters in Triangle cities spend more than 30 percent of their income on rent—meaning they are "cost-burdened" or "housing stressed," in the language of housing policy. For renters with higher incomes, this means they can't save enough money for a down payment. For low-wage workers, high rent compared to their incomes often means they must choose between paying the rent or the utility bill, or choosing rent over food or essential car repairs. Partly as a result, each of the Triangle's core cities also face significant homelessness problems.

It goes without saying that Texas must continue to encourage its cities and counties to maintain a light regulatory approach to housing development so that housing supply can keep up with demand. But more must be done, especially in the core of the Triangle's cities. Access to jobs and public transit (vital for essential low-wage workers) is excellent in these core locations—yet the very people who benefit most from access to jobs and transit are being displaced to inconvenient locations by rising housing costs. Texas and the Triangle cities can help counteract this displacement problem in part by using underutilized land assets in our urban cores—land owned by government agencies, churches, large institutions, parking entities—to provide moderately priced housing for our essential workers. Community land trusts are one way to operationalize this idea, but Texas must also focus on opportunities to expand homeownership as well.

Health

Perhaps no other state has such an impressive array of health and medical resources at its disposal. Houston in particular is the world's leading center for clinical medical care. And yet Texas has by far more residents without health insurance than any other state in the nation—well over six million people, or more than 20 percent of the overall population.

At the same time that Texas has more uninsured residents than any other state, it is also the largest state that has declined to expand Medicaid to those above the federal poverty line, as is permitted under the Affordable Care Act. Most other populous states with Republican leadership have expanded Medicaid. While this expansion has cost those states some money, it has also shifted care for uninsured low-income residents away from expensive emergency rooms, where the cost is borne primarily by property-tax payers. Texas should follow the lead of other large Republican-led states and expand Medicaid.

Texas should also fund the expansion of preventive care–focused clinics in "urban health deserts"—those lower-income urban neighborhoods where private clinics typically do not operate. In addition, Texas can also expand low-cost medical care by permitting retail pharmacies to open insurance-accepting clinics—open nights and weekends—staffed by nurse practitioners rather than doctors. This practice is currently not widely permitted in the state but would increase care for those in need at a fraction of the cost of emergency rooms and urgent care facilities.

Updating the State's Infrastructure

Texas has a lot of work to do in modernizing the infrastructure of the Triangle cities as economic platforms for the future.

In the utility sector, the power needs of oil refineries, automotive plants, and heavy manufacturers continue to be significant, but modern industries, like semiconductor fabs and data centers, are fueling demand growth today. The state's interconnected energy grid, ERCOT, reports unprecedentedly low surplus power during peak load times during hot Texas summers.[3]

Meanwhile, all the major Triangle cities rank in the top forty for traffic congestion, according to the US Census Bureau's American Community Survey—with Houston leading the way at number sixteen. Each metro will have to think about a full spectrum of mobility choices. This means continued state investments in highways and municipal investments in city streets as well as federal and local investments in rapid transit and more extensive bus systems. It means attention to safe bicycle lanes and micromobility systems. And it means focusing on mobility technologies of the future: the large-scale integration of rideshare on demand with public transit, bus rapid transit systems, and still more innovative technologies now on the drawing board. The state's role is critical as Triangle transportation systems continuously adapt to rapid growth, autonomous vehicle technologies, growing land-use densities, and changing ridership habits. To be sure, the Texas Department of Transportation must broaden its focus to include all transportation modes and technologies rather than focusing just on highways.

Beyond transportation, the Texas Triangle metros will need to invest in the infrastructure of flood-control systems, particularly in Houston after the experience of Hurricane Harvey. Houston is ranked as one of the US cities most susceptible to ocean rise associated with climate change, especially because of the vulnerability of the massive refineries on the Houston Ship Channel.[4]

Attention to other forms of traditional infrastructure must include the reduction of fuel emissions from electric generation, waste disposal, water adequacy, and airport expansions. Under the rubric of smart city infrastructure, the Triangle cities will need to study many new technologies: renewable energy generation, inter-active power grids, efficient street lighting accessorized with traffic monitoring and crime prevention devices, extended broadband communications, water and power conservation devices, build-ing control systems, and handheld data interactivity with local governments to improve basic city services, among many others.

Finance

All these investments to create cities with a good quality of life will require capital. Sources of capital for public-sector priorities include property taxes, sales taxes, utility fees, and special charges. A significant part of the capital needed to support public projects enhancing the quality of life in each of the Triangle metros will also come from private sources in the form of business transactions, long-term private investments, and private philanthropy. Federal funding is a major source of capital as well, in the form of military spending for key facilities, financing of interstate highways, edu-cation programs, and federal grants to the biosciences.

Although Texas has never viewed state-funding questions through the prism of the state's urban needs, state funding is critical to build the highways, public schools, health clinics, and public postsecondary institutions that are needed to strengthen the metropolitan engines that, in turn, will power the state's budget. The necessary step here is not to increase taxes or impose a state income tax—Texas' prosperity depends in part on low taxes—but to ensure that the Triangle's urban and metropolitan needs are pri-oritized in the state budget much more than in the past. Although Texas' property taxes are high, recent efforts to restrain property tax rates make it much more difficult for local governments to meet important needs.

Bridging the Political Divide

As we have explored previously, the "New Texas"—bigger, more urban, and more sophisticated—requires a new approach to politics and policy, and the "Old Texas" way of doing business won't be enough. The challenges listed earlier must be addressed by the state in a systematic way rather than with the traditional patchwork response we see during every legislative session in reaction to emergencies, court orders, or woeful underperformance. The process of transformation to a new Texas will require research to describe the implications of the changes in clear terms so that the public leadership of the state can assess it. But it will also require a more bipartisan approach.

Like the rest of the country, Texas has experienced seemingly endless partisan struggle between Democrats and Republicans in recent decades.

In recent legislative sessions, the Republican leadership has taken a largely unconstructive approach toward the priorities of large cities. For example, the legislature has reduced cities' powers of annexation, which have played an important role in the growth and economic health of some leading cities, and sparred over the role of urban police departments in enforcing federal immigration laws. On annexation as well as on immigration enforcement, voting patterns that have made the Triangle cities islands of "blue" amid oceans of suburban and rural "red" have created political targets too tempting to resist.

In order to stay ahead of the state's major changes, Texas Republicans face important questions. How can they adapt the small-government values they've long championed in ways that meet the needs of the new Texas? How can the state reconcile all competitive advantages it derives from its small-government, antitax tradition with the imperative of addressing critical infrastructure and education needs?

Democrats too must address fundamental questions. For better or worse, they have long believed that they can simply ride the crest of the demographic wave—particularly the growing Hispanic population share in the state—to ultimate political dominance in

Austin. But simply waiting for Texas to tip "blue" is proving to be a questionable strategy, as many Hispanic and African American voters have become open to Republican values of light-touch regulation and restrained taxes. To be sure, Democrats are likely to stand their ground on hot-button social issues. But they should also anticipate the state's economic changes and become champions of a pragmatic economic agenda to create the quality jobs, higher wages, small business starts, and educational improvements to which Texans aspire.

In other words, *both* Republicans and Democrats must move beyond the current partisan paralysis in order to ensure that Texas pursues policies and investments that recognize the critical role that cities and metropolitan areas will play in the state's future.

Spreading Prosperity across Texas

As in other states, many Texans in smaller communities and rural areas feel the state's powerful economy is leaving them behind—and with good reason. According to a recent Brookings Institution report, "Why Rural America Needs Cities," between 2010 and 2018 the Texas Triangle metros have grown more than 16 percent, while rural Texas grew only 0.3 percent, with more than half of the rural counties losing population.[5] As the Brookings report points out, rural communities in states like Texas "have lower shares of residents with college degrees, digital skills and specialized knowledge-based jobs, all of which are crucial determinants of durable success in the modern era."

The Triangle will dominate the state in terms of population growth and economic expansion, but the politics of Texas will become further bifurcated and contentious if the state does not craft its public investments to share that economic momentum with other Texas cities beyond the Triangle as well as with rural and small-town areas of the state. Thus the practical challenge facing the state today is to keep the modern economic engine of the Texas Triangle running at full momentum *while at the same time* linking its assets and resources to the state's other cities and rural areas. Texas is fortunate that the Triangle is positioned by geography, history, and its institutions to serve that role.

The state budget will become a powerful driver of equitable prosperity across Texas. In the years ahead, the budget will become ever more dependent on taxes generated in the Triangle metros. As we have indicated, the state must invest in the Triangle in return to ensure ongoing prosperity. But the state can also use investments and policies to support small towns and rural Texas as well:

- Spreading prosperity to rural Texans must include careful attention to road and transportation improvements, including as passenger rail systems are developed. For example, the Texas Central High Speed Railway between Dallas and Houston has very deliberately planned a stop in College Station in order to link the growing momentum generated by one of the largest universities in the nation, Texas A&M, and the agricultural expertise of the Brazos River Valley with the urban resources of Houston and Dallas.

- The state can also influence regional economic development through targeted investment in K–12 and postsecondary education. For example, the public university systems could assure Texans that they will invest a reasonable share of statewide revenues in building up the knowledge base of smaller metros and rural areas by focusing on such UT campuses in El Paso, Tyler, and the Rio Grande Valley and A&M campuses in places like Kingsville, Laredo, Commerce, and Canyon.

- Another area in which Texas could deploy world-class assets from within the Texas Triangle to help the rest of the state is health care. Each of the five Texas Triangle metros has world-class medical centers, including premier hospital systems, medical schools, nursing schools, research operations, home health-care networks, and biomedical companies. Partnerships spanning the state—including both telemedicine and in-person medical care—could enhance both health care and local economies around the state.

- Similarly, Triangle-based manufacturers, banks, engineering firms, and business-service providers could locate branches and engage suppliers from midsized cities and rural areas to access capable entrepreneurs and massive investments of capital in the infrastructure needed for water adequacy, conservation strategies, green ecosystem developments, and bio-based inputs in manufacturing. Triangle-based equipment manufacturers, transport firms, broadband enterprises, environmental engineering firms, and capital providers can solidify the natural business strengths of rural areas.

Texas could also ease the divide between rural Texas and the state's larger metros by promoting intangible bonds—for example, by encouraging Texans to create quality-of-life amenities in smaller communities. In view of the professed love many Texans have for wide-open spaces, the land, cowboy values, and country lifestyles, more Texans might choose to stay in or move to smaller communities to raise their families if they could more easily access well-paying work and the comforts of modernity. Already the numbers who commute from bucolic places like the counties west of Fort Worth or southwest of Austin to booming Triangle job centers are large and growing.

If the state can make progress with its mobility puzzles, offer competitive education in smaller towns, and provide connections to the global economy, even more Texans just might choose the less crowded, less congested, and less pressurized lifestyle of small-town Texas. Smaller towns and rural areas might see a resurgence as they revive the social virtues of "Main Street" life and move on from the current era of loss, decline, and desperation. These are big "ifs," but Texas values just might show the way toward renewed connections between urban and rural places and demonstrate how to spread the benefits of modern technology and global connectivity beyond the obvious leading metro areas.

Rural development in many regions of the state might benefit from fresh state policies toward traditional industries like oil and gas, farming, and ranching. For example, aggressive state support for oil and gas production in the Eagle Ford and Permian Basin oil fields in recent years has not only propelled Texas into becoming a leading force for national energy independence but also breathed unexpected economic life into some of the poorest communities in the state.

The Stakes Are High

While the future looks bright for the Texas Triangle, an objective analysis must take into consideration factors that could derail this outlook. We see a variety of possible obstacles, ranging from economic recessions to political strife to long-term concerns like climate change and extreme weather events.

Economic Recessions

To start with, the Triangle metros—like all cities in the world—are vulnerable to deep global economic downturns. Such downturns ripple in short order through our entire society, and the COVID-19 crisis has certainly left no city unscathed, least of all those in the Triangle. Global economic realities come to the Texas Triangle through its ports, its airports, and its trucking routes. The Triangle economies are more diversified than ever before and less vulnerable to downturns in sectors like oil and gas, but no urban economy is immune to severe recessions.

Failure to Invest in Infrastructure

In the longer term, one of the most serious threats to the Triangle's prosperity is the risk that Texas fails to invest in needed infrastructure. For example, a wide range of mobility improvements is necessary—from walkable neighborhoods to bicycle lanes to city streets and highways to advanced transit and rail solutions—in every corner of the Texas Triangle. Other forms of needed infrastructure include adequate water supplies, reasonably priced power, well-wired broadband communication networks, and functioning basic municipal services.

High Housing Costs

Policies that contribute to spiraling home prices are causing talented young people and businesses to abandon otherwise thriving metros like San Francisco, San Jose, and New York, especially after the COVID-19 outbreak. The Texas Triangle has done well in housing production, yet prices continue to rise relative to incomes. Accelerating growth in housing supply in high-opportunity areas and restoring greater affordability are essential components to the continuing growth of the Texas Triangle cities. They are, in essence, another critical piece of economic infrastructure for the megaregion.

Political Strife

Another threat is political. As we have stated, the perception is growing that state leaders in the legislature are unsupportive of—or even hostile to—the interests of the state's large cities. Other legislative measures include restrictions on city budgets, taxing powers, local referenda, and other municipal powers. The unfortunate net effect of these measures could be the disabling of the Triangle metros in their efforts to keep up with the economic growth they are experiencing and thus a reduction of the economic returns to Texas as a whole from Triangle growth.

Lack of Cooperation

Especially in Texas, there can be sharp political differences between cities and suburbs. Thus it will be important to develop a consensus on the basic elements of the Triangle growth agenda: jobs, incomes, quality education, worker training, infrastructure investment, the social safety net, inclusive governance, entrepreneurial opportunities, and fair access to upward mobility. Failure to accelerate the scale and pace of investment in human capital can become a limiting factor in the Triangle's future.

Climate Change

Partly due to climate change, each of the corners of the Texas Triangle confronts growing weather-related challenges. These will become more severe in their human impact, disruptive power, and financial cost because of increasing population and expanding land uses. Houston's experience with hurricanes and flooding, such as the destructive power demonstrated by Hurricane Harvey in 2017, is likely to be repeated in years to come in all cities in the Triangle. The interaction between climate-related events and unprecedented population growth requires thoughtful preparation, both to mitigate the risks from possible events as well as to react in emergencies and speed up recovery in their aftermath.

Unexpected Challenges

The experience of the COVID-19 crisis in 2020 has brought to the surface a number of unexpected challenges. Like the federal government and all other states, Texas found itself woefully unprepared for the pandemic, despite years of warnings from public-health experts. The early days of "social distancing" and "shelter-in-place" guidelines saw repeated conflicts among state, county, and local authorities—with many of the disputes tinged with all-too-typical red-blue partisan sniping. On the other hand, the cutting-edge medical centers of the Triangle demonstrated their sophistication and agility in their rapid response to the health crisis. The Triangle must move beyond the partisan approach. Sober leadership within each metro and in the state can weigh the probabilities, determine the costs of action or inaction, and proceed accordingly.

Texas' Future

In a larger context, Texas is likely to find that the federal government will have limited resources to address the challenges we outline in this book and support the Texas Triangle's growth. Enormous fiscal packages aimed at fighting the COVID-19 crisis and rescuing the US economy have left the federal government indebted to an unprecedented extent. Federal spending on Social Security and federal health-care programs will devour more and more of the federal government's available resources. The years ahead are likely to see fiscal consolidation in Washington. Consequently, the future of Texas will depend more on the state's own decisions than many appreciate. More than at any time in the last one hundred years, the future of Texas is in the hands of the state's political, business, education, and community leaders. Fresh policies to address the state's growing challenges are becoming urgently important.

As Texas leaders from every part of the state contemplate the measures needed to sustain the state's progress in the face of the new realities we document in this book, they should recognize that the growing size and economic might of the Texas Triangle are powerful assets for the state. The Texas Triangle is an economic engine that is generating benefits for all of Texas. The growth of the Triangle will raise the stature of Texas on the national and global stages, and it will make Texas an economic force in the world that no one can ignore.

ACKNOWLEDGMENTS

The Texas Triangle has many friends. They are anyone who recognizes that Texas is a state where the concentrated urban population and its economy add up to a global force stronger than the state's spread-out rural economy. This can be anyone, regardless of where they live. This does not diminish the Texas rural population or its economy, which is the largest rural community in the nation.

This book benefited from people who understand the dimensions of the Texas Triangle and who assisted the authors with their knowledge. Our thanks go to Lloyd Potter, Texas state demographer, and his staff at the Texas Demographic Center at the University of Texas at San Antonio's downtown campus. The center's staff maintains an encyclopedia of accessible online data about Texas now and in the state's future.

Surely the largest repository of Texas economic information is maintained by the Federal Reserve Bank of Dallas. We thank Keith Phillips, a senior economist based at the San Antonio Federal Reserve branch who is also the bank's foremost expert on Texas labor markets and an award-winning forecaster. Several Dallas Fed publications provided critical background for this book.

A wealth of valuable information is compiled and offered by the Real Estate Center at Texas A&M University in College Station. Jim Gaines, the center's chief economist, was generous with his time for several interviews.

Catherine Nixon Cooke, a San Antonio writer, assisted with the narrative flow for portions of this book. Her other publications include *In Search of Tom Slick*, published by Texas A&M University Press, and her collaboration with the former San Antonio mayor, the late Lila Cockrell, in *Love Deeper Than a River*.

Other experts who gave interviews were Carlton Schwab, CEO and president of the Texas Economic Development Council in Austin, and Mario Hernandez, a former council chairman and retired president of the San Antonio Economic Development Foundation. Thanks also go to Trey Jacobson, an economic development specialist and consultant and a former chief of staff for San Antonio Mayor Ron Nirenberg.

Other valuable interviews came from Bernard Weinstein, economist and associate director of SMU's Maguire Energy Institute in Dallas, and Noel Poyo, executive director in San Antonio for the National Association for Latino Community Asset Builders. Also, Celina Moreno, CEO and president, and Hector Bojorquez, director of operations and educational practice, both at the IDRA in San Antonio, were generous with their time and expertise. William Tipton of Compart Maps in Ventura, California, prepared the book's maps.

The authors also appreciate the talented staff at the Texas A&M University Press in College Station, led by Dr. Jay Dew, director, and Thom Lemmons, editor in chief.

APPENDIX 1

Texas Fortune 500 Companies (2019)

With ranking by revenue

Dallas–Fort Worth Metropolitan Area

1. ExxonMobil (2)
2. McKesson (7)
3. AT&T (9)
4. Energy Transfer (59)
5. American Airlines Group (68)
6. Southwest Airlines (142)
7. Fluor (164)
8. Kimberly-Clark (171)
9. Tenet Healthcare (172)
10. HollyFrontier (175)
11. D. R. Horton (194)
12. Texas Instruments (199)
13. Jacobs Engineering Group (208)
14. J. C. Penney (261)
15. Pioneer Natural Resources (333)
16. Vistra Energy (337)
17. GameStop (346)
18. Yum China Holdings (362)
19. Alliance Data Systems (390)
20. Dean Foods (393)
21. Builders FirstSource (394)
22. EnLink Midstream (396)
23. Celanese (426)

Houston Metropolitan Area

1. Phillips 66 (23)
2. Sysco (54)
3. ConocoPhillips (86)
4. Enterprise Products Partners (89)
5. Plains GP Holdings (94)
6. Halliburton (127)
7. Occidental Petroleum (167)
8. EOG Resources (181)
9. Waste Management (213)

10. Kinder Morgan (224)
11. Anadarko Petroleum (237)
12. Group 1 Automotive (272)
13. Huntsman (276)
14. Quanta Services (283)
15. CenterPoint Energy (299)
16. Targa Resources (302)
17. Calpine (330)
18. Westlake Chemical (352)
19. National Oilwell Varco (357)
20. Cheniere Energy (383)
21. Apache (411)
22. Marathon Oil (456)

San Antonio Metropolitan Area

1. Valero Energy (24)
2. USAA (101)
3. iHeartMedia (456)

Austin Metropolitan Area

1. Dell Technologies (34)

Source: Fortune magazine

Top Texas Triangle Tourism Destinations

San Antonio Metropolitan Area

1. The River Walk
2. The Alamo
3. Natural Bridge Caverns
4. New Braunfels Gruene Historic District

Austin Metropolitan Area

1. Texas State Capitol

Houston Metropolitan Area

1. Johnson Space Center and Mission Control
2. Galveston Beaches
3. Moody Gardens and Aquarium
4. Strand Historic District
5. Houston Museum of Fine Arts
6. Houston Museum of Natural Science

Dallas–Fort Worth Metropolitan Area

1. Sixth Floor Museum
2. Fort Worth Stockyards

Source: Planetware.com

Top Texas Triangle Amusement Parks

San Antonio Metropolitan Area

1. Six Flags Fiesta Texas
2. SeaWorld San Antonio
3. Morgan's Wonderland
4. Schlitterbahn Waterpark New Braunfels
5. Natural Bridge Caverns
6. Seguin's ZDT's Amusement Park

Austin Metropolitan Area

1. Pflugerville's Typhoon Texas
2. San Marcos' Wonder World Cave & Adventure Park

Houston Metropolitan Area

1. Kemah Boardwalk
2. Schlitterbahn Galveston Island Waterpark

Dallas–Fort Worth Metropolitan Area

1. Arlington's Six Flags Over Texas
2. Richland Hills' NRH2O Family Water Park
3. Fair Park
4. Grapevine's Great Wolf Lodge Waterpark

Source: Tripadvisor.com and author research

Selected Texas Triangle Public and Private Universities

Dallas–Fort Worth Metropolitan Area

Public universities

University of Texas at Dallas
University of Texas at Arlington
University of Texas Southwestern Medical Center at Dallas

University of North Texas
University of North Texas at Dallas
University of North Texas Health Science Center
Texas Woman's University

Private universities

Southern Methodist University
Texas Christian University
University of Dallas

Dallas Baptist University
Dallas Christian College
Dallas International University

Houston Metropolitan Area

Public universities

University of Houston
University of Houston–Clear Lake

University of Houston–Downtown
Prairie View A&M University
Texas Southern University

Private universities

Rice University
University of St. Thomas
North American University

Strayer University
Houston Baptist University

San Antonio Metropolitan Area

Public universities

University of Texas at San
  Antonio
UT Health San Antonio

Texas A&M University–San
  Antonio

Private universities

Trinity University
University of the Incarnate
  Word
St. Mary's University

Our Lady of the Lake
  University
Texas Lutheran University

Austin Metropolitan Area

Public universities

University of Texas at Austin

Texas State University

Private universities

St. Edward's University
Concordia University
Huston-Tillotson University
Southwestern University

APPENDIX 5

Texas Triangle Community College Systems

Dallas–Fort Worth Metropolitan Area

Dallas County Community
    College District
Collin College

Tarrant County College District
Weatherford College

Houston Metropolitan Area

Houston Community College
Brazosport College
Galveston College
Lone Star College System

San Jacinto College
Wharton County Junior
    College

San Antonio Metropolitan Area

Alamo Community Colleges

Austin Metropolitan Area

Austin Community College

APPENDIX 6

Passenger Rail Travel in the Texas Triangle

Amtrak provides the only passenger rail service into, out of, and inside Texas. Amtrak operates two routes in Texas, known as the Texas Eagle and the Sunset Limited. The three corners of the Texas Triangle are all served by Amtrak, but no Amtrak passenger service exists directly between Houston and the Dallas–Fort Worth areas.

Texas Eagle

This route stretches between Chicago and Texas and to Los Angeles. In Texas, Amtrak's Texas Eagle route stops at these fifteen Texas train stations:

Dallas
Fort Worth
Austin
San Antonio
El Paso
Alpine
Cleburne
Del Rio

Longview
McGregor
Marshall
Mineola
San Marcos
Sanderson
Taylor

Annual Texas Eagle ridership: 306,321 (2016 fiscal year)

Sunset Limited

This route operates between Los Angeles and New Orleans. In Texas, the Sunset Limited service stops at these six Texas train stations:

Houston   Alpine
San Antonio   Beaumont
El Paso   Del Rio

Annual Sunset Limited ridership: 98,079 (2016 fiscal year)

Source: Amtrak.com

International Flights to and from Texas Triangle Airports

The Texas Triangle airports connect the area to nearly all parts of the world with these nonstop flights to destinations outside the fifty United States. Some flights are seasonal. The list was compiled before the 2020 COVID-19 pandemic. Any route cancellations could eventually be restored as the airline industry recovers.

Dallas / Fort Worth International Airport

Frankfurt, Germany
Amsterdam, Netherlands
Munich, Germany
Beijing, China
Dubai, United Arab Emirates
Shanghai, China
London, United Kingdom
Madrid, Spain
Rome, Italy
Toronto, Canada
Dublin, Ireland
Seoul, South Korea
Doha, Qatar
Hong Kong, China
Montreal, Canada
Tel Aviv, Israel
Tokyo, Japan

Cancún, Mexico
Mexico City, Mexico
Vancouver, Canada
Sydney, Australia
São Paulo, Brazil
Bogotá, Colombia
Calgary, Canada
Lima, Peru
Auckland, New Zealand
Santiago, Chile
Punta Cana, Dominican
    Republic
Buenos Aires, Argentina
Guadalajara, Mexico
Nassau, Bahamas
San Juan, Puerto Rico
Monterrey, Mexico

Puerto Vallarta, Mexico
Santo Domingo, Dominican
   Republic
Montego Bay, Jamaica
San José del Cabo, Mexico
Oranjestad, Aruba
San Salvador, El Salvador
Belize City, Belize
Liberia, Costa Rica
George Town, Cayman Islands
Providenciales, Turks and
   Caicos Islands
Quito, Ecuador
Saint Thomas, US Virgin
   Islands
Guatemala City, Guatemala
Querétaro, Mexico
Guayaquil, Ecuador
Guanajuato, Mexico

Ciudad Chihuahua, Mexico
San Pedro Sula, Honduras
Mazatlán, Mexico
Zihuatanejo, Mexico
Saint Kitts, Saint Kitts and
   Nevis
Roatan, Honduras
Cozumel, Mexico
Huatulco, Mexico
Tegucigalpa, Honduras
Morelia, Mexico
Acapulco, Mexico
Oaxaca, Mexico
Aguascalientes, Mexico
Durango, Mexico
Torreón, Mexico
San Luis Potosí, Mexico
Zacatecas, Mexico

Houston Bush Intercontinental Airport

Mexico City, Mexico
Monterrey, Mexico
Toronto, Canada
Guadalajara, Mexico
San Salvador, El Salvador
Cancún, Mexico
León, Mexico
Querétaro, Mexico
Guatemala City, Guatemala
Panama City, Panama
San José, Costa Rica
San José del Cabo, Mexico
Aguascalientes, Mexico
Amsterdam, Netherlands
Bogotá, Colombia

Belize City, Belize
Frankfurt, Germany
Puerto Vallarta, Mexico
San Luis Potosí, Mexico
Tokyo, Japan
Montreal, Canada
San Pedro Sula, Honduras
Acapulco, Mexico
Buenos Aires, Argentina
Ciudad Chihuahua, Mexico
Doha, Qatar
Dubai, United Arab Emirates
Havana, Cuba
Lima, Peru
Mérida, Mexico

Morelia, Mexico
Oaxaca, Mexico
Paris, France
Puebla, Mexico
Port of Spain, Trinidad and
   Tobago
Rio de Janeiro, Brazil
Coxen Hole, Honduras
São Paulo, Brazil
Santiago, Chile
Sydney, Australia
Tampico, Mexico
Tegucigalpa, Honduras
Taipei, Taiwan
Quito, Ecuador
Veracruz, Mexico
Edmonton, Canada
Vancouver, Canada
Ixtapa, Mexico

Istanbul, Turkey
Beijing, China
Manchester, United Kingdom
Managua, Nicaragua
Munich, Germany
Lomé, Togo
Nassau, Bahamas
Cozumel, Mexico
Mazatlán, Mexico
Bonaire, Caribbean
   Netherlands
Grand Cayman, Cayman
   Islands
Montego Bay, Jamaica
Punta Cana, Dominican
   Republic
Saint Thomas, US Virgin
   Islands
Monzanillo, Mexico

Houston Hobby Airport

Cancún, Mexico
San José del Cabo, Mexico
Belize City, Belize
Liberia, Costa Rica
Puerto Vallarta, Mexico
San José, Costa Rica
San Juan, Puerto Rico

Montego Bay, Jamaica
Aruba, Dutch Caribbean
Grand Cayman, Cayman
   Islands
Punta Cana, Dominican
   Republic

Austin Bergstrom International Airport

Amsterdam,
   Netherlands
Calgary, Canada
Cancún, Mexico
Frankfurt, Germany

London, United Kingdom
   (Heathrow)
London, United Kingdom
   (Gatwick)
Ontario, Canada

Paris, France

San José del Cabo, Mexico

Mexico City, Mexico

Toronto, Canada

San Antonio International Airport

Mexico City, Mexico

Guadalajara, Mexico

Monterrey, Mexico

Cancún, Mexico

Source: Airport websites (2019)

Triangle Counties

The 35 Texas counties listed here, out of the statewide total of 254 counties, comprise the Texas Triangle. If they were a nation, the combined economies of these counties would be the fifteenth-largest nation in the world in economic size.

Austin MSA

Travis
Bastrop
Caldwell

Hays
Williamson

Dallas Metropolitan Division

Dallas
Collin
Denton
Ellis

Hunt
Kaufman
Rockwall

Fort Worth Metropolitan Division

Tarrant
Hood
Johnson

Parker
Somervell
Wise

Houston MSA

Harris
Austin

Brazoria
Chambers

Fort Bend
Galveston
Liberty

Montgomery
Waller

San Antonio MSA

Bexar
Comal
Bandera
Atascosa

Guadalupe
Kendall
Medina
Wilson

NOTES

Chapter 1

1 Terry Maxon, "Southwest Airlines Co-founder Rollin King Passes Away," *Dallas Morning News*, June 27, 2014, https://www.dallasnews.com/business/airlines/2014/06/27/rollin-king-the-original-southwest-airlines-founder-passes-away.

2 "The Texas Way of Urbanism," Center for Opportunity Urbanism, 2017, https://urbanreforminstitute.org/wp-content/uploads/2016/12/TheTexasWayOfUrbanismReport-8.pdf.

3 See the database at the US Bureau of Economic Analysis, https://www.bea.gov/data/gdp/gdp-state.

4 Robert W. Gilmer and Samuel Redus, "Texas Triangle: Economic Engine of the Southwest," Texas A&M University Real Estate Center, Publication 2091, February 16, 2015, https://assets.recenter.tamu.edu/documents/articles/2091.pdf.

5 Gilmer and Redus.

6 Cassandra Pollock, "Texas House Speaker Dennis Bonnen Won't Seek Reelection after Recording Scandal," *Texas Tribune*, October 22, 2019, https://www.texastribune.org/2019/10/22/Dennis-Bonnen-to-not-seek-reelection-to-Texas-House/.

7 These numbers include only boardings, not through passengers changing at airports. Both D/FW and Bush are major hub airports where passengers change planes.

Chapter 2

1 See, for instance, Richard Florida, "The Real Powerhouses That Drive the World's Economy," Bloomberg CityLab, February 28, 2019, https://www.bloomberg.com/news/articles/2019-02-28/mapping-the-mega-regions-powering-the-world-s-economy.

2 "Automation and the Future of Work," McKinsey Global Institute, October 29, 2018, https://www.mckinsey.com/featured-insights/future-of-work/ai-automation-and-the-future-of-work-ten-things-to-solve-for#.

3 Adam McCann, "Most Diverse Cities in the U.S.," WalletHub, April 10, 2019, https://wallethub.com/edu/most-diverse-cities/12690/.

4 Alberto Alesina and Eliana La Ferrara, "Ethnic Diversity and Economic Performance," *Journal of Economic Literature* 43, no. 3 (September 2005): 762–800.

5 Available at Moody's website, https://www.moodys.com/sites/products.

6 See the Opportunity Atlas website, https://www.opportunityatlas.org.

7 Data on metropolitan-area poverty rates are from the US Census Bureau, American Community Survey. Data on population shares in the middle class are from "America's Shrinking Middle Class: A Close Look at Changes within Metropolitan Areas," Pew Research Center, May 11, 2016, https://www.pewsocialtrends.org/2016/05/11/Americas-shrinking-middle-class-a-close-look-at-changes-within-metropolitan-areas/.

8 "14th Annual Demographia International Housing Affordability Survey: 2018," Demographia, 2018, https://www.demographia.com/dhi2018.pdf.

9 Available at Moody's website, https://www.moodys.com/sites/products.

10 Data provided by the O'Neil Center for Global Markets and Freedom, Cox School of Business, Southern Methodist University.

11 See Moody's business cost index, https://www.moodys.com/sites/products.

12 Joseph Gyourko, Albert Saiz, and Anita A. Summers, "A New Measure of the Local Regulatory Environment for Housing Markets: The Wharton Residential Land Use Regulatory Index," University of Pennsylvania, Samuel Zell and Robert Lurie Real Estate Center Working Paper No. 558, October 22, 2006, http://realestate.wharton.upenn.edu/wp-content/uploads/2017/03/558.pdf.

13 See the Trust for Public Land website, https://www.tpl.org/parkscore.

14 Available upon request.

Chapter 3

1 Author calculations; https://www.bea.gov.

2 "GDP," World Bank, 2020, https://data.worldbank.org/indicator/NY.GDP.MKTP.CD.

3 "Basic Data Selection," United Nations, accessed December 10, 2020, https://unstats.un.org/unsd/snaama/Basic.

4 "Global Metro Monitor," Brookings, January 22, 2015, https://www.brookings.edu/research/global-metro-monitor/.

5 "America's Top 20 Export States," World's Top Exports, accessed December 10, 2020, https://www.worldstopexports.com/americas-top-20-export-states/.

6 "Top 50 Metropolitan Area Export Tool," International Trade Administration, accessed December 10, 2020, https://www.trade.gov/data-visualization/exports-top-50-metropolitan-areas-united-states.

7 Author calculation.

Chapter 4

1 "Urban Texas," Texas Demographic Center, August 2017, http://demographics.texas.gov/Resources/publications/2017/2017_08_21_UrbanTexas.pdf.

2 Pia Orrenius, Alexander T. Abraham, and Stephanie Gullo, "Gone to Texas: Migration Vital to Growth in the Lone Star State," Federal Reserve Bank of Dallas, 2018, https://www.dallasfed.org/research/swe/2018/swe1801b.

3 "New Census Bureau Population Estimates Show Dallas-Fort Worth-Arlington Has Largest Growth in the United States," US Census Bureau, March 22, 2018, https://www.census.gov/newsroom/press-releases/2018/popest-metro-county.html.

4 "Texas Keeps Getting Bigger," US Census Bureau, March 22, 2018, https://www.census.gov/library/visualizations/2018/comm/popest-texas.html.

5 https://www.census.gov/data/datasets/2017/demo/popest/counties-total.html (no longer extant).

6 "Census Bureau Reveals Fastest-Growing Large Cities," US Census Bureau, May 24, 2018, https://www.census.gov/newsroom/press-releases/2018/estimates-cities.html.

7 "Texas Population Estimates Program," Texas Demographic Center, accessed December 10, 2020, http://txsdc.utsa.edu/Data/TPEPP/Estimates/.

8 "2018 Conference," Texas Demographic Center, May 23–24, 2018, http://txsdc.utsa.edu/AnnualConference/Content.

9 "Introduction to Texas Domestic Migration," Texas Demographic Center, April 2016, http://demographics.texas.gov/Resources/Publications/2016/2016_04-13_DomesticMigration.pdf.

10 Orrenius, Abraham, and Gullo, "Gone to Texas."

11 "U-Haul Names Top 50 Growth States for 2018," U-Haul, January 2, 2019, https://www.uhaul.com/Articles/About/16389/U-Haul-Names-Top-50-Growth-States-For-2018/.

12 Laura Begley Bloom, "Vermont Wants to Pay You $10,000 to Move There and Work," *Forbes*, June 3, 2018, https://www.forbes.com/sites/laurabegleybloom/2018/06/03/vermont-wants-to-pay-you-10000-to-move-there-and-work/?sh=2960533711c9.

13 "Quick Facts," US Census Bureau, accessed December 10, 2020, https://www.census.gov/quickfacts/fact/table/VT,US/PST045217.

14 Mick Normington, "Listening to the Marketplace," Texas Workforce Commission, February 22, 2017, http://tawb.org/wp-content/uploads/2017/03/Austin-Texas-Economic-Development-Council-SLIDES-Feb-2017.pdf.

15 Emily Foxhall, "What's a Texas Town without a Dairy Queen?," *Houston Chronicle*, 2018, https://www.houstonchronicle.com/news/houston-texas/texas/article/What-s-a-Texas-town-without-a-Dairy-Queen-13011433.php?cmpid=gsa-chron-result.

Chapter 5

1 Jason Saving, "Why Texas Grows Faster: The Role of Smaller Government," in *Ten-Gallon Economy: Sizing Up Economic Growth in Texas*, ed. Pia M. Orrenius, Jesús Cañas, and Michael Weiss (New York: Palgrave Macmillan, 2015).

2 Marta Tienda, "Texas' Education Challenge," in *Ten-Gallon Economy*.

3 "2018 Conference," Texas Demographic Center, May 23–24, 2018, http://txsdc.utsa.edu/AnnualConference/Content.

4 "The History of the Texas Franchise Tax," Fiscal Notes, Office of the Texas Comptroller, 2015, https://comptroller.texas.gov/economy/fiscal-notes/2015/may/franchisetax.php.

5 "#1 Texas," Chief Executive, 2018, https://chiefexecutive.net/texas-18/.

6 Dale Buss, "Five States to Watch," Chief Executive, May 2, 2018, https://chiefexecutive.net/5-states-to-watch-texas-florida-indiana-colorado-and-alabama/.

7 "Small Business Policy Index 2018," Small Business & Entrepreneurship Council, 2018, http://sbecouncil.org/resources/publications/small-business-policy-index-2018/.

8 Jon Prior, "Piper Jaffray's Private Equity Arm Eyes Texas Deals with New $130 Million Fund," *San Antonio Business Journal*, October 11, 2018, https://www.bizjournals.com/sanantonio/news/2018/10/11/piper-jaffrays-private-equity-arm-eyes-texas-deals.html.

9 Jordan Blum, "Permian Will Outpace All OPEC Nations except Saudis," *Houston Chronicle*, June 14, 2018, https://www.chron.com/business/energy/article/Permian-will-outpace-all-OPEC-nations-except-12992184.php.

10 Mick Normington, "Listening to the Marketplace," Texas Workforce Commission, February 22, 2017, http://tawb.org/wp-content/uploads/2017/03/Austin-Texas-Economic-Development-Council-SLIDES-Feb-2017.pdf.

11 "150 Best Places to Live in the U.S.," *U.S. News & World Report*, 2018, https://realestate.usnews.com/places/rankings/best-places-to-live.

12 Kali McFadden, "America's Biggest Boomtowns," MagnifyMoney, August 6, 2018, https://www.magnifymoney.com/blog/news/americas-biggest-boomtowns/.

Chapter 6

1 "2010 Census Results Give Texas Four Additional Seats in Congress," *Dallas Morning News*, December 22, 2010, https://www.dallasnews.com/news/local-politics/2010/12/22/2010-census-results-give-texas-four-additional-seats-in-congress.

2 "No Change in Apportionment Allocations with New 2016 Census Estimates but Greater Change Likely by 2020," Election Data Services, December 20, 2016, https://www.electiondataservices.com/wp-content/uploads/2016/12/20161220-NR_Appor-16wTablesAndMaps.pdf.

3 "Rust Belt Losing Steam in the Next Census," *U.S. News & World Report*, May 22, 2017, https://www.usnews.com/news/best-states/articles/2017-05-22/rust-belt-losing-steam-in-the-next-census.

4 "Historical Presidential Elections," 270towin, accessed December 10, 2020, https://www.270towin.com/historical-presidential-elections/.

5 "Donald Trump Won in Texas," Politico, December 2, 2020, https://www.politico.com/2020-election/results/texas/.

6 Alan Peppard, "John Connally, JFK Shared a Complicated History before Assassination," *Dallas Morning News*, November 20, 2018, https://www.dallasnews.com/news/jfk/2018/11/20/john-connally-jfk-shared-complicated-history-before-assassination.

7 "2010 Census Urban and Rural Classification and Urban Area Criteria," US Census Bureau, December 2, 2019, https://www.census.gov/programs-surveys/geography/guidance/geo-areas/urban-rural/2010-urban-rural.html.

Chapter 7

1 Robert W. Gilmer, "The Texas Triangle as Megalopolis," Houston Business, Federal Reserve Bank of Dallas, April 2004.

2 Robert W. Gilmer, "The Simple Economics of the Texas Triangle," Houston Business, Federal Reserve Bank of Dallas, January 2004, https://www.dallasfed.org/~/media/documents/research/houston/2004/hb0401.pdf.

3 Richard Florida, *The New Urban Crisis* (New York: Basic Books, 2017).

4 Cecil Harper Jr., "Bryan, John Neely (1810–1877)," Handbook of Texas, accessed December 10, 2020, https://tshaonline.org/handbook/online/articles/fbran.

5 "At the Heart of Texas," Federal Reserve Bank of Dallas, February 2016, 17.

6 "History," State Fair of Texas, accessed December 10, 2020, https://bigtex.com/about-us/history/.

7 Bill Minutaglio and Steven L. Davis, *Dallas 1963* (New York: Twelve, 2013), 19.

8 Michael Philips, *White Metropolis: Race, Ethnicity, and Religion in Dallas, 1841–2001* (Austin: University of Texas Press, 2006).

9 Jim Schutze, *The Accommodation: The Politics of Race in an American City* (New York: Citadel Press, 1987).

10 https://dallasnews.com/news/news/2012.03/10/from-beyond-the -grave-j-erk-j (no longer extant).

11 Adam McCann, "Most Diverse Cities in the U.S.," WalletHub, April 10, 2019, https://wallethub.com/edu/most-diverse-cities/12690/.

12 Conor Shine, "D/FW Airport Slips on List of World's Largest Airports despite Passenger Traffic," *Dallas Morning News*, April 9, 2018, https:// dallasnews.com/business/dfw-airport/2018/04/09/dfw-airport-slips -list-worlds-largest-despite-passenger-traffic.

13 Jane Jacobs, *The Death and Life of Great American Cities* (New York: Random House, 1961).

14 Edward Glaeser et al., "Growth in Cities," NBER Working Paper No. 3787, 1992.

15 "Voters Support Part—but Not All—of $3.7B Dallas ISD Bond Election," WFAA, updated November 4, 2020, https://www.wfaa.com/article/ news/politics/elections/results-dallas-isd-bond-election/287-09a46c8d -b9d1-4f6c-9ae6-3a02b9d0cb3a.

16 Cullum Clark, Sarah Beth Luckey, and Kristin Spanos, "Eds and Meds: The Economic Contribution of Anchor Institutions to Dallas and Other Cities," *Economic Development Journal*, Spring 2020.

17 Data from "16th Annual Demographia International Housing Afford- ability Survey: 2020 Edition," Demographia, accessed December 10, 2020, http://www.demographia.com/dhi.pdf.

18 Joseph Gyourko, Albert Saiz, and Anita A. Summers, "A New Measure of the Local Regulatory Environment for Housing Markets: The Wharton Residential Land Use Regulatory Index," University of Pennsylvania, Samuel Zell and Robert Lurie Real Estate Center, Working Paper No. 558, October 22, 2006, http://realestate.wharton.upenn.edu/wp-content/ uploads/2017/03/558.pdf.

19 "US Metropolitan Area Economic Freedom Index," O'Neil Center for Global Markets and Freedom, accessed December 10, 2020, https://www .smu.edu/cox/Centers-and-Institutes/oneil-center/research/U,-d-,S,-d -,-Metropolitan-Area-Economic-Freedom-Index.

20 See the Opportunity Atlas, https://www.opportunityatlas.org.

21 Data from Wendell Cox, Demographia.

22 "1 in 3 Children in Dallas Lives in Poverty," Dallas Child Poverty Action Lab, accessed December 10, 2020, https://childpovertyactionlab.org.

23 City of Dallas 2019 Water Conservation Plan, April 24, 2019, https:// dallascityhall.com/departments/waterutilities/DCH%20Documents/ pdf/Water%20Conservation%20Plan.pdf.

24 Charles L. Marohn Jr., *Strong Towns: A Bottom-Up Revolution to Rebuild American Prosperity* (Hoboken, NJ: Wiley, 2020).

Chapter 8

1 Janet Schmelzer, "Fort Worth," Texas Handbook Online, accessed December 10, 2020, https://tsaonline.org/handbook/online/articles/hdf01.

2 https://web.archive.org/web/20070927222718/http://www.bell helicopter.com/en/training/index.cfm?content=bout%2Fhistory.cfm& g_folder=header_4 (no longer extant).

3 Max Baker, "How the F-16 Fighter Jet Put Fort Worth on the Aerospace Map," *Fort Worth Star-Telegram*, November 24, 2017, https://www.star -telegram.com/news/business/aviation/article186288298.html.

4 From the Office of Economic Development, Arlington, Texas, https://arlingtontx.gov/business.

5 Richard Florida, "The Fastest-Growing U.S. Cities Aren't What You Think," Bloomberg CityLab, August 21, 2019, https://www.bloomberg .com/news/articles/2019-08-21/america-s-fastest-and-slowest-growing -cities.

6 "Fort Worth, Texas," BestPlaces, accessed December 10, 2020, https://www.bestplaces.net/cost_of_living/city/texas/fort_worth.

7 "Looking for Small Business Friendliness? Head to Fort Worth," *Dallas Business Journal*, August 31, 2019, https://www.wtol.com/article/news/local/tarrant-county/fort-worth-is-the-second-friendliest-city-in -the-country-for-small-businesses-study-says/287-47c2f0d0-ae28-4046 -8cf2-1fb8cc8b4e21.

8 "Renaissance Heights in Fort Worth, TX Joins Purpose Built Communities Network," Purpose Built Communities, April 27, 2015, https://purposebuiltcommunities.org/network-member-updates/renaissance -heights-fort-worth-tx-joins-purpose-built-communities-network/.

9 "Project Studies: Fort Worth District," Texas Department of Transportation, accessed December 10, 2020, https://www.txdot.gov/inside-txdot/projects/studies/fort-worth.html.

10 http://fortworthtexas.gov/uploadedFiles/Planning_and_Development/Planning_and_Design/Comprehensive_Plan/2015-progress-and -priorities.pdf (no longer extant).

Chapter 9

1 Lisa Grey, "Indian-American K. P. George Takes Historic Place as Fort Bend County Judge," *Houston Chronicle*, December 30, 2018, https://www

.chron.com/news/houston-texas/houston/article/Indian-American-K
-P-George-takes-historic-place-13498873.php.

2 "Houston Regional Market Profile," Greater Houston Partnership,
accessed December 10, 2020, https://www.houston.org/sites/default/
files/2019-11/Houston%20Regional%20Market%20Profile.pdf.

3 https://web.archive.org/web/20060809124347/http://usinfo.state
.govxarchives/display.html?p=washfile-english&y=2003&m=November
&x=20031121162843yeroc9.75003e-02 (no longer extant).

4 "Talking Points, Q3/18," Greater Houston Partnership, accessed December 10, 2020, https://www.houston.org/houston-data/talking-points.

5 Alan Berube, Sarah Crump, and Alec Friedhoff, "Metro Monitor 2020,"
Brookings, March 5, 2020, https://www.brookings.edu/interactives/
metro-monitor-2020.

6 "Measuring Inclusion in America's Cities," Urban.org, September 15, 2020,
https://apps.urban.org/features/inclusion/index.html?topic=map.

7 Bill Gilmer, "How Houston Survived the Great Oil Bust of 2015–16,"
Forbes, July 24, 2018, https://www.forbes.com/sites/uhenergy/2018/
07/24/how-houston-survived-the-great-oil-bust-of-2015-16/.

8 Bill Gilmer, "How Houston Dominates the Oil Industry," *Forbes*, August 22,
2018, https://www.forbes.com/sites/uhenergy/2018/08/22/proximity
-counts-how-houston-dominates-the-oil-industry/?sh=173c77016107.

9 "Houston Industries," Greater Houston Partnership, accessed December 10, 2020, https://www.houston.org/business/infrastructure.html.

10 "Best Colleges in Texas," *U.S. News & World Report*, accessed December 10,
2020, https://www.usnews.com/best-colleges/tx.

11 "HBCU Ranking 2018: Texas Southern University," HBCU Colleges,
accessed December 10, 2020, https://hbcu-colleges.com/texas-southern
-university.

12 "Texas Economic Snapshot," Office of the Texas Comptroller, accessed
December 10, 2020, https://comptroller.texas.gov/economy/economic
-data/nasa/snapshot.php?utm_source=tw&utm_medium=en-social&
utm_campaign=gft-nasa&utm_content=motion-vid.

Chapter 10

1 The score for Dallas–Fort Worth is a weighted average of the separately
calculated scores for Dallas and Fort Worth, weighted by population.

2 "Capitol Myths and Legends," Texas State Preservation Board, accessed
December 10, 2020, https://tspb.texas.gov/prop/tc/tc-history/myths
-legends/index.html.

3 "Estimates of the Total Populations of Counties and Places in Texas
for July 1, 2018, and Jan. 1, 2019," Texas Demographic Center, accessed

December 10, 2020, https://demographics.texas.gov/Resources/TPEPP/Estimates/2018/2018_txpopest_place.pdf.

4 "Facts & Figures," University of Texas at Austin, accessed December 10, 2020, https://www.utexas.edu/about/facts-and-figures.

5 Data from the Texas A&M Real Estate Center, https://www.recenter.tamu.edu/.

6 Philip Jankowski, "Now That Voters Have Said Yes, Project Connect's Real Work Starts," *Austin American Statesman*, November 6, 2020, https://www.statesman.com/story/news/local/2020/11/06/now-that-voters-have-said-yes-project-connectrsquos-real-work-starts/43010655/.

Chapter 12

1 "About," US Census Bureau, accessed December 10, 2020, https://www.census.gov/programs-surveys/metro-micro/about.html.

2 "Texas Population Estimates Program," Texas Demographic Center, accessed December 10, 2020, https://demographics.texas.gov/Data/TPEPP/Estimates/.

3 Database at US Bureau of Economic Analysis, https://www.bea.gov.

4 Frederick L. Briuer, "Fort Hood," Handbook of Texas, accessed December 10, 2020, https://tshaonline.org/handbook/online/articles/qbf25.

5 "Who We Are," Central Texas College, accessed December 10, 2020, https://www.ctcd.edu/sites/ctcd/assets/File/About%20Us/quick-data-reference.pdf.

6 "USAG Fort Hood Fact Sheet," Killeen Chamber of Commerce, March 3, 2017, https://killeenchamber.com/assets/uploads/docs/Fact_Sheet_March_2017.pdf.

7 "Scott and White Memorial Hospital," Handbook of Texas, accessed December 10, 2020, https://tshaonline.org/handbook/online/articles/sbs06.

8 Christopher Long, "Belton, TX," Handbook of Texas, accessed December 10, 2020, https://tshaonline.org/handbook/online/articles/heb06.

9 "About UMHB," University of Mary Hardin-Baylor, accessed December 10, 2020, https://go.umhb.edu/about/history.

10 "Quick Facts," US Census Bureau, accessed December 10, 2020, https://www.census.gov/quickfacts/fact/table/US/PST045219.

11 Database at US Bureau of Economic Analysis, https://www.bea.gov/.

12 Roger N. Conger, "Waco, TX," Handbook of Texas, accessed December 10, 2020, https://tshaonline.org/handbook/online/articles/hdw01.

13 "History," Baylor University, accessed December 10, 2020, https://www.baylor.edu/about/index.php?id=88778.

14 Joe Holley, "As the 'Fixer Uppers' Move on, Will Hometown Stay Fixed Up?," *San Antonio Express-News*, January 17, 2017, D1 and D6.

15 "Quick Facts."

16 "History of the University," Texas A&M University, accessed December 10, 2020, https://tamu.edu/about/history.html.

17 "Accountability," Texas A&M University, accessed December 10, 2020, https://accountability.tamu.edu/.

18 "About," Texas A&M University, accessed December 10, 2020, https://www.tamus.edu/system/about/.

19 T. G. Webb, *Battle of the Brazos: A Texas Football Rivalry, a Riot, and a Murder* (College Station: Texas A&M University Press, 2018).

20 "The Little Creamery," Blue Bell Creameries, accessed December 10, 2020, https://www.bluebell.com/the-little-creamery/.

21 "Quick Facts."

22 "About Us," Round Top Festival Institute, accessed December 10, 2020, http://festivalhill.org/about.

23 "Shakespeare at Winedale," University of Texas at Austin, accessed December 10, 2020, https://liberalarts.utexas.edu/winedale/.

Chapter 13

1 Database at US Bureau of Economic Analysis, https://www.bea.gov/.

2 "Mexico Population," Population City, accessed December 10, 2020, http://population.city/mexico/.

3 "At the Heart of Texas: Cities' Industry Cluster Drive Growth," Federal Reserve Bank of Dallas, December 2018.

4 University of Texas Rio Grande Valley, https://www.utrgv.edu/sair/data-reports/.

5 "Fort Bliss," MyBaseGuide, accessed December 10, 2020, https://www.mybaseguide.com/search/?s=fort%20bliss.

6 "Spring Enrollment Reaches Record in 2018," UTEP Campus Newsfeed, accessed December 10, 2020, https://www.utep.edu/newsfeed/campus/Spring-Enrollment-Reaches-Record-in-2018.html.

7 "Fact Book 2019," Texas Tech University Health Sciences Center-El Paso, accessed December 10, 2020, http://elpaso.ttuhsc.edu/oire/fact-book/default.aspx.

8 "El Paso Community College," Community College Review, accessed December 10, 2020, https://www.communitycollegereview.com/el-paso-community-college-profile.

9 Charles D. Vertress, "Permian Basin," Handbook of Texas, accessed December 10, 2020, https://tshaonline.org/handbook/online/articles/ryp02.

10 Marissa Luck and Erin Douglas, "Big Oil's Investments in Permian Pay off as Earnings Soar," *San Antonio Express-News*, February 3, 2019, B2.

11 "At the Heart of Texas."

12 "Quick Facts," US Census Bureau, accessed December 10, 2020, https://www.census.gov/quickfacts/.

13 Irina Slav, "Permian Oil Reserves May Be Twice as Big as We Thought," Oil Price, December 7, 2018, https://oilprice.com/Energy/Crude-Oil/USGS-Doubles-Permian-Oil-Reserves-Estimate.html.

14 "2016 U.S. Port Rankings by Cargo Tonnage," American Association of Port Authorities, accessed December 10, 2020, http://aapa.files.cms-plus.com/PDFs/2016%20U.S.%20PORT%20RANKINGS%20BY%20CARGO%20TONNAGE.pdf.

15 "Economic Impact Study," Port Corpus Christi, accessed December 10, 2020, http://portofcc.com/about/financials/economic-impact-study/.

16 "Naval Air Station Corpus Christi," Office of the Texas Comptroller, accessed December 10, 2020, https://comptroller.texas.gov/economy/economic-data/military/nas-corpus.php.

17 "No. 1 Inland Port along US-Mexico Border," Laredo Economic Development Corporation, accessed December 10, 2020, https://www.laredoedc.org/site-selection/international-trade/.

18 See the Laredo Economic Development Corporation website, https://www.laredoedc.org/.

Chapter 14

1 "2010 Census Urban and Rural Classification and Urban Area Criteria," US Census Bureau, December 2, 2019, https://www.census.gov/programs-surveys/geography/guidance/geo-areas/urban-rural/2010-urban-rural.html.

2 https://gis-portal.data.census.gov/arcgis/apps/MapSeries/index.html.

3 "Resident Population Data," US Census Bureau, accessed December 10, 2020, https://web.archive.org/web/20101225031104/http://2010.census.gov/2010census/data/apportionment-pop-text.php.

4 https://www.icip.iastate.edu/tablrs/population/urban-pcy-states (no longer extant).

5 Ernest R. Parisi, "Fast Facts about Rural Texas," University of North Texas, accessed December 10, 2020, https://govinfo.library.unt.edu/chc/resources/slide/parisi_rural_tx_fastfacts.html.

6 Felix Rohatyn, *Bold Endeavors: How Our Government Built America, and Why It Must Rebuild Now* (New York: Simon & Schuster, 2009), 138.

Chapter 15

1 http://blog.nola.com/times-picayune/2007/08/whats_houston_got _that_no_does.html (no longer extant).

2 "Reports of Missing and Deceased Aug. 2, 2006," Louisiana Department of Health and Hospitals, accessed December 10, 2020, https://web.archive .org/web/20120211020954/http://www.dhh.louisiana.gov/offices/page .asp?ID=192&Detail=5248.

3 http://www.cnn.com/2011/US/08/12/katrina.houston/index.html (no longer extant).

4 Mark Reagan, "Transplanted San Antonians Reflect on Hurricane Katrina 10 Years Later," *San Antonio Current*, August 26, 2015, https://www .sacurrent.com/sanantonio/transplanted-san-antonians-reflect-on -hurricane-katrina-10-years-later/Content?oid=2463900.

5 Richard Thompson, "Tidewater Latest to Move HQ, Jobs from New Orleans, Offshore Services Company Headed to Houston," *Advocate*, May 12, 2018, https://www.theadvocate.com/new_orleans/news/ business/article_408ca026-53de-11e8-bfc0-577515eb921d.html.

6 "Largest Employers in the Dallas Fort Worth Area," Destination DFW, accessed December 10, 2020, http://www.destinationdfw.com/Largest -Employers-in-Dallas-Forth-Worth-Texas.

7 Brian Womack, "AT&T's Headquarters Will Feature a Massive Screen, Other Amenities," *Dallas Business Journal*, May 21, 2018, https://www .bizjournals.com/dallas/news/2018/05/21/at-ts-headquarterswill -feature-a-massive-screen.html.

8 "Major Employers," Greater Oklahoma City Chamber Economic Development, accessed December 10, 2020, https://www.greateroklahomacity .com/index.php?submenu=_employers&src=employers&srctype=major _employers_map.

Chapter 16

1 "S.A. Faces Housing Crisis," *San Antonio Express-News*, September 5, 2018.

2 Arren Kimbel-Sannit, "Where Are D-FW Houses below $150,000 and Apartments for under $800? Curious Texas Investigates," *Dallas Morning News*, July 24, 2018, https://www.dallasnews.com/life/curious-texas/2018/07/ 24/d-fw-houses-150000-apartments-800-curious-texas-investigates.

3 Raj Chetty, John Friedman, and Nathaniel Hendren, "The Opportunity Atlas: Mapping the Childhood Roots of Social Mobility," Executive Summary, Opportunity Insights, US Census Bureau, January 2020, https:// www.nber.org/papers/w25147.

4 David DeMatthews and David S. Knight, "Texas Needs to Fund Its Public Schools Differently," UT News, October 9, 2018, https://news

.utexas.edu/2018/10/09/texas-needs-to-fund-its-public-schools
-differently/.

5 "Fast Facts," National Center for Education Statistics, accessed December 10, 2020, https://nces.ed.gov/fastfacts/display.asp?id=372.

6 Maria "Cuca" Robledo Montecel, "No Place for Complacency in Educating Poor Children," MySanAntonio.com, January 26, 2019, https://www.mysanantonio.com/opinion/commentary/article/No-place-for-complacency-in-educating-poor-13562899.php.

7 Aliyya Swaby, "Teacher Raises and All-Day Pre-K: Here's What's in the Texas Legislature's Landmark School Finance Bill," *Texas Tribune*, May 24, 2019, https://www.texastribune.org/2019/05/24/texas-school-finance-bill-here-are-details/.

8 Krista Torralva, "Study: Students in San Antonio's Pre-K 4 SA Program Did Better on State Tests," *San Antonio Express-News*, January 28, 2019, http://www.express-news.com/news/education/article/Study-students-in-San-Antonio-s-Pre-K-4-SA-13567760.php.

9 "60x30TX, Texas Higher Education Strategic Plan: 2015–2030," Texas Higher Education Coordinating Board, July 23, 2015, https://reportcenter.highered.texas.gov/agency-publication/miscellaneous/60x30tx-strategic-plan-for-higher-education/.

10 Raymund A. Paredes, "Legislature, Colleges Together Can Reach 2030 Goal," *San Antonio Express-News*, July 8, 2018, F1.

11 "Texas Clear Lanes and Congestion Relief Task Force Committee Activity," Texas Department of Transportation, September 26, 2018.

12 "Report Card for Texas' Infrastructure," Texas Section of the American Society of Civil Engineers, 2017, 28, https://www.infrastructurereportcard.org/wp-content/uploads/2016/10/FullReport-TX_2017_web.pdf.

13 Ray Leszcynski, "Here's What Is Ahead for the Proposed Houston-to-Dallas High-Speed Rail including Potentially Traumatized Butterflies," *Dallas Morning News*, August 31, 2018, https://www.dallasnews.com/news/transportation/2018/08/31/ahead-proposed-houston-dallas-high-speed-rail-including-potentially-traumatized-butterflies.

14 Jesus Jimenez and Nataly Keomoungkhoun, "How Many Landowners Are Fighting Eminent Domain in the Bullet Train Project? Curious Texas Investigates," *Dallas Morning News*, March 9, 2020, https://www.dallasnews.com/news/curious-texas/2020/03/08/how-many-landowners-are-fighting-eminent-domain-in-the-bullet-train-project-curious-texas-investigates/.

15 "Transit Vote Not Required, but Welcome," *San Antonio Express-News*, October 9, 2018, A10.

16 "Texas COVID-19 Case Data," Texas Health and Human Services Commission, October 12, 2020, https://hhs.texas.gov/services/health/coronavirus-covid-19; "Texas Population Estimates Program," Texas

Demographic Center, accessed December 10, 2020, https://demographics
.texas.gov/Data/TPEPP/Estimates/; author calculations.

17 "Texas' Most Vulnerable Populations," Texas Demographic Center, September 2020, https://demographics.texas.gov/Resources/publications/
2020/20200918_ACS2019Brief_TexasMostVulnerablePopulations.pdf?dt
=20200922.

18 "Local Area Unemployment Statistics: Unemployment Rates for Metropolitan Areas," US Bureau of Labor Statistics, accessed October 2020,
https://www.bls.gov/web/metro/laummtrk.htm.

19 "The AEI Housing Center's Nowcast: Reopening of 40 Metro Area Economies, COVID-19 Data through Week 42, Foot Traffic Data through Week
41," American Enterprise Institute, October 21, 2020, https://www.aei
.org/reopening-of-metro-area-economies/.

20 Harvey Leifert, "Dividing Line: The Past, Present and Future of the 100th
Meridian," *Earth*, January 22, 2018, https://www.earthmagazine.org/
article/dividing-line-past-present-and-future-100th-meridian.

Chapter 17

1 "Texas Population Projections 2010 to 2050," Texas Demographic Center,
January 2019, https://demographics.texas.gov/Data/TPEPP/Projections/.

2 "Texas Population Projections 2010 to 2050," Texas Demographic Center,
2019, https://demographics.texas.gov/Resources/publications/2019/
20190925_PopProjectionsBrief.pdf.

3 "New Census Bureau Estimates Show Counties in South and West Lead
Nation in Population Growth," US Census Bureau, April 18, 2019, https://
www.census.gov/newsroom/press-releases/2019/estimates-county
-metro.html.

Chapter 18

1 Author research.

2 "Education Spending per Student by State," Governing the Future of
States and Localities, https://governing.com/gov-data/education-data/
state-education-spending-per-pupil-data.html.

3 Robert Walton, "ERCOT Reserves Drop below 2,300 MW, Forcing Texas
Grid to Call for Energy Emergency," Utility Dive, August 14, 2019,
https://utilitydive.com/news/ercot-reserves-drop-below-2300-mw
-forcing-texas-grid-to-call-for-energy-e/560833.

4 "Risky Business: The Bottom Line on Climate Change," Risky Business
Project, 2015, https://riskybusiness.org/, 87.

5 "Urban Texas," Texas Demographic Center, August 21, 2017, https://
demographics.texas.gov/Resources/publications/2017/2017_08_21
_UrbanTexas.pdf.

INDEX

Page numbers followed by f *and* t *refer to figures and tables, respectively.*